PICTORIAL HISTORY
OF WORLD WAR II

The graphic record of your Armed
Forces in action throughout every
phase of the global conflict

Volume 2

The War in the Pacific

1952

ACKNOWLEDGEMENTS

All photographs are official Department of Defense, U.S. Coast
Guard, U.S. Air Force, U.S. Army, U.S. Marine Corps or U.S.
Navy except as follows:

ACME NEWSPICTURES, INC.: 7 (lower), 9, 10, 36, 37, 370.   ODHAMS PRESS: 13, 14, 15, 16, 17, 18, 19, 20, 21, 66, 67, 171.

INTERNATIONAL NEWS PHOTOS: 382.   PRESS ASSOCIATION, INC.: 12, 359.

WIDE WORLD PHOTOS, INC.: 24.

Printed in the United States of America

WE ARE GRATEFUL!

To the 15,000,000 gallant men and women of the Armed Forces who served heroically in the defense of their country over land, sea, and in the air from the dismal day at Pearl Harbor to the final, unconditional surrender of the Axis Powers in 1945.

These volumes are humbly dedicated.

CONTENTS

Page

YOUR NAVY IN ACTION by Admiral of the Fleet Ernest J. King   1

THE WAR IN THE SOLOMONS by Lieutenant General Oscar W. Griswold   34

The U.S. COAST GUARD IN WORLD WAR II by Admiral Russell R. Waesche   65

TARAWA by Lieutenant General Julian C. Smith   112

THE WAR IN THE CENTRAL PACIFIC by Lieutenant General Robert C. Richardson   142

THE WAR IN THE CBI by Major General Frank D. Merrill   182

THE MARIANAS CAMPAIGN by General Holland M. Smith   188

THE WAR IN THE SOUTHWEST PACIFIC by Lieutenant General Robert L. Eichelberger   244

SUPERFORT WARFARE IN THE PACIFIC by Major General Curtis E. LeMay   311

THE OKINAWA CAMPAIGN by General Lemuel C. Shepherd, Jr.   315

THE SURRENDER OF JAPAN by Admiral of the Fleet William F. Halsey   350

INDEX   389

COLOR PLATES

Page

THE EYES OF THE FLEET—PATROL PLANES - - - - - - - - - - - 59

THE WAR IN THE PACIFIC—AT SEA - - - - - - - - - - - 60

A WELCOME SIGHT—A WELCOME BACK - - - - - - - - - - 93

SNJ'S OVER EL CENTRO - - - - - - - - - - - - - 94

FIGHTING ON DISTANT, TROPIC SHORES - - - - - - - - - - 159

THE WAR IN THE PACIFIC—AIR - - - - - - - - - - - 160

BATTLE FOR TARAWA - - - - - - - - - - - - - 193

AT KWAJALEIN AND GUAM - - - - - - - - - - - - 194

THE LONG ROAD BACK—ISLAND BASES - - - - - - - - - - 227

FLAG RAISING ON SURIBACHI - - - - - - - - - - - 228

NEARING JAPAN—IWO JIMA AND OKINAWA - - - - - - - - - 261

THE WAR IN THE PACIFIC—BORNEO - - - - - - - - - - 262

FLAME THROWER ASSAULT - - - - - - - - - - - - 295

ATOMIC DEVASTATION—NAGASAKI - - - - - - - - - - 296

UNCONDITIONAL SURRENDER - - - - - - - - - - - - 329

THE WAR IN THE PACIFIC—OCCUPATION - - - - - - - - - 330

YOUR NAVY IN ACTION

By Admiral of the Fleet Ernest J. King, USN

I CAN best stress the importance of the U.S. Navy to the American people when I state that without sea power on our side the United States would never have become a nation, would not have continued to exist as a nation, and even more specifically would not have won the great conflict successfully concluded in 1945. The destruction of British commerce by our commerce raiders, plus the timely control of the Chesapeake Bay by the French Fleet that made Washington's victory at Yorktown possible, insured our independence. Our similar destruction of British commerce in the War of 1812, plus our naval victories on Lake Erie and Lake Champlain, forced Britain to concede us an equal peace without the great loss of territory which at first seemed inevitable. Our Navy's blockade of the Southern Confederacy and control of the river highways into the heart of the South tore the Confederacy to pieces and preserved the Union. Our naval victories in the Spanish-American War were the greatest factor in winning that war. The combined sea power of the United States and Great Britain in the first World War made possible our tremendous army in Europe which turned the tide of victory for the Allies. And in the recent war the Navy repeated the identical job in Europe and at the same time crushed the Japanese Navy and brought about the surrender of Japan while Army and Air Forces were still largely intact.

Sea power is not the combat Navy alone, but also includes merchant ships, bases, naval air power —all the things that allow a country to gain control of the sea for its own purposes and to deny that use of the sea to the enemy. In its essence you can call it "Our Navy." And the purpose of these volumes is to tell in part the story of that Navy.

By its attack on Pearl Harbor Japan attempted to erase the greatest threat to her hoped-for-victory—our Navy. And that attack, demobilizing for a year or more our most powerful warships through bomb and torpedo damage, was a terrible blow. It left Japan with a superior navy in the Pacific, even if we had brought all our remaining ships from the Atlantic to help—something we could not do because of our other enemies on the Atlantic side, the Axis Powers of Europe.

THE JOINT CHIEFS OF STAFF

IN THAT trying time our President formed for the first time that unique organization for directing all our military effort—the organization of the Joint Chiefs of Staff.

The Joint Chiefs of Staff was composed of the Chief of Staff of the Army, the Chief of Naval Operations of the Navy, the Commanding General of the Army Air Forces, and the Chief of Staff of the President (Commander-in-Chief of the Army and Navy). Meeting together in Washington, those four men, with the help of their own service staffs, coordinated and directed the whole course of our military operations: the Battle of the Atlantic, the invasion of Africa, Italy, France, and Germany; the vast battle of the Pacific with all its numerous operations — the Coral Sea, Midway, Guam, Saipan, conquest of the Philippines, the Battles of the Philippine Sea and Leyte Gulf that broke the Japanese Fleet — the blockade by air, submarine, and surface ships that strangled Japan— Okinawa, and the final bombing of Japan that shattered the last remnants of Japan's will to resist.

In the Joint Chiefs of Staff each member had an equal voice, and no plan could be made or put into effect without the common consent of all four members. Each man on it was an expert in his own field, and not until his agreement was obtained that a thing could be or should be done was that thing attempted. Frequently proposals were made that did not obtain that unanimous approval—there was not a member who at one time or another did not advocate things that would have been great mistakes. When, as on some few occasions, a dead-lock occurred on a vital matter, the decision was made by the President after hearing the proponents and the opponents. But always decisions were made, and those decisions proved correct.

When once a decision was made, the plan was turned over to be executed by that member whose branch of the service was best fitted to carry it out. If it was primarily an Army job, like the invasion of Europe, it was placed under Army supervision, and the Army commander on the spot, like General Eisenhower, was in complete control not only of the Ground forces but of the Naval forces and the Air forces that were necessary to convoy the troops, crack open the beachhead, land the troops, and then see that they were safeguarded from enemy attack. A similar instance was the invasion of the Philippines where, as it was primarily an Army ground forces job, General MacArthur was in supreme command, and the Navy and Air forces gave their support. Conversely if it was primarily a Naval job, like the operations of Midway, Kwajalein, Guam, Saipan, Iwo Jima, and Okinawa, the Navy's Admiral Nimitz was in overall command, even though the Army and Air Force supported him.

Thus the final victory over the Axis Powers was not that of any one service alone but that of all the services, cooperating and working together as fellow Americans with teamwork for the common good.

INTERNATIONAL LIAISON

ANOTHER function of the Joint Chiefs of Staff was coordinating our war effort with those of the other United Nations—chiefly with Great Britain, but also with Russia, China, Canada, Australia and New Zealand, Holland, the South American Republics, etc. Our Joint Chiefs of Staff worked closely with the military leaders of all those other nations and developed the plans for the combined attack of all the United Nations on the Axis enemy.

The part of the U.S. Navy alone in this war was stupendous. And I wish here to acknowledge our debt not only to the men and women of the United States Navy, Marine Corps, Coast Guard, and their several Women's Reserves, but also to all those innumerable civilians who aided the Navy's war effort.

The day after Pearl Harbor our Navy's position in the Pacific was extremely grave. The bulk of our major ships had been put out of commission for a year; only our small Asiatic Fleet under Admiral Hart in the Philippines and portions of the Pacific Fleet that had been absent from Pearl Harbor on the day of the attack were in fighting condition in the Pacific. Even Hawaii might be attacked and overrun at any moment. And in the Atlantic the Axis submarines were destroying a tremendous tonnage of our shipping within sight of our very shores.

THE DECISION

THEN, even at the lowest of the war tide, the decision was made, and correctly: first fight for time, especially in the Pacific—and then assemble the might to conquer first Italy and Germany, and then inevitably Japan must succumb.

It was a difficult decision. Japan swept through Malaya to Singapore, then overran Burma; she battered at the Philippines; she overran the Dutch East Indies, and threatened Australia and New Zealand and even India itself.

Distressful though it was, it was realized immediately that with our Pacific Fleet shattered, and no western Pacific bases left to operate from, we could give no help either to our Army in the Philippines or our Allies in Singapore—we could not even evacuate them. But our little Asiatic Fleet fell back, sacrificing themselves in innumerable battles against overwhelming enemy forces until only the remnants staggered into Australian ports. But they had gained time. And instead of challenging our enfeebled forces in American waters and attacking Hawaii, Alaska, and Panama, or cutting our supply lines in those waters, the Japanese Navy wasted time in serving as a mere adjunct to the Army in its land conquest.

But our shipyards, our ordnance plants, our scientists were working. Radar was perfected, new sonic devices invented, planes and warships built by the thousands, escort carriers and landing craft constructed, and millions of men recruited and trained in all forms of fighting and war effort. The escort carrier, the destroyer, radar and other electronic devices defeated and then smashed the submarine menace. Our Navy transported and safeguarded the invasion forces to Africa and Europe, and then smashed the enemy beachheads to afford them a landing. Our still small forces in the Pacific turned back the threat to our lifeline to Australia at the Coral Sea battle, and then drove the first entering wedge into the Japanese conquered empire at Guadalcanal. At Midway we hurled back the first real Japanese threat at Hawaii, Alaska, and the West Coast. Our ever growing Navy and Marine Corps, and Naval Flying Forces bombed and then seized the stepping stone islands—Tarawa, Kwajalein, Guam, Saipan. We guarded the landings that reconquered the Philippines, our carrier forces seized control of the air everywhere it was needed, and our Fleet broke the back of the Japanese Navy in the great naval battles of the Philippine Sea and of Leyte Gulf. Our submarines destroyed the majority of the Japanese merchant marine, as well as innumerable Japanese naval combat ships. When we seized Okinawa, we seized a point just off Japan from which we could, and did, destroy the remnants of the Japanese Navy and bomb the Japanese homeland into final submission—a submission that would inevitably have come anyway from the strangling blockade we had thrown around Japan. With a greater army and more planes than she had at the time of Pearl Harbor, Japan surrendered—because with the destruction of her Navy and merchant marine she could not obtain from outside those necessities without which Japan could not even live, much less fight.

Nor is the Navy content to rest on its present laurels. Long a leader in invention and research, our Navy is always studying new weapons, new methods—the atomic bomb and guided missiles, for instance. Whatever new weapons, or defenses against new weapons, science can develop, the U.S. Navy intends to incorporate them into itself, to make sure that the Navy shall always be strong enough to perform its historic function of defense of our own country and of offense against enemy countries.

It is to be hoped that every American will exert his effort and influence to see that that goal is achieved—that the U.S. Navy will always remain, as it is today, the world's greatest sea power.

Ernest J. King

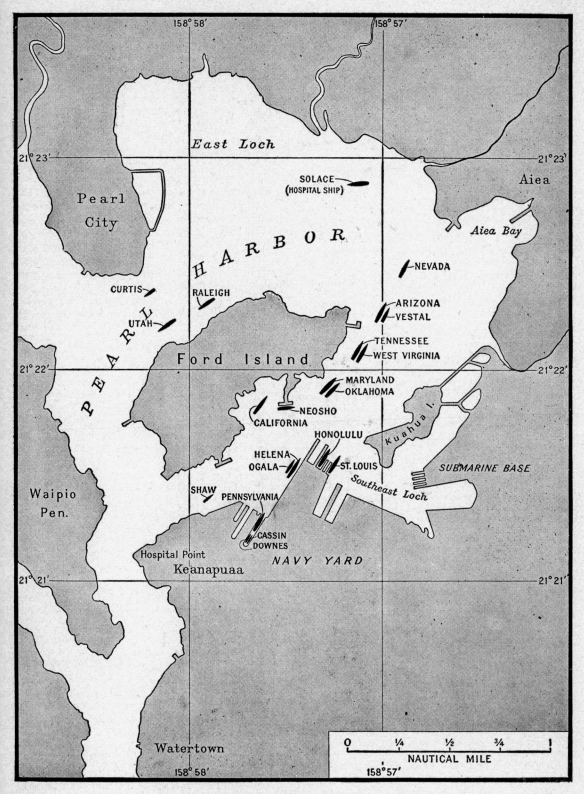

Map showing the disposition of the fleet at Pearl
Harbor on 7 December 1941.

JAPAN ENTERS WAR IN TRUE AXIS FASHION. At dawn on the morning of Sunday, December 7, 1941, a force of approximately 150 Japanese bombers and torpedo-carrying planes launched a surprise attack on Pearl Harbor, the chief U.S. Naval Base in the Pacific. Hits were scored on several naval vessels lying at anchor in the harbor and two battleships, the "Oklahoma" and the "Arizona," were sunk. Other

military objectives on the island, including Hickam Field, U.S.
Army air base, were attacked and considerable damage was
done. The casualties amounted to 4,500; 2,300 of which were
fatal. It was not until later in the day that the formal declaration of war against the U.S. and Great Britain was made.
ABOVE. One of the best combat photographs of all time, this
photo depicts the magazine of the USS "Shaw" exploding.

UNDER ATTACK. The photograph (upper) is one captured from the Japanese. It was taken by a Jap aviator almost directly overhead during the early part of the attack on Pearl Harbor. The white splashes alongside the ships are made by the dropping bombs. Ford Island appears in the lower right hand corner. The three outboard ships from left to right are the "Vestal," the "West Virginia," and the "Oklahoma." Inboard from left to right are the "Nevada," the "Arizona," the "Tennessee," and the "Maryland." LOWER. The "Nevada," sustaining minor damage, gets up steam and pulls away from the other burning ships. The "Nevada" was the only battleship to get under way during the attack.

SUNDAY MORNING. UPPER. Undergoing routine availability in Dry Dock Number One, Navy Yard, Pearl Harbor, the USS "Pennsylvania," 33,100-ton flagship of the Pacific Fleet, rests on keel blocks in company with the 1,500-ton destroyers, USS "Downes" and USS "Cassin" (lying on her side). Preparations were being made to hold mass on the battleship's quarterdeck. Suddenly and with complete surprise, Japanese dive-bombers and torpedo planes came roaring down out of the high overcast. Repeated attempts to torpedo the caisson of the drydock failed. The enemy strafed ships and surrounding dock areas severely. A medium bomb struck the starboard side of the "Pensy's" boatdeck, bursting inside casement nine, and wiping out the crew of the 5"/51. The destroyers took hits and were seriously damaged, the intensity of the fires in the "Downes" exploding her fuel tanks. On deck at least two warheads of her armed torpedoes went off with a mighty roar, capsizing the "Cassin" and showering that section of the harbor with metal fragments. A portion of a torpedo tube weighing nearly a thousand pounds settled on the "Pennsylvania's" forecastle. LOWER. The "West Virginia," moored outboard of the "Tennessee" at Ford Island, bore the brunt of the attack which swept down from Merry's Point. Two bombs and six torpedoes left her main deck awash. The "Tennessee" shot down five attacking Japanese bombers. But she herself received hits in two turrets. The steel decks grew white hot from the oil blazing on the water; and the "Tennessee," restricted in movement, churned the water with her props to keep the flames away.

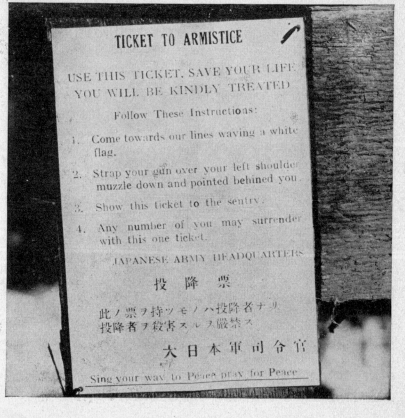

PRELUDE TO DISASTER. UPPER. View of Clark Field, Luzon, shortly before arrival of 9 B-17D's led by Maj. Emmett O'Donnell, pioneering an aerial route from Hawaii, Midway, Wake, Port Moresby, Darwin to Manila. These were followed by 27 more, led by Col. Eugene Eubank, who became head of the Bomber Command under Gen. Brereton. In early December, owing to the critical situation, Maj. O'Donnell based 16 of the Flying Fortresses at Del Monte, Mindanao, the remaining 20 being at Clark Field. The Japanese struck in the Philippines at noon, December 8th, with a heavy force of land and carrier-based airplanes, first at Gen. George's fighter base at Iba Field, then at Nichols Field and Clark Field, destroying all but 72 of the 290 planes based in the Islands. The B-17s at Del Monte were saved, and evacuated to Australia, to fly long range bombing missions against the enemy in the Philippines. During January and February they operated from Java. RIGHT. One of thousands of propaganda leaflets dropped by the Japanese on Bataan, early 1942.

TICKET TO ARMISTICE

USE THIS TICKET. SAVE YOUR LIFE. YOU WILL BE KINDLY TREATED

Follow These Instructions:

1. Come towards our lines waving a white flag.

2. Strap your gun over your left shoulder muzzle down and pointed behined you.

3. Show this ticket to the sentry.

4. Any number of you may surrender with this one ticket.

JAPANESE ARMY HEADQUARTERS

投 降 票

此ノ票ヲ持ツモノハ投降者ナリ
投降者ヲ殺害スルヲ厳禁ス

大 日 本 軍 司 令 官

Sing your way to Peace pray for Peace

DEFENSE OF THE ISLANDS. One of a battery of coastal defense guns on Corregidor, the rocky fortress in Manila Harbor, which aided in staving off the Japanese before surrendering to repeated enemy pounding. American and Filipino forces continued to resist the invaders for months from this island stronghold after Manila was evacuated. The Japanese, however, greatly outnumbered them and they were forced to capitulate, beaten and exhausted, on May 6, 1942.

THE JAPANESE DRIVE FOR MANILA. Almost immediately after Pearl Harbor, the Japanese bombed our bases in the Philippines and by December 10 had landed invasion troops. Our little Asiatic Fleet fought a desperate delaying action until the remnants reached Australia. Our remaining ships and planes hung on, knowing that no possible help could come. Slow patrol planes of Navy Patrol Wing Ten tackled new Japanese fighters; Lieut. Bulkeley's little squadron of PT boats attacked everything from Japanese troop carriers to cruisers. Our submarines fought their way out when nothing was left to fight with. Our remaining naval forces and Marines joined the Army as a naval brigade and fought as land soldiers through the whole campaign to Bataan and Corregidor. ABOVE. This picture, one of the first brought out of the Philippines after the war began, shows barges in the U.S. Navy Yard at Cavite burning fiercely after the Japanese bombing of December 12, 1941. The raid cost many lives.

A HOPELESS FIGHT. Within 24 hours of Pearl Harbor, Guam, two-thirds of the way from Hawaii to the Philippines, was bombed, and the next morning the Japanese poured ashore to overwhelm the small American garrison. RIGHT. This photograph was taken from a Japanese propaganda booklet "Victory on the March" published in December, 1942. The photograph was captioned "The Naval Ensign being hoisted over the former American base." Guam was to remain in Jap hands until July, 1944.

GALLANT DEFENSE. Four hours after Pearl Harbor the Japanese attacked Wake Island. For two weeks the brave defenders fought, shooting down planes, repulsing attacks, and even sinking Japanese destroyers and cruisers. With the final enemy thrust on December 22, the Marines transmitted their last signal: "Urgent!" Enemy on island. The issue is in doubt!" Then silence. ABOVE. The picture shows the Wake airstrip under later attack by our planes. In the foreground lie wrecks of Japanese ships, mementos of the heroic American defense and of the hopelessness of the fight.

JAPANESE SUCCESS IN CHINA. On Christmas Day, after resisting Japanese attacks for seven days, and rejecting three demands for surrender, the British colony of Hong Kong capitulated. The garrison of British, Canadian and Indian troops fought heroically against overwhelming odds under the leadership of Sir Mark Young, the Governor. The decision to surrender was made only after important reservoirs had fallen into enemy hands, leaving only one day's supply of water. ABOVE. A Japanese artillery unit lobs shells on the city.

FIGHTING IN LUZON. The Japanese landed a force of 100,000 men in the Lingayen Gulf area of Luzon after failing in their first attempts to gain control of the Philippines, on December 22, 1941. Landings were also made on Mindanao, second largest of the island group, where fighting took place in Davao. On this day, too, the small garrison of 400 Marines at Wake Island, the U.S. naval base situated in the Marshalls, surrendered after an heroic defense lasting 14 days. The pictures (above) show the crumbled ruins of buildings and streets in San Pablo, near Manila, after a Christmas Day bombing.

LUZON ADVANCE. Overwhelmed by superior numbers, American and Filipino forces were compelled to evacuate Cavite and the Philippine capital, and to fall back to shorter lines as tanks and dive bombers scattered their ranks. The island fortress of Corregidor continued resistance. UPPER. Japanese tank units enter the capital at 3 P.M. on December 31, where they found the evacuees had destroyed all military stores. LOWER. The Intramuros section of Manila ablaze.

FIGHTING BEGINS IN BURMA. Japanese and Thai (Siamese) troops crossed the frontier into Burma on January 20, 1942, and fighting raged north of Myawaddi, 60 miles east of Moulmein. Faced with numerically superior forces, the British were obliged to fall back to Moulmein. The enemy employed powerful air units to support this offensive, but the R.A.F. and

American Volunteer Group (commanded by General Claire Chennault) inflicted heavy losses. ABOVE. A single file of Japanese infantry crosses a temporary bridge somewhere in Burma. The main structure had previously been destroyed by the retiring British. Subsequent to this action, the Japanese continued on unchecked to capture Moulmein and Rangoon.

END OF AN HEROIC DEFENSE. The Army's stubborn defense of Bataan, conducted with heart-warming gallantry by military personnel, as well as civilians, occupied considerable numbers of the enemy for several months. Unfortunately it could not prevent the Japanese from establishing bases in the Philippines for future use. Maj. Gen. Edward King's 78,000 troops were down to ⅓ rations as the enemy began a final push on April 3, that resulted in the surrender of the starving remnants on April 9. Thus the U.S. and Filipino forces on the Bataan Peninsula of Luzon were overcome by the Japanese, bringing to an end the epic resistance of four months. Then began the Death March out of Bataan, during which prisoners, without food or water, were forced to march 85 miles to the Japanese prison camp. Some Americans, including 3,500

Marines, succeeded in escaping to Corregidor. Continual pounding of that Island fortress by Japanese big guns neutralized it, and the Japs began their landings on the night of May 5. Two days later, General Jonathan Wainwright surrendered Corregidor's 10,000 troops. Capitulation came only after complete physical exhaustion. UPPER LEFT. Japanese forces on Bataan passing blazing oil dumps set afire by the defenders before surrendering. LOWER LEFT. Two Jap soldiers, killed in combat, lie where they fell. UPPER RIGHT. A group of freshly-captured Japanese prisoners of war, stripped of their uniforms, are kept in line by American and Filipino soldiers on the way to a compound. LOWER RIGHT. The thoroughness of Jap artillery is clearly manifested in the destruction of this Bataan village. Nothing remains.

PACIFIC THEATRE OF WAR. An outline of the progress of the War in the Pacific from the outbreak of hostilities to the Japanese occupation of the Andaman Islands on March 23, 1942, is depicted above. During this period, Malaya was overrun, and Borneo, Java, Sumatra, and Celebes had been

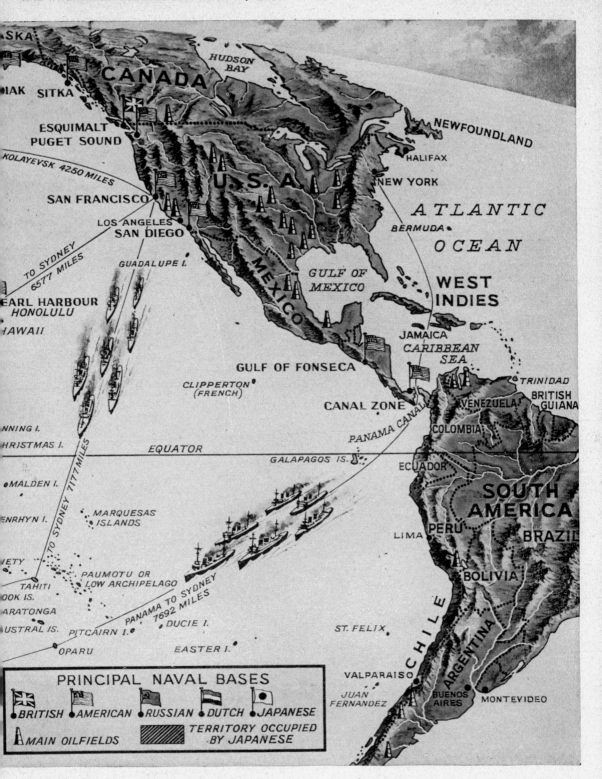

PRINCIPAL NAVAL BASES

● BRITISH   ● AMERICAN   ● RUSSIAN   ● DUTCH   ● JAPANESE

⚑ MAIN OILFIELDS   TERRITORY OCCUPIED
                              BY JAPANESE

occupied. Fighting was currently in progress in New Guinea where Japanese landings had taken place following enemy occupation of the adjacent islands of New Britain and New Ireland. In Burma, British forces were retreating towards Mandalay. Japan's entry cut the supply route to Russia.

TAKE-OFF FOR TOKIO. In April, 1942, the United States and the world at large was electrified by an announcement by President Roosevelt that American fliers had carried the Battle of the Pacific to the heart of the Japanese empire with a surprising and daring raid on military targets at Tokio, Yokohama, Osaka, Kobe and other industrial centers of the Rising Sun. The attack was made by 16 B-25 Mitchell medium bombers and led by Lt. Col. James H. (Jimmy) Doolittle. Eighty officers and men of the AAF volunteered for the dangerous mission, making up the flight crews. They took off from the deck of a sea-buffeted 27,000-ton aircraft carrier, USS "Hornet." A Naval flight officer had trained the pilots to simulate carrier take-offs during which heavily loaded B-25s were flown off strips bounded by white lines marking off equivalent distances. ABOVE. Lt. Col. (later Lt. Gen.) Doolittle wires a Japanese medal to

the fin of a 500-pound bomb, soon to be returned to its Nipponese makers in a blast of destruction. UPPER RIGHT. "Off we go"—the Air Corps song was never more appropriate than here as a B-25 soars off the flight deck of the "Hornet" on its way to Tokio and other industrial cities to give the Japanese their first taste of bombs dropping on their own soil. Main strategic effect of the raid was not the very real but limited damage inflicted, but the psychological effect of driving home to the Japanese high command and people generally their vulnerability from the air. Hundreds of planes were withdrawn from the Asiatic and South Pacific fronts for "inner Empire" defense. LOWER RIGHT. Decoration of Tokio pilots by Madame Chiang Kai-shek at Chungking, China, in June, 1942. Three years later, Gen. Doolittle was on Okinawa with a force of B-29s bombing Japan again.

THEY WERE EXPENDABLE. Bataan had fallen on the 9th of April, and the epic resistance which had lasted for four months ended. Those of the American-Filipino forces who had not been killed or captured escaped to the island of Corregidor, where they continued to hold out. It was another great stand. The Japanese batteries on the mainland subjected Corregidor to intense artillery fire at point-blank range. This, together with heavy aerial bombardment, inflicted heavy casualties on the defenders and destroyed many of the island's military installations. Then came the 5th of May. After a particularly severe bombardment which swept away the beach defenses, Japanese troops crossed the narrow channel that separates Corregidor from the mainland and assaulted the island. Although outnumbered six to one, the defending forces succeeded in inflicting 60,000 casualties on the enemy. It was only after the defenders were physically exhausted by days and nights of continuous fighting that they finally gave up (above).

RETIRING BEFORE THE JAPANESE. One of the greatest feats achieved by an American soldier was General Joseph Stillwell's 140-mile march from Burma, which began May 1, and terminated in Imphal, Assam, on May 20. From the time the heroic band left Wunthe until they reached the Chinwin River, they were out of communication with the world. In the spring of 1942 the Allies took what the General called a "hell of a beating" in Burma, which they lost to the Japanese. Stillwell, who was chief of staff to Generalissimo Chiang Kai-shek, prophesied Burma could and would be retaken from the Japanese.

JAP CARRIERS HIT. While Japanese planes were attacking the American carriers "Lexington" and "Yorktown" during the Battle of the Coral Sea, May 8, U.S. Navy planes from these ships were scoring hits on the home carriers of the enemy fliers. The task forces were about 170 miles apart at the time. The two Jap carriers, "Ryukaku" and "Shokako," had as escorts a battleship or very large cruiser, three heavy cruisers, and four destroyers. Our planes made repeated hits with both bombs and torpedoes, but subsequent developments showed that neither carrier had gone down. The "Shokako," however, was seriously damaged and might have been sunk if it had not been lost in the heavy overcast. No part of the Battle for the Coral Sea was as dramatic as the fight put up by the 33,000-ton U.S. Aircraft Carrier "Lexington," first against attacking Japanese planes, and then against terrific internal explosions which several times were brought under control and then broke out again. UPPER. The "Shoho" takes a torpedo hit from a U.S. Navy plane. In the action of May 7 this Japanese carrier was at first mistaken for the "Ryukaku." Bomber and torpedo planes from both the "Lexington" and the "Yorktown" scored many times on the "Shoho," approaching the ship closely through the smoke resulting from the first attack. Within a few minutes the enemy carrier slid under the surface. LOWER. Twisting and turning in a giant "S" maneuver, the Japanese carrier "Shokako" attempts to avoid torpedoes dropped by U.S. Navy planes. Spray from the near-misses of Navy bombs showers her flight deck.

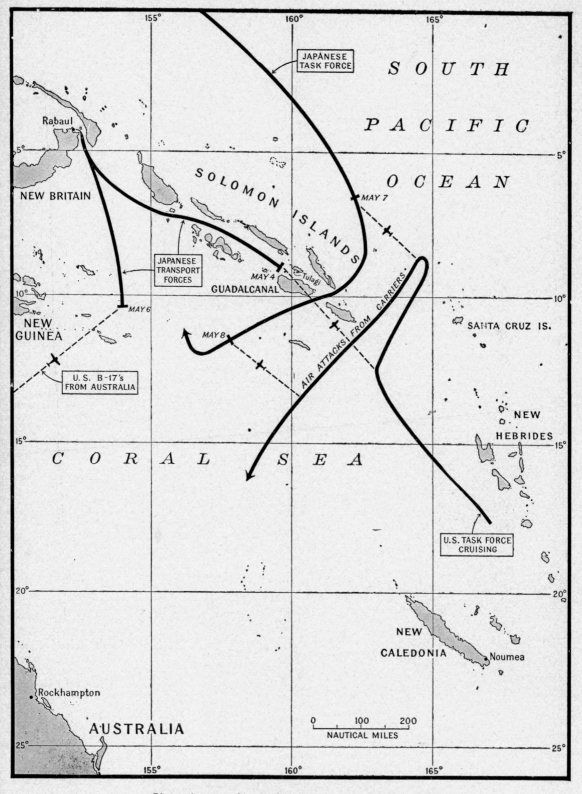

Chart showing the tracks of Japanese and American
forces in the Battle of the Coral Sea.

BATTLE OF THE CORAL SEA. One of the most significant sea battles in naval history was fought May 8, 1942. While U.S. aircraft were still in action against the Japanese Fleet in the Coral Sea the enemy launched a counter-attack and scored several hits with bombs and torpedoes on the 33,000-ton U.S. Aircraft Carrier "Lexington." Several hours after the battle, while steaming at 20 knots, the "Lexington" was rocked by a terrific internal explosion, probably caused by the ignition of gasoline vapors from leaks in the gasoline lines. As the flames grew the captain ordered the crew to aban-

don ship. Ninety-two per cent of the ship's company were rescued and reached port safely. The last man to leave the ship was her commanding officer, Captain Sherman. As he slid down a line into the water, a torpedo in the warhead locker exploded, and the "Fighting Lady" sank soon afterwards. The attack of the U.S. Fleet in the Coral Sea cost the enemy the aircraft carrier "Shoho," three heavy cruisers, one light cruiser, two destroyers, several transports, and damage to a second carrier. U.S. losses included the "Lexington," the destroyer "Sims" and the 25,000-ton tanker "Neosho."

HOT SPOT OF BATTLE. Tiny Midway knew what it was to be the center of a battlefield those June days in 1942 when fierce fighting raged over it and around it for hundreds of miles. From its runways American planes took off to hurl themselves through Japanese flak and fighter screens to get at the ships beyond. And down at the runways and oil tanks and other installations Japanese planes came diving from above with bombs and incendiaries in return. UPPER. A general view of the damage done on Midway Island by the Japanese air attack. LOWER. A view of the oil storage tanks hit and burning after the Japanese attack on the island. The gooney birds in the foreground seem undisturbed.

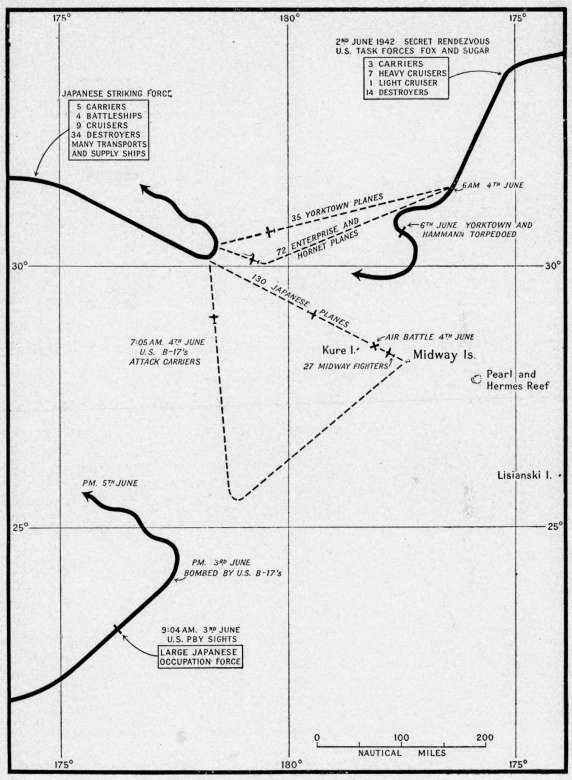

2ND JUNE 1942 SECRET RENDEZVOUS
U.S. TASK FORCES FOX AND SUGAR

3	CARRIERS
7	HEAVY CRUISERS
1	LIGHT CRUISER
14	DESTROYERS

JAPANESE STRIKING FORCE

5	CARRIERS
4	BATTLESHIPS
9	CRUISERS
34	DESTROYERS
	MANY TRANSPORTS
	AND SUPPLY SHIPS

6 AM 4TH JUNE

35 YORKTOWN PLANES

6TH JUNE YORKTOWN AND
HAMMANN TORPEDOED

72 ENTERPRISE AND
HORNET PLANES

130 JAPANESE PLANES

AIR BATTLE 4TH JUNE

Kure I.

Midway Is.

27 MIDWAY FIGHTERS

7:05 AM. 4TH JUNE
U.S. B-17's
ATTACK CARRIERS

Pearl and
Hermes Reef

Lisianski I.

PM. 5TH JUNE

PM. 3RD JUNE
BOMBED BY U.S. B-17's

9:04 AM. 3RD JUNE
U.S. PBY SIGHTS

LARGE JAPANESE
OCCUPATION FORCE

0   100   200
NAUTICAL   MILES

Chart showing the tracks of the Japanese and
American forces in the Battle of Midway.

AIRCRAFT CARRIER "YORKTOWN" SINKS. Two large Japanese fleets approached Midway Island, U.S. naval and air base in the Pacific, on June 3, 1942. As soon as enemy contact was reported a strong force of U.S. Army bombers set out to locate the Japanese fleet, and in the attack that followed direct hits were scored on eight enemy ships. Meanwhile, a force of about 180 Japanese carrier-borne planes raided the airfields, docks, and harbor installations on the island, but succeeded in causing only minor damage. The strength of the U.S. attack forced the enemy to withdraw with tremendous losses, their greatest since the war began. This amounted to four aircraft carriers sunk, two battleships damaged, two heavy cruisers sunk and three damaged, one light cruiser damaged, and three destroyers sunk. The U.S. lost one aircraft carrier, the "Yorktown" (above), and the destroyer "Hammon." Military strategists later interpreted the attack as a preliminary thrust, the ultimate objective of which was the Hawaiian islands with the complete neutralization of the U.S. base at Pearl Harbor. This defeat of the Japanese fleet was the stroke that equalized the strength of the American and Japanese navies, and permitted the former to drop the defensive role maintained since Pearl Harbor. At Midway there was no exchange of fire between the big guns of the opposing fleets.

DUTCH HARBOR BOMBED. On the morning of June 3, 1942, Japanese planes raided the U.S. naval and air base at Dutch Harbor, Unalaska, in the Aleutians. High explosives and incendiary bombs were dropped, but damage was slight. A few barracks and warehouses at Ft. Mears and Dutch Harbor were bombed and set afire, and a Navy patrol plane, which was about to take off with mail, was strafed. In the picture (above), bombs from Jap planes drop harmlessly into the bay. The ship in the background staved off the enemy attack with machine-gun fire. In the harbor at the time of the attack were three U.S. destroyers, an Army transport, a mine-sweeper, and a Coast Guard cutter. The "Northwestern," which had been beached for use as a barracks, was also subjected to the Jap attack.

THE WAR IN THE SOLOMONS

By Lieutenant General Oscar W. Griswold

ON that Sunday the Japanese struck from the air at Pearl Harbor the average American had probably never even heard of such places as Guadalcanal, Lunga Point, Rabaul, Munda and Bougainville. But they were destined to learn about them—and many of our men were destined to die there—for they marked the first miles on that long, hard, and bloody road back to the Philippines.

Immediately after Pearl Harbor the indefatigable Japs busied themselves with continuous aggression. They took Wake and Guam, captured Rabaul on New Britain, advanced in New Guinea and the Solomons, and fortified numerous other islands and areas.

At the same time, we too—as far as meager preparation would permit—rushed our forces overseas to reinforce such garrisons as we and our Allies still held. We sent troops to the Fiji Islands, Australia, New Caledonia, Samoa, the Society Islands and other points. Bases were established on Efate and Esperitu Santos.

While this was going on an organization of Allied forces in the Pacific was developed. It was divided into three major independent area commands: the Pacific Ocean Area under Admiral Chester W. Nimitz, the Southwest Pacific Area under General Douglas MacArthur, and the South Pacific area under Admiral William F. Halsey, who reported directly to Admiral Nimitz. A new Army headquarters — U.S. Army Forces in the South Pacific Area — was established under Major General Millard F. Harmon.

After the Japanese suffered Naval defeats in the Coral Sea and Midway, the change in the balance of sea power, together with the threat posed by the Japanese infiltration down the Solomon Islands, prompted our Joint Chiefs of Staff to speed plans for assuming the initiative. Accordingly, on 2 July 1942, they ordered the Southwest and South Pacific Areas to mount an offensive through the Solomons and New Guinea and recapture Rabaul. The opening phase of the campaign was to be the capture of the island of Guadalcanal and Tulagi in the Solomons.

This invasion was launched by the 1st Marine Division on 7 August, and there ensued for several months some of the bitterest and bloodiest fighting of the war. American forces were not able to prevent the Japs from pouring new troops onto the island, and our men were confined to a small perimeter around Henderson Field. By October, the situation had become increasingly critical, and the 164th Infantry Regiment of the American Division was dispatched to the area, and played a major role in repelling enemy assaults.

By December the 1st Marine Division was exhausted and evacuated from the island. Command then passed to Major General Alexander M. Patch, commander of the Americal Division and later of the XIV Corps. General Patch's command contained the Americal Division, the 25th Division, the 147th Infantry Combat Team, the 2nd Marine Division and several artillery battalions. With this force, about 25,000 troops of the Japanese 17th Army were routed by 9 February 1943, and Guadalcanal was completely in our hands.

Meanwhile, we were busy with plans to take the next step on the long road to the Philippines — the capture of Munda in the Solomons —as a preliminary to the assault of Bougainville and Rabaul. All these operations were under the overall command of Admiral William F. Halsey.

On 21 February elements of the 43rd Division seized the Russell Islands, where construction of airfields and a Naval base was begun immediately.

In June this same Division, reinforced, under the Tactical Command of Admiral Turner, landed on Rendova Island, and at Wickam's Anchorage, Segi, and Viru of the New Georgia Group. Later the 43rd effected a shore-to-shore assault from Rendova against the coast of New Georgia just south of Munda airfield. Swinging north and west on the heavily jungled terrain, the Division met fierce resistance, and it was necessary to commit major elements of the 25th and 37th Infantry Divisions to the battle. I had replaced General Patch as commander of the XIV Corps, and on orders from General Harmon I assumed command of the land operation on 15 July. Munda fell on August 6, and the mopping up of New Georgia proper was completed by the 14th. A detached force consisting of a Marine Raider Regiment — less one battalion — reinforced by a battalion from the 37th Division, had been landed by Admiral Turner at Rice's Anchorage on the north coast of New Georgia, across the island from Munda. This force fought magnificently, but was unable to defeat decisively the enemy in its front. They were relieved by elements of the 25th Division, which cut through difficult terrain in its mopping up.

Remaining islands in the New Georgia Group were seized in the next six weeks; Baanga and Arundel were captured by the 43rd Division after savage and sustained fighting; Vella Lavella was taken by units of the 25th Division and the 3rd New Zealand Division. By-passed Kolombangara was evacuated by the Japs and was occupied in early October by our troops without opposition.

Next step on the road that led to the Philippines and Nippon was reduction and seizure of the enemy bases on Bougainville and its outlying islands. These bases were strongly held, but we had to have them to put fighter planes in range of Rabaul, which the Joint Chiefs of Staff had decided to neutralize rather than capture.

With General MacArthur's concurrence, Admiral Halsey decided to by-pass heavily-defended southern Bougainville and the Shortlands, in favor of a landing at Cape Torokina at Empress Augusta Bay on the west coast of Bougainville. All the Bougainville airfields lay within 65 miles of the cape and Rabaul was but 215 miles distant.

As a preliminary to the main effort, veteran New Zealand troops captured the Treasuries on 27 October, while a Marine parachute battalion staged a diversionary raid on Choiseul Island. Elements of the 93rd Infantry Division soon replaced the Marines on the Treasuries.

On 1 November the reinforced 3rd Marine Division of the I Marine Amphibious Corps landed at Cape Torokina, quickly established a beachhead, and seized its major objectives. Construction of bomber and fighter fields was begun at once. The 37th Infantry Division, in corps reserve, began moving ashore on 8 November. Strong defenses were set up. The 37th Division expanded and held the left side of the line, the 3rd Marine Division the right. On 15 December the XIV Corps, under my command, relieved the I Marine Amphibious Corps on Bougainville, and in December and January the Americal Division replaced the 3rd Marine Division.

In order to secure a fighter-plane base to support a projected invasion of the Japanese base at Kavieng, New Ireland, north of Rabaul, forces of the South Pacific, including New Zealand units, landed on Green (Nissan) Island on 15 February 1944. By March a fighter strip was in operation.

In March the plan to seize Kavieng was cancelled by the Joint Chiefs of Staff, who had decided to neutralize both Kavieng and Rabaul with minimum forces. Admiral Halsey, who had prepared plans to take Kavieng, sent his forces instead against the St. Matthias Group northwest of New Ireland. On 20 March, Marines landed unopposed on Emirau of the St. Matthias Group. These troops were first relieved by the 147th Infantry and later by elements of the 93rd Infantry Division. The seizure of Torokina, Green, and Emirau, coupled with simultaneous operations by forces of the Southwest Pacific on New Britain and in the Admiralties, sealed off Rabaul and Kavieng.

The construction of airfields at Treasury, Cape Torokina, Green, Emirau and the Admiralties had made possible an increase in the tempo of the air offensive against Rabaul. Land-based planes of both the South and Southwest Pacific Areas, in conjunction with Admiral Halsey's carrier task forces, pounded the objective relentlessly. By February 1944, Rabaul, as an air and naval base, was impotent. Its well-trained, well-equipped garrison—of Japan's 60,000 troops of 8th Area Army—was isolated, unable to take any further effective part in the war.

The Japanese on Bougainville had been unable to offer any effective resistance to the Allied landing or airfield construction at Cape Torokina. Although isolated from Rabaul and from their homeland, they determined to challenge the American grip on the small beachhead. Laboriously hauling weapons, ammunition, and supplies through the mountainous, jungled interior, they assembled about 15,000 men for a counter-offensive. By 8 March 1944 they were ready to attack.

The Japanese 6th Division, reinforced, operating under the 17th Army, struck violently against the XIV Corps' perimeter. The attack was carefully planned and savagely executed, but it was suicidal. The well-trained, disciplined troops of the Americal and 37th Divisions held firmly, though at times losing small portions of territory which were promptly regained by counter-attacks. The enemy did some damage with his artillery, but failed to interrupt Allied air operations. The Japanese infantrymen, attacking repeatedly against prepared postions, were slain in great numbers. We counted more than 8,000 dead before they pulled back broken and cut to pieces at the end of March.

The March counter-offensive had marked the end of major ground operations by American troops in the South Pacific Area. Their mission—a share in the neutralization of Rabaul to preserve the life-line to Australia—had been magnificently accomplished. Fighting in steaming, tropical jungles against a relentless, savage foe, they demonstrated a superiority over the enemy and a resistance to hardship that will always redound to the credit of American arms.

We had learned a great deal in these campaigns. We had come to grips with the enemy— if not on his own ground, at least on ground which he had greedily and capably entrenched himself. We drove him out. We conquered him on the first lap of the journey, and we knew then that we could conquer him or by-pass him all the way on the long road back.

Oscar W. Griswold

THE INFANTRY DOGGEDLY MARCHES ON. A group of
weary but resolute GI's start down a New Guinea road to
initiate a flanking movement against the Japanese. Both
American and Australian troops repeatedly proved their

mettle over mud-covered, jungle terrain in their operations
against the aggressors. Their campaign to push the Japanese
back to the sea met with success despite such hardships as
malaria, unfamiliar terrain, torrential rain, oppressive heat.

LANDING OPERATION. A true Marine Corps landing operation is executed on the tip of Guadalcanal as these soldiers of the sea come ashore from their landing craft during the preliminary fight to establish a beachhead on this South Pacific outpost. These Marines formed part of the famed Raider battalions which were used with great success in landing operations in the South Pacific campaigns. An expeditionary force comprising the U.S. First Marine Division, reinforced with elements of the Americal Division, plus a protective convoy, arrived off the Solomon Islands on August 6, and at dawn on August 7, split into two forces. One proceeded to the vicinity of Tulagi and the second to Guadalcanal. The approaches to the areas of operation were fortunately under cover of an overcast sky that made enemy aerial reconnaissance difficult. On the night of August 6-7 the weather cleared, but the expeditionary forces along with their supporting craft proceeded to their assigned positions undetected, and the Japanese were taken by surprise. By nightfall of August 9, unloading operations had been completed and cargo ships left the area. By noon of August 10, they were fully involved and had consolidated their positions on the islands of Guadalcanal, Tulagi, Gavutu, Tanambogo, and portions of Florida Island.

ASHORE TO STAY. Back in Washington, Commandant Holcomb told fellow Americans that the Guadalcanal amphibious landing was "a difficult and hazardous affair." It was that. After a steak, eggs and potato meal at 2 A.M. on the 7th, general quarters sounded at 5:25 aboard the transports and supporting fighting units of the large Naval task force which served as escort and beach softener. While Marines stood by to lower boats, hell broke loose on the large island as planes and ships poured death ashore. At Tulagi, Marines went ashore at 8 A.M. The landing boats circled and moved on Guadalcanal to land Col. Leroy P. Hunt's Combat Group A, and later Col. Clifton B. Cates' Combat Group B. Scattered rifle shots told of movement inland as the troops fanned out through the high grass, looking for Japs who had taken to the hills. More troops poured ashore and by four o'clock that afternoon Division Headquarters was set up in a palm grove near the east branch of the Ilu River. RIGHT. Marines rest momentarily en route to the front. LOWER. Others push forward on patrol missions as the tropical sun casts shadows during the late afternoon.

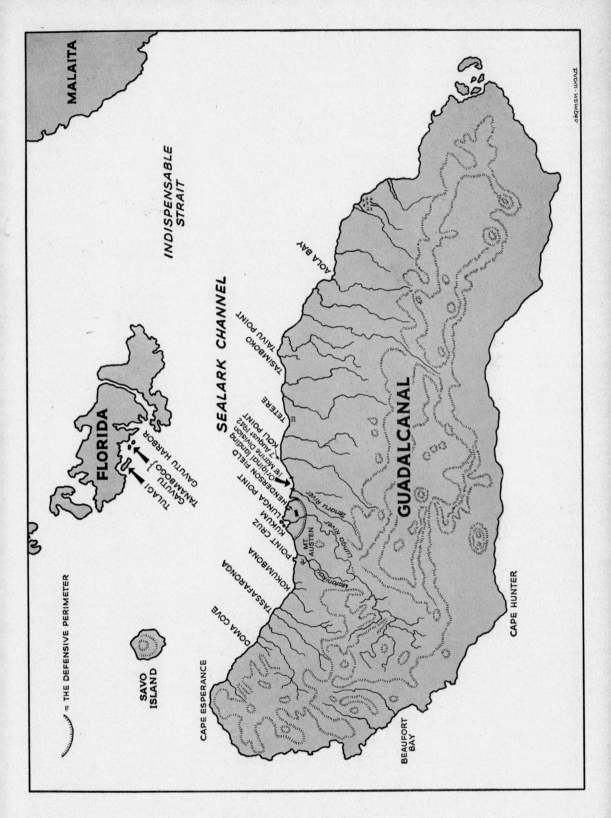

First offensive action of World War II

HERE TO STAY. UPPER. Marine tanks patrol the beach at Guadalcanal. LOWER. Marines move toward the rear area with a wounded buddy. The hundreds of Jap defenders on Tulagi, Gavutu and Tanambogo died rather than surrender, although some prisoners were taken who were wounded. Radios were used by the Japs to maintain contact with their companions, holed up in caves which served as their final tombs in many cases. One Jap kept firing for three days after his companions had died and his food and water played out. As many as 40 Japs defended each cave; when one was killed at a machine gun or automatic weapon another would move up. Long after organized resistance had ceased, snipers caused trouble from trees, caves or hidden holes in the ground. This operation set the pattern of resistance and Marines learned much throughout the Solomons which was the proving ground for our doctrines of jungle warfare, and served as the laboratory for testing not only our supplies and weapons but also our stamina. For a while the Marines were long an stamina and short on supplies. Tanks had to be used on Tanambogo, one of which the Japs knocked out with a gasoline bomb, killing most of the crew. A scene that was to take place repeatedly all over the Pacific for the next three years took place late the first day when Marines raised the Stars and Stripes from a Gavutu hilltop while a bugler blew colors and Marines paused long enough to watch a scene with which they were to become all too familiar. During the first week of hostilities, the enemy occupied himself with harassing actions: snipers at night, bombers at noon, and subs shelling occasionally. Jap troops comprised labor units and veterans who had seen action in the Philippine and Singapore campaigns.

A MESSAGE FOR THE JAPANESE. ABOVE. An 80 mm
mortar crew in action during the fighting on Guadalcanal.
Of the 19,000 troops employed in the assault on the island,
the First Marines suffered approximately 1,200 casualties,
while the American Division lost a total of 550 men,

NO PARADE GROUND. Combat correspondent Jim Hurlbut wrote of the early "mopping up" phase: "This is no parade ground bunch of Marines. The pretty blue uniforms are all back home and the green dungaree field uniforms are torn and dirty. The boys are rough, tough and nasty and they are plenty mad." UPPER LEFT. A Marine patrol takes a break at a captured communications command post. LOWER LEFT. Later, at the dedication of the cemetery, the last rites are said by chaplains in a ceremony that was also due for sad repetition. UPPER RIGHT. Capt. S. F. "Pappy" Moran, so-called because he was old enough to be father to most of the Marines on the island, escorts a dejected Jap flier to the prison compound. "Pappy" was an ace interpreter and talked to the Japs like a "Dutch Uncle." LOWER RIGHT. Asleep in death, these Japanese troops were victims of a futile attack on strongly held positions along the Tenaru River. The Japanese lost almost a whole battalion when they streamed across this sandy spit on the night of Aug. 20th, and ran into machine gun fire and strands of barbed wire. Their annihilation was completed the next day by the Marines.

GUADALCANAL'S AIRFIELD. ABOVE. Henderson Field was named after one of the heroes of the Battle of Midway, Major Lofton R. Henderson, a Marine squadron commander who died at Midway. The Japanese had been rushing construction on the airfield at Guadalcanal at the time the Marines landed, and had already graded and surfaced almost all of the 3,778-foot landing strip which was about 160 feet wide. The Marines completed the job and eventually added a fighter strip. In the early stages the runways were hazardous from rain and enemy bombing.

LIFE IN THE FIELD. LEFT. Palm fronds and coconut logs serve as good camouflage for this Marine crew of a 50 caliber machine gun guarding one of the possible avenues of Japanese approach. LOWER. A mortar crew is setting up shop in a defiladed position on the reverse slope of a Guadalcanal gulch. First order of business was the mortars, already dug in. Next came the shelter halves which would serve as partial protection against the sun and rain. Once in place, the mortars were on call for fire missions beyond the front lines at any point suspected of harboring Japs. Planes, artillery, mortars, machine guns and rifles all were used to help repel the first serious Jap thrust at the airfield in mid-September. The Raiders under Col. Merritt A. Edson, to whom had been attached the remainder of the Parachute Battalion, met the brunt of the attack in positions which had been given them as "rest areas." For 18 hours the Japs attacked, some even reaching the Division Command Post area. "Red Mike" Edson was up and down his ridge, adjusting his lines and taking personal charge in an action which won him the Congressional Medal of Honor. More than 600 Japs were killed in the Ridge area.

FOREVER ALERT. Constant vigilance, day and night, was a necessary Marine habit on Guadalcanal. Although the wily Jap specialized in surprise attacks at night, the dense tropical jungle of this island offered excellent concealment for daylight sniping. Moreover, the tactics of the enemy called for continual harassment of the invading forces. Hence, night-long activity to keep the Marines awake. Here as battle-weary, mud-caked Americans take a dip in a turgid stream, they never cease to be aware of the possibility of a sudden enemy attack. The machine gunner on guard not only watches the shoreline, but he scans the water too, in case a Jap might try to place a demolition charge under the foot bridge. The guard is ready to nail the first Jap who shows his head. The Guadalcanal operation stopped the Japanese advance in the direction of Australia and New Zealand, and saved the situation in the South Pacific.

COMMUNICATIONS ON GUADALCANAL. UPPER. Stretching into the distance, this million dollar telephone line goes up on Guadalcanal. The poles, made of mahogany, were estimated at $180 each and carried the communications network through jungles and across plains and rivers. The "cat" tractor helps speed up the detail by hauling the wire. LEFT. In a communications tent, these Marines cheerfully carry out hazardous missions under a sign which clearly indicates their capacity. A bearded tech. sergeant is recording a message coming in over the field telephone. These Marines of the Second Division were reinforced with an additional regiment on Guadalcanal early in November, 1942, when the 8th Marines landed, accompanied by artillery units and the Army's Americal Division. As more troops arrived on Guadalcanal and the American defense area was pushed forward through patrol action and the occupation of additional ground, communications became increasingly vital. Frequently the Japs would cut communication lines or plug in on Marine circuits, giving false commands in perfect English and hampering operations.

THE SAVAGERY OF WAR. Bodies of Japanese who succeeded in crossing the mouth of the Tenaru River, Guadalcanal, during attempts to dislodge U.S. Marines from the
island, are strewn along the sand the day after the battle.
Losses on both sides were heavy. LOWER. Believing surrender dishonorable, many Japanese preferred 'hara-kiri,'' or
suicide. Here, two Japs had placed the muzzles of their
rifles against their foreheads and released the triggers with
their toes. As the South Pacific campaigns progressed, more
and more of the Emperor's warriors decided to forego "hara-
kiri" and readily allowed themselves to be taken prisoner.

REFLECTIVE POW'S. In contrast to the treatment accorded
Americans and British seized in the engagements in the
Pacific, this group of Japanese prisoners receive fair treatment. ABOVE. They are marched off to an enclosure in a
POW camp on Guadalcanal to be treated with honors
compliant with those decided on at the Geneva Convention. Allied prisoners who were fortunate enough to escape
from the Japs said that no such care was tendered them,

MARINES IN MOTOR VEHICLES. Jeeps and armored cars loaded with Marines, course their way through freshly-made roads in the jungles situated near the Guadalcanal front.

RAID AT MAKIN. The surprise Raider landing from submarines on Butaritari island, Makin atoll, was led by Lt. Col. Evans F. Carlson. Everything possible went wrong. Yet the operation succeeded because plans were changed and adaptations made. The Marines went ashore from the Nautilus and Argonaut in rubber boats at dawn on August 17, 1942, and were met by enemy troops who engaged them in a fire fight. The President's son, Maj. James Roosevelt, was Executive Officer under Col. Carlson. It was a weird battle. The subs set afire two Jap transports full of the enemy. Jap planes bombed and strafed for an hour and failed to hit a Marine. Getting back to the subs through the rough swells cost 7 lives for a total of 30 dead. UPPER. Col. Carlson, exponent of "Gung Ho" (work together), poses with his men. LEFT. Here, Col. Carlson, holding a Jap flag, talks to officers upon his return. Later hit while aiding a wounded Marine on Saipan, Col. Carlson was retired as a Brigadier. He died shortly after the war ended.

ROTTING JAP SHIPS. Naval and air attacks on enemy ships attempting to reinforce their Guadalcanal troops made the area a graveyard for Jap shipping. UPPER LEFT. Some American ships were also lost in fierce fighting. This Navy PT boat was beached behind Jap lines after a fight with Jap destroyers. The next day our own ships demolished it to deny its use to the enemy. LOWER LEFT. During the naval Battle of Guadalcanal in November, 1942, this Jap troop ship, the "Kinugawa Mauru," was beached by the Japs after being hit, and was then pounded by our ships. UPPER RIGHT. Her landing boats strewn along the beach, this enemy transport lies broken and gutted by fire following the November 13-15 battle off Savo Island. LOWER RIGHT. Scuttled by her own crew, this two-man Jap submarine was raised from 20 feet of water by the Seabees and rusts away near the rotting hulk of the "Yamazuki Mauru," a transport. In the three-day Battle of Guadalcanal the Japanese forces suffered major blows. They lost 2 battleships, 6 heavy cruisers, 2 light cruisers, 6 destroyers, and 12 transports sunk; plus 2 battleships, 1 cruiser and 7 destroyers damaged. American forces lost 2 light cruisers and 7 destroyers. Hopelessly outnumbered, we had struck a paralyzing blow to the Jap fleet coming in for the kill. In this brilliant naval action, Admiral Callaghan had run his small force under cover of darkness between parallel columns of the Japanese ships, firing to port and starboard while going full steam ahead. Two days later, two Jap divisions were lost as their transports were bombed, shelled and sunk. The naval Battle of Guadalcanal meant the beachhead was finally secured.

PROGRESS, WEATHER AND U.S.O. UPPER LEFT. A line of jeeps moves through the inescapable mud to the front lines of Guadalcanal. The last jeep is laying a temporary telephone line. CENTER LEFT. Landing craft are beached and battered on a Guadalcanal waterfront during a tropical hurricane. The numbers on the trees are guides to boat crews unloading supplies. LOWER LEFT. During the storm the roads leading to this bridge were washed out, but the bridge stood solid across the Tenaru River. UPPER RIGHT. Gen. Francis Mulcahy, Marine Wing Commander, greets Joe E. Brown as the actor puts on a show for the Marines. LOWER RIGHT. Actor Ray Bolger performs a solo jitterbug dance for the troops as part of a U.S.O. show. With him was Little Jack Little. The two entertainers acted as their own stage hands and put on a two hour entertainment for the men. By this time things were going much better. More planes were operating off Henderson Field; Joe Foss ran his plane total to 26 Nips in Jan. 1943, and our warships began the softening-up of New Georgia. On Feb. 9, 1943, the conquest of Guadalcanal was officially announced. In bringing the operation to a successful end, Marine, Navy and Army air units brilliantly backstopped the Marine and Army infantry and the fighting ships of the Navy. Planes operated against Munda, the Bougainville area and the other Jap-held islands from vital Henderson, now enlarged. The final offensive began on Jan. 15th. Upon its completion some 6,000 Japs had been killed and more than 100 prisoners captured. The Marines' total casualties numbered 1,242 dead and 2,655 wounded in the operation that lasted six months.

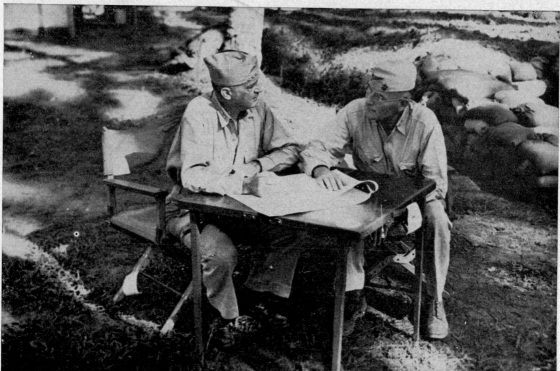

THE COMMANDANT CHECKS UP. UPPER. Pipe in hand, Gen. Holcomb, Marine Commandant, jockeys along the Guadalcanal "roads" on an inspection trip. Gen. Vandegrift is in the back left seat of the jeep. Seated next to him is Col. Edson. America sent such men against the Jap Gumbatsu or military clique. These leaders rewrote the plans for the Greater East Asia Co-Prosperity Sphere, and began retaking Japan's empire. LOWER. Wearing three stars, Gen. Vandegrift visits Maj. Gen. Charles Barrett on Guadalcanal in 1943, this time as Corps Commandant.

FROM THE BLUE OF ICE TO THE BLUE OF OCEAN. UPPER. A Catalina flying boat patrols its lonesome way over the frozen wastes of the North. LOWER. A seaplane tender "mothers" PT boats as well as seaplanes. A Catalina is tied up astern and three PT boats are moored alongside. The tender has provisions for refueling, replenishing, and minor repairs, as well as an opportunity for the crews to relax in more spacious quarters.

PRACTICE SALVO. One of the tensest moments in the shakedown of a new ship is when she first fires her guns. The stresses arising from the terrific concussion often do slight structural damage which must be rectified before the ship is ready to join the fleet and participate in action. But modern ship designers are able to allow for all but the most minor effect. ABOVE. The USS "Missouri" fires a round of 16-inch shells during her shakedown cruise. The shells which have just left the guns can be seen in the air in the upper left portion of the picture.

"ZEROS AND BETTYS OVERHEAD! LET'S GO!!"
This squadron of 14th (The Flying Tiger) Air Force fighter
pilots snapping into action, running for P-40s for a go at
the Japs might very well have been a group of the original
"Flying Tigers," the American Volunteer Group, former
AAF, Navy and Marine pilots who even before Pearl
Harbor were privately at war with Japan, under the daring
leadership of Colonel Claire Chennault. They had earlier
models of this same Curtiss P-40, and Chennault, who knew
all about Jap aircraft and pilot tactics, kept drumming into
them: "If you take the best characteristics of your plane
and fight with them, never letting the enemy fight with the
best characteristics of his plane, then you can lick him."
Under Chennault's guidance the AVG, during the period
from December 18, 1941 to July 4, 1942, when they disbanded, piled up the astonishing total of 297 confirmed
air victories, accounting for some 1500 Jap pilots and crew
members, with never more than 55 flyable planes at hand.
The next step was the activation of the China Air Task
Force (then a part of the 10th in India) on July 4, 1942,
composed of 34 battered P-40s mostly from the AVG
(whose pilots out of loyalty to Chennault stayed on a while
with the new outfit), under Col. Bob Scott of the 23rd

Fighter Group, and 7 B-25 Mitchell bombers under Col.
Caleb V. Haynes. Chief assets of the CATF were the highly
efficient Chinese ground-observer aircraft warning net, and
the battle-tested theories of air warfare, both evolved by
Chennault himself. They developed bases at Kunming to
receive supplies from over the Hump and help defend the
route, in Kweilin and Hengyang. By saving up gas, bombs
and ammunition for special drives, Chennault would work
a change of pace and shunt his bombers and fighters around
from base to base so quickly the Japs never knew what hit
them, and where they would be hit next. October 25, 1942
was a red letter day, with an attack on a big enemy task
force enroute to the Solomons which had been assembled
in Victoria Harbor between Kowloon and Hong Kong.
Shipping, docks and oil tanks were smashed, and 17 Jap
planes destroyed. Defending fighters back at Kunming broke
up a big Jap raid on Burma. That night two more attacks
were carried out, one against Canton airfield and the other
destroying the power station at Hong Kong. The CATF then
"evaporated" in the tremendous expanse of China, and
turned up in a different spot later when it had built up
another stock of supplies. Thus it went until March 1943,
at which time the Fourteenth Air Force was activated,

PARATROOPERS SPREADEAGLE JUNGLE. One offshoot of
the Japanese plan to slash the all-important supply line from
the United States to Australia was to strike for control of
southeastern New Guinea. A distinct foothold was achieved
in this campaign when, following the landing of troops, the
Nips drove on to the very doors of Port Moresby situated

amid the Gulf of Papua and the Coral Sea. ABOVE. Paratroopers landing behind the enemy's lines in New Guinea in
an attempt to regain lost ground. The airborne troops, employing their surprise tactics to advantage, played a significant role in the retaking of New Guinea from the Japanese.
This flight bailed out from a particularly hazardous altitude.

ABANDON SHIP. By rope and net, U.S. soldiers clamber down the sides of the USS "President Coolidge" after the 22,000-ton transport struck a mine and sank on December 12 while on a war mission in the South Pacific. The proximity of the island in the background, coupled with prompt and efficient rescue methods, restricted the casualties to two men. At the opening of the war the greatly expanding fleet necessitated a like increase in auxiliaries, such as attack transports and cargo ships. The "President Coolidge" was chartered from the American Lines to be operated as a transport for the Army by the War Shipping Administration. Double inner-spring mattresses gave way to four high iron bunks, cream colored walls became steel gray, and the ballroom became a storage room for oil-soaked machinery.

THE U.S. COAST GUARD

IN WORLD WAR II

By Admiral Russell R. Waesche, USCG

THE Coast Guard had become part of the Navy only a month before Pearl Harbor, but its larger cutters had already been armed and were soon protecting our convoys from enemy submarines in the Atlantic. The "Campbell" rammed one of a wolf pack after depth charging five others, picked up survivors and was towed to St. John's with a flooded machinery compartment. The "Spencer" and "Icarus" brought theirs to the surface and captured their crews before they sank. Dozens of other submarines never reached the surface again after Coast Guard depth charges found their target. One of the large cutters, the "Alexander Hamilton," was torpedoed off Iceland. A smaller one, the "Acacia," was sunk in the West Indies, while a third, the "Escanaba," was blown up while returning from Greenland.

It was in Greenland that the Coast Guard established a patrol and ultimately destroyed Weather Stations which the Germans had set up there, depriving our foes of advanced weather information on the European battle fronts.

As the war progressed Coast Guardsmen who had gained invaluable experience in the handling of small boats in surf, were sent to man the strange new landing craft which the transports first carried to Guadalcanal. Later these men helped land the Marines and Army in the Gilberts, the Marianas, the Marshalls, the Admiralties, on New Guinea, in the Halmaheras, the Carolines, the Philippines, and finally at Iwo Jima and Okinawa. They also manned landing craft at the invasions in North Africa, Sicily, Italy, Normandy, and Southern France. Continuing the life saving tradition of the Coast Guard, thousands of lives were saved when troop ships were torpedoed in the Atlantic, and on D-day in Normandy the 83-footers saved nearly 1500 lives.

THE RESERVE

MEANWHILE at home new recruits, Temporary Reservists and Spars were freeing the fighting Coast Guard from home security patrols. As beach patrols relaxed in 1944, with the driving of the German submarines farther from our shores, thousands of these fighting men were released to man Navy attack transports, destroyer escorts, frigates, LST's LCI(L)'s, and Army freight and service boats and tugs that were coming down the shipways. Coast Guardsmen were fighting off submarine attacks in the Mediterranean or shooting down Japanese suicide planes in the Pacific. Some of them died but more of them piloted thousands of Marine and U.S. Army troops safely to enemy-held beaches. Their deeds of heroism are legion.

While nearly half the 173,000 Coast Guardsmen were in the thick of battle, the other half were performing equally important if less spectacular tasks at home and abroad. It was the Coast Guard that built and manned LORAN stations on many a lonely island in the Pacific. As the offensive mounted, hundreds of newly garrisoned islands had to be serviced by Coast Guard manned Army boats. At home the millions of tons of newly constructed merchant shipping were being inspected by the Coast Guard, their officers licensed and their seamen certificated, while merchant marine hearing units, established throughout the world, aided merchant marine personnel. The lights on our coasts had to be blacked out or dimmed. Ice was broken on the Great Lakes to permit earlier spring movements of iron ore to the steel mills. Thousands of vessels were loaded with explosives under expert Coast Guard supervision. Shipyards were guarded and waterfront property protected from sabotage and fire. Finally with the upsurge of ocean flying, Air-Sea Rescue called for Coast Guard planes and cutters. "On the eve of the return of the Coast Guard to the Treasury" said a recent message from the Chief of Naval Operations "I desire to commend the officers and men of the Coast Guard for their superb performance of duty through the war."

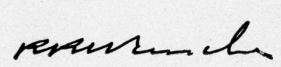

JAP RESISTANCE ENDS AT BUNA. Six weeks of the bitterest fighting imaginable preceded Allied seizure of Buna, New Guinea. It took place amid jungles and reeking swamps, in one of the world's worst climates. The last Japanese defenders clung to a small pocket west of a swollen creek. After holding out for several days against an Australian force which had taken the government station, the Japs were cut off by Americans. On the last day, 650 Japs died at Buna. Blood and sweat mingled with constant floods of rain. When some of the enemy swam out to sea they were raked by Kittyhawk fighter planes. All organized resistance on Buna ended January 3. Isolated nests of snipers remained to be blotted out one by one. A few miles west of Buna, small Japanese forces still showed resistance at Sanananda Point. Here, sheets of rain which overflowed the swamps held back Allied ground movement for many days. But on January 17 U.S. forces cut a main road in two places behind the enemy's rear. This split the Japanese into three separate clusters. By the next day two headlands on either side of Sanananda Point had been captured. The enemy was now hemmed into a 500-yard strip of beach, along with a few surrounded pockets inland. Despite continued tropical rains Allied forces were able to wrest all remaining positions from the Japanese on Sanananda Point by January 22. The reconquest of the Papuan part of New Guinea was complete. About 750 Japanese were killed in the final attack, and great piles of military equipment were captured. RIGHT. Japanese shot or drowned on the beach at Buna Mission. A smashed landing boat lies in the background.

OCCUPATION OF THE RUSSELLS. Moving north, Marine Raiders landed in the Russell Islands late in February, 1943, to find the enemy gone. UPPER. Operating in rubber boats, they go ashore unchallenged. LOWER. Moving in for another landing, this boatload of Marines is standing upright, evidently expecting no enemy fire. Unable to hold Guadalcanal, the Jap had moved his forces northeast to New Georgia. On February 4, 1943, the First Division, Reinforced, including several Second Division units and the Army's Americal, was cited by the President,

BOOMTOWN, SOUTH PACIFIC. UPPER. This strip in the Russells, the most advanced in the Pacific in February, 1943, was used by Marine piloted "Corsairs" and bombers during the New Georgia and Bougainville campaigns. A sign near the strip reads: "Welcome to Boomtown — Drive Carefully." Marine Press Relations Officer Penn Kimball wrote: "Civic pride runs high in this amazing jungle encampment. Its reason for existence is the grim business of shooting Japs out of the sky." LOWER. Struck by Jap bombs, this burning LST was saved and restored to duty.

NORTH PACIFIC FIGHTING. The Japs were very busy in the months following Pearl Harbor. Their aggression and seizure of bases brought them to Attu and Kiska in the Aleutian Islands in June, 1942. Presence of the enemy on these Alaskan approaches to the United States was alarming, and preparation was made to drive them off. First they were pounded from our advanced air bases on Adak and Amchitka. Then on May 11, 1943, ground troops under command of Major General Eugene M. Landrum—portions of the 7th Infantry Division, a battalion of the 4th Infantry, and Alaska Scouts—landed at two points on Attu. UPPER LEFT. Troops and supplies hitting the beach at Attu. Note the rugged coastline and the numerous boats shuttling back and forth between troop transport and shore. LOWER LEFT. When landing barges reached the beach men grabbed the ammunition and headed for cover to engage the enemy. Men here can be seen carrying 105 howitzer ammunition to supply guns already going into position. In background, other landing barges can be seen through the fog, coming in to land. The Japs were located in such inaccessible positions that artillery fire was necessary for blasting them out. UPPER RIGHT. A 105 howitzer lets go with some big ones at Holtz Bay, Attu, on May 12, 1943. LOWER RIGHT. A general view of the ridge between Red Beach, where American forces landed, and Holtz Bay itself. With their usual capability, the Japs had gun emplacements at strong points all over the island, and it was not taken until fierce fighting reduced such points. Though it was May, spring had not come to Attu, and our assaults were waged in the bitterest sort of weather. The weather itself claimed casualties.

SCRATCH ONE ISLAND. By the end of May, 1943, Attu
was in our hands. Japs not killed or captured chose to
kill themselves. UPPER LEFT. Old Glory is erected on the
deck of an abandoned Jap landing boat on the beach where
our foothold was gained. LOWER LEFT. On near-by Kodiak
Island, crew of a 37 mm anti-aircraft gun on the alert
and en route to its position. Troops were here to block
further Jap advances. ABOVE. On May 20, 1943, elements
of the 4th Infantry moved to the front to relieve forces
which had been in the line since the assault began. The
troops shown here have just landed, and are moving up
an incline that leads to a high knoll overlooking the bay.

CATCH JAPS LOOKING THE OTHER WAY. Dawn of June 30 glimmered over a shrewdly conceived and wrought landing on Rendova Island. Here Marine and Army units mass on the beach while landing boats shuttle briskly from ship to shore, manned by Coast Guardsmen. Enemy shore batteries woke up only after the invaders had dug in. Purpose of the feat, as part

of the overall assault on the Japanese stronghold of New
Georgia, was to close in on Munda airfield. From Rendova artillery arched shells into installations at the field, eight miles
away. From offshore the Navy threw in the power of its heaviest guns. Farther progress afoot, however, was neither neat
nor easy. It took five punishing weeks to win all of Munda,

NEW GEORGIA CAMPAIGN. One of the almost forgotten campaigns of the Pacific and yet the scene of considerable fighting, the New Georgia operation lasted more than three months and resulted in the capture of five enemy airfields which led Marine Press Relations Officer Charles Mathieu to write: "Let the Japs build more Henderson and Munda airdromes —we'll use them." From the occupation of the Russells to the landings of Army and Marine troops in the New Georgia area on June 30, 1943, was a period of getting troops ready, while continuing air and sea attacks up and down the island chain. UPPER LEFT. A troop transport unloads its Army combat troops off Rendova for the June 30th offensive. UPPER CENTER. Soldiers hit the beach and keep moving at Rendova. LOWER LEFT. The new LCI's (Landing Craft, Infantry) pull up to the beach and allow troops to wade ashore from ramps. The unopposed landing on Rendova, an island adjacent to Munda, was made by the Army's 172nd Regimental Combat Team. The Army's 103rd Artillery and the Marines' 9th Defense Battalion came ashore the first day.

RENDOVA ISLAND. Attacking at early morn, these Army troops (upper right) take cover on the beach as rain poured from the skies. LOWER RIGHT. At Rendova the Navy had another new ship available that was to go wherever American forces landed, the LST (Landing Ship, Tank). Here it is unloading its cargo during the early operations as Marines of the Ninth Defense Battalion patiently wait for an opportunity to unload their weapons and supplies on the already overcrowded beach. The LST, sometimes referred to as a "Large, Slow Target," was the workhorse of the Pacific and could come right up to a beach because of her shallow draft and allow Marines to drive tanks, trucks, amphibian tractors and other vehicles right into action, fully loaded with ammunition and weapons. Many of these seagoing vessels were credited with Jap planes shot down. In addition to the ship's weapons, the troops aboard generally set up their anti-aircraft guns for possible use, as did these Marines here. The LST's could carry some 2,000 tons and 200 Marines, and shuttle from beachhead to loading areas almost continuously.

BATTLE FOR MUNDA. The Allies needed Munda airfield for use as a base for future operations. They got it—but not easily. The 43rd Division, effecting an assault against the coast of New Georgia just east of Munda, met stiff resistance. It was necessary to commit elements of the 25th and 37th Infantry Divisions. Even then, progress was slow, but Munda was to fall. UPPER LEFT. Landing boats loaded with infantry and medics make a landing on the Choi River beach, New Georgia. LOWER LEFT. These men of the 169th Infantry were wounded on July 10 in the battle for Munda. ABOVE. Soldiers of the 172nd Infantry slowly ford a stream through the jungle terrain.

BOMBING MUNDA. Made while flying through enemy ack-ack fire, this picture (upper) shows the bombed Munda airstrip at left, the Lambeti plantation at right. When Munda finally fell on August 5, 1943, most of the enemy survivors had disappeared. This was the beginning of a long series of evacuations from island to island as the Japanese withdrew from one hopelessly defended position after another. RIGHT. In one of the most difficult Pacific operations, Marine Raiders, after landing at Segi Point nine days before the D-day landing of June 30th, moved through slime and stench of the jungle to attack Jap troops from the rear at Viru Harbor. Although the terrain included deep rivers and swamps the Marines got to their objective only one day late, achieved tactical surprise and gained their assigned positions. Lt. Biggerstaff, Marine PRO, in describing the aftermath of a Raider patrol action, wrote: "We were a horrible sight. The Seabees and Sailors coming ashore thought so, too. They took one look, trotted to their quarters, opened their sea-bags and brought us their extra clothing. They literally gave us everything. Then their cooks took over. . . ."

NEW GEORGIA NIGHTMARE. "There are few places more desolate than Dragon's Peninsula and few campaigns more vicious than the battle which raged across it through July, 1943." That's how combat correspondent Jim Lucas described the action of the Raiders against Triri, Enogai and Bairoko on New Georgia. UPPER. Raiders, bent on closing the back door to Munda, landed at Rice Anchorage some 15 miles to the north and moved through a land that God forgot, against continual efforts of the Jap to make it a place the invaders would never forget. Under command of Marine Lt. Col. Sam Griffith, the First Raiders had teamed up with two Army battalions from the 145th and 148th Infantry Regiments to form a "Northern Landing Force" under Col. Harry Liversedge. This group moved slowly through almost impassable terrain. At one place, 1,200 men crossed the Tamakau River on a fallen log. The crossing took six and a half hours. On July 7th, Triri fell after a brief fire fight and as Griffith related: "Our doctors cared for the wounded. Fathers Redmond and Murphy conducted a dignified service for our dead." LEFT. Ruins of Munda atop Kokengolo Hill.

SHELLING MUNDA. At Munda the Japs got a good lesson on what happens when the Army, Navy and Marines
team up for action. UPPER. This spectacular picture shows
the Navy shelling Munda at 3 o'clock in the morning of
July 12. LOWER. In a shell hole overlooking Munda airfield shortly before it was taken these members of Company D, 169th Infantry, take a break. Munda was to be in
Allied hands shortly after this picture was made on August
3, 1943, but was then the scene of bitter fighting between
American and Japanese troops.

CLEANING OUT A PILL BOX. UPPER. Infantrymen cover a Chemical Warfare soldier with a flame thrower (third from right) as they move toward a Jap pill box near Munda airfield. These flame throwers were death on Japs. LOWER. Riflemen of the 43rd Infantry Division charge a smoking pill box after the Chemical Warfare soldier has done his job. This pill box was one of a great many Japs had built along the beach near the field. This trial by fire was developed into the easiest and cheapest method of dislodging the enemy. Otherwise, it was almost impossible to get them out,

MORE HEAT TREATMENT. Still more Japs get the heat
treatment (upper left) as flame throwers of the 43rd Chemical Warfare Service pour fire into a Jap pill box near Munda
field in the closing days of action there. LOWER LEFT.
But all the dead were not Japanese. This is a view of Munda
Cemetery No. 1, near Laiana Beach, New Georgia. Men
are re-burying the bodies of soldiers removed from Leaf
Cemetery. ABOVE. Knee deep in water and mud, Engineers "bulldog" logs into place for a corduroy across a
swamp on New Georgia. Roads had to be built and rebuilt before artillery could be transported here. This bridge
formed a portion of what the men called "Wilderness Road,"

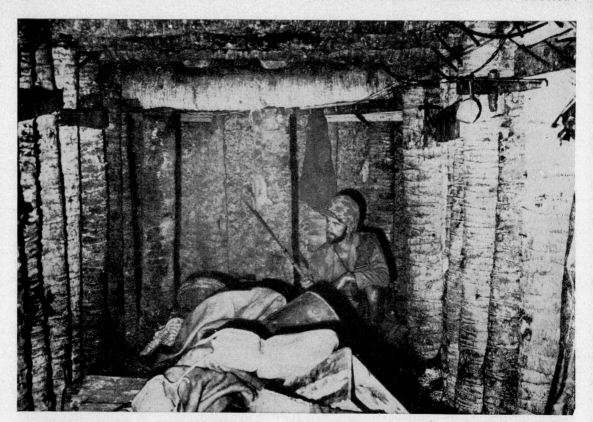

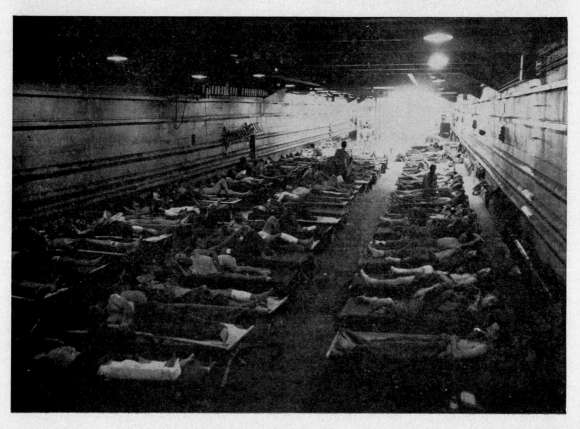

AFTERMATH OF MUNDA. The two pictures on the opposite page might be labeled "cause" and "effect." UPPER LEFT. A Marine raider, his beard showing lack of attention for many days, investigates this tunnel inside Kokengolo Hill which both allowed the defenders to maintain communication between units and to withstand air and artillery attacks. From such tunnel or cave positions the Munda Japs inflicted heavy casualties on the troops attacking them. Evacuated to the tank deck of an unloaded LST (lower left), which has been converted into a makeshift hospital ward, wounded Marines and Soldiers are ably administered to by overworked Navy doctors and corpsmen. UPPER RIGHT. Guadalcanal veterans felt right at home in the New Georgia mud, but the ubiquitous Seabees performed with their usual incredible speed in constructing roads. This one leads from Munda Airport to the Seabee camp. LOWER RIGHT. New Georgia Marines had their own "Washing Machine Charlie" and here dive for their poncho-covered fox hole as the alert warning sounds. Writer Jim Lucas commented: "Charlie would come promptly at 4 A.M., gunning his motors so that we would know he had arrived. He would air his troubles and then depart. But he was fooling no one. Within 10 minutes—always 10—he was back, this time to dive on us. Occasionally he would drop his bombs. Not often. Just enough to keep us guessing. Then he would be away again. The third time he would sneak back, his motors dead. We could expect bombs the third run. Charlie would keep this up to 7 A.M., and then disappear."

NIGHT ACTION OFF VELLA LAVELLA. The Japanese in the Solomons were faltering. Desperately the "Tokyo Express" attempted to supply and reinforce their beleaguered garrisons in Vila and elsewhere in the Kula Gulf. Under the cover of night, their destroyers, piled high with men and materials, tried to run through our naval defenses and then withdraw quickly. Although a destroyer is limited in its capacity, and therefore cannot transport as many troops and as much equipment as might be desired, the Japanese counted on the destroyer's speed and mobility for success in these desperate missions. At times they were successful. In order to stop these blockade runners, our Naval Command dispatched Group X to make a sweep of Vella Gulf and to engage any enemy encountered. Group X was composed of about five destroyers. One night in August they picked up four Japanese ships steaming in column — three were destroyers, the fourth was a cruiser, designed to afford heavier gun protection to the gauntlet-running ships. Group X took them by surprise. Apparently the Japanese did not make as efficient use of radar as our ships did. Group X closed in for the kill. On the command to fire, twenty-four torpedoes went racing through the dark waters, leaving thin strategic lines of white wake behind. Balls of red flame went shooting skyward. Violent explosions followed which blew two enemy destroyers to pieces. The cruiser burst into a mass of flame. The waters reflecting this eerie light outlined the third Japanese destroyer which had escaped severe torpedo damage and was now pitifully attempting to elude its attackers. The destroyers in Group X trained their guns on it and sank the ship within minutes. The entire battle had lasted only a half-hour. Vella Lavella was one of the many actions which contributed to the decimation of the Japanese Navy. LEFT. A destroyer of Group X bellows a flash of hot flame from one of the guns which sank that last Japanese destroyer.

SHUTTLING AROUND END. First phase of the northward drive through the Solomon Islands ended with capture of the airfield at Munda, on the island of New Georgia. Now bent on seizing Bougainville, the largest of the Solomon Islands, U.S. forces first had to contend with intervening Japanese garrisons situated on Kolombangara and Vella Lavella. These smaller islands, respectively, lay northwest of New Georgia. During August, 1943, the waters around these islands boiled with the traffic of Japanese and U.S. naval units in pursuit of each other. U.S. strategists decided to bypass the ten thousand or so Japanese troops on Kolombangara. In the photograph (above) Paramarines push off on the end run to Vella Lavella. This island fell to an amphibious assault on September 3. The Japanese garrison on Kolombangara then languished uselessly until partly evacuated by night, under naval bombardment, to Bougainville and another sizable island to the north, Choiseul. September 23rd witnessed the arrival of Marine fliers at the captured field on Kolombangara. Then, late in October, 1943, a Marine parachute battalion landed on Choiseul to divert attention from the forthcoming invasion of Bougainville.

"BIG BUKA" NEXT STOP. The mission on Bougainville was similar to Guadalcanal. It required establishing a landing, setting up a perimeter, scratching out an airfield, holding the area against counter-attacks, and employing the new strip to pound Rabaul. UPPER. As the transports as-sembled to take the Third Marine Division to its baptism of fire on November 1, 1943, the Navy sent along protectors. Their carrier planes coupled with those of the Army and Marines neutralized enemy air. LOWER. Safe from air attack, transports move into Empress Augusta Bay, Bougainville.

D DAY LANDING. Huddled inside their landing craft, Marines of the Third Division (upper) approach a Bougainville beach. Boats landed in waves and were numbered visibly like this one so that units would land as close together as possible. Landing techniques were now almost perfected, although new doctrines were necessary for later operations against defended atolls with protecting coral reefs. LOWER. Early assault waves are already on the Bougainville beaches while others come ashore and are soon swallowed up in the jungle. The beach marked "C" is easily seen by incoming boats, and troops are thus landed where they belong, making unnecessary a lateral movement up or down a beach to rejoin units. This landing craft is spitting spray from its propellers as the coxswain holds his craft solid on the beach. Navy censors scratched original negative to efface the numbers on the back of the boat. The black mark hides the number of the transport from which the craft came as well as the number of the small boat itself. Marines are standing on this beach so it appears that there is little enemy resistance in this area. No supplies have yet been landed to clog the beach, and no vehicles are ashore so this is a very early wave of assault troops. As the landing progressed at Cape Torokina, Marines received fire from two small islands in the Bay, Puruata and Torokina, which were soon silenced by fast shooting Raiders. An estimated 300 Japanese opposed the original landings of the 3rd and 9th Regiments from well dug in positions and caused some confusion and casualties before troops got ashore and silenced the weapons and their operators.

THE BOSS OF THE LANDINGS. When the strike is over and the flight returns to its home carrier, no man aboard is more important than the Landing Signal Officer. It is his job to guide the planes in for a perfect landing, indicating their way to the center of the runway. When the approach is faulty or a plane is crippled, he must quickly recognize the situation and coach the plane in for the best possible landing under adverse conditions.

MARINES ALOFT. A formation of scouting and training planes (SNJ's) flies over the rugged terrain near the Marine Corps Air Station at El Centro, California (above). Marine Corps aviation expanded rapidly during World War II and at one time almost one third of Corps strength was in aviation. The early victories in the Solomons campaigns were never surpassed because of the nature of future operations. However, at war's end the Corps had four Air Wings with squadrons and groups based throughout the Gilberts, Marshalls, Admiralties, Philippines, Ryukyus, Marianas and many other island groups of the Pacific.

MUD AND JAPS. In their camouflage uniforms, Marines (upper) return fire from an unseen sniper. First Amphibious Corps Commander Vandegrift had told his men: "Be alert, and when the enemy appears, shoot calmly, shoot fast and shoot straight." Good advice! LOWER. The Bougainville mud trot is demonstrated here as an alert photographer snaps a patrol in the gooey mud. The front man crosses over to keep from falling, others plow on through, not wasting any effort but pushing steadily forward. At the column's end a high stepper in canvas puttees exerts extra effort.

LIFE ON BOUGAINVILLE. "Fatigue hangs over the men like the almost ceaseless rain," a photographer captioned his picture (upper). Rain was constant and so were enemy bombing and strafing raids. These Marines are returning from the front lines after making the initial landing. What appear to be Jap Samurai swords at first, actually are tree limbs being carried back for cooking some hot chow from field ration cans. LOWER. A rocket platoon, one of the first in the Pacific, moves along the "corduroy" road of the East-West trail on Bougainville.

ACTION AND BOREDOM. The Jap had lots of tricks and here he used the body of a dead Marine (upper) to stage an ambush along a trail. The running Marine has emptied his weapon and is moving back under covering rifles of his patrol. The tank has been thrown sideways from an explosion and the woods are probably full of unseen Japs who fight and then fade away into the jungle in approved fashion. LOWER. The bored crew of the "Swamp Angel," christened appropriately, moves slowly through the rough terrain with supplies and ammunition for the troops operating inland. These buffaloes, an improvement on the earlier alligator model, also move the wounded back to the beach to field hospitals or floating hospital wards from their first stop at battalion aid stations. The component parts of this team which included the Army's 37th Infantry Division and the Raider Regiment had heard Vandegrift's valedictory just prior to the operation. He told them: "It is not the individual that counts, nor the individual service. It is the Marines, the Navy, the Army, the Coast Guard, and our Allies that matter —all of them—working toward a common interest—victory." Vandegrift was to turn the First Marine Amphibious Corps over to Gen. Geiger after the first few days of the Bougainville operation, but he left behind his formula for leadership: Know your subject. Be sure in your own mind that your mission is correct. Always believe, no matter how hard the going, that you will come through successfully. If you have any doubts of that, keep them to yourself. He believed that when men had knowledge of the common objective, and assurance of ammunition, food and medical aid, "they will repay you ten times over."

ONE MORE ISLAND. After Munda came Bougainville in the northern Solomons — and plans were made to take it and use it as a base for pounding the very dangerous Jap base at Rabaul, 215 miles away. With General MacArthur's concurrence, Admiral Halsey, in immediate command, decided to strike at Empress Augusta Bay, on the west coast of Bougainville. Prior to this effort, New Zealand troops landed in the Treasuries (27 October, 1943) and Marines raided Choiseul Island. On November 1 Marines landed at Cape Torokina. The 37th Infantry Division moved in a week later, and strong defenses were set up. While Bougainville did not match Guadalcanal as a slugging match intense, hard fighting took place here. Allied forces took advantage of sea and air superiority, "contained" the enemy and cut his supply lines to Rabaul by occupying Green (Nissan) Island to the north of the Solomons. But it was not easy going on Bougainville. UPPER LEFT. A detachment of American troops on patrol in Bougainvill's jungles. In single file the men have entered a tangle of trees and vines when a Jap mortar shell drops just ahead. The explosion blows mud and vegetation high into the air. At the same time, snipers are busy. LOWER LEFT. These men are on the alert for Jap snipers at the bottom of bitterly-contested Hill 700 on the defense perimeter of Bougainville. UPPER RIGHT. Men of Company F, 129th Infantry, on the alert for Japs on Bougainville. LOWER RIGHT. Behind a tank, Yanks mop up on Bougainville. The wily Japs, hard-pressed, filled these woods.

MOPPING UP. At night on Bougainville the Japs would infiltrate American lines. At dawn, the Yanks went out and killed them. UPPER. GIs mopping up in March, 1944. Note man at right leaving fox hole; another fires, still another crawls forward. Action was hot and close. LOWER. A GI blasts away at a Jap. The enemy made furious attacks in March, but in 18 days of bitter fighting more than 7,000 Japs bit the dust. Many of the dead were members of the Japanese Sixth Division, which led the Rape of Nanking. In mopping up Bougainville, fighting was sticky.

THE JAPS WON'T QUIT. Following a Jap infiltration of U.S. lines these men of the 129th Infantry move up a flame thrower and rifles to knock out a nearby position (upper). Note the dead Japs to the left of the flame thrower. LOWER. A soldier of the 37th Division grimaces and bites his tongue as he flings a grenade toward a Jap pill box that has just been located during mopping up operations on Bougainville. Soldier at left is merely watching. For many days, even after they were beaten, the Japs persisted in their infiltration tactics. Always they were beaten and subdued.

FINAL PHASES. The Japanese counter-offensive on Bougainville, launched in March, had been suicidal. The Americal and 37th Divisions held firmly against everything they threw. Their infiltration tactics, while troublesome, were of no great significance. By the end of March, Bougainville was ours, and the Japs left in the Solomons were isolated. ABOVE. Members of the 148th Infantry, mopping up, move cautiously while tanks of the 754th Tank Battalion stand guard. UPPER RIGHT. Yanks of the 37th Division firing on a pill box occupied by infiltrating Japanese. LOWER RIGHT. Members of Companies G and E, 132nd Infantry, cross a bomb-shattered area during their advance.

KEEN EYES AND KEENER NOSES. From homes in the United States scores of lithe, powerful dogs were recruited to serve with the Army and Marines in island combat. For the most part they remained with their original trainers, men with a professed yen and talent for this type of duty. As may be seen in this picture (left), Doberman Pinschers and German Shepherds predominated among the breeds represented. Taught to seek out concealed snipers, these loyal allies saved many a human life while often surrendering their own. They ran messages as well, often through dense foliage and across distances which would have bogged down a man. Their masters at home were entitled to hang out service flags for these dogs, either blue or gold. After retraining, most of them were returned to their owners.

RABAUL BOUND. As a Marine fighter returns from an air strike, road graders put the finishing touches to the Toro-kina Point fighter strip (above). Operation "Cherry Blossom" was proceeding according to form and already the lines of fighters and dive bombers (upper right) had come to roost. Propeller to tail (center right), this air armada of Marine "Corsairs," Navy "Hellcats" and New Zealand P-40's is about to be flown off the metal strips for the first great fighter sweep against Rabaul. Here the Jap was hoarding his first line planes for defense, after having lost an estimated 2,000 pilots and planes since the original Guadalcanal landing. A little later (lower right), heavier planes took off with these 2,000 pounders, being examined here by two Marine bomb men in a Bougainville dump. The Japs were known to have had from 300 to 600 planes at Rabaul, New Britain, which refused to engage Allied fliers in offensive operations. The SCAT planes of MAG 25 were also busy, landing the first day the strip was open to take out wounded. In all, they teamed up with the Army's Thirteenth Air Force to remove 1,200 casualties from Bougainville and to deliver 840 tons of priority supplies. Air-ground support tactics were given their first real work-out here, thanks to Marine Lt. Col. John Gabbert, the Division Air Officer. He had established an air support school and trained officers from all regimental and battalion headquarters prior to the landing on Bougainville. Enlisted men had familiarized themselves with portable radios and learned to communicate with planes. It was during this period that Marine fighters caused trouble to enemy night bombers and probably restricted some of their activities. Historian John DeChant reported close air support was requested on four occasions: the original beachhead landing, a November 9th mission by 18 torpedo bombers (TBF's) over Piva Village, a strike on "Hellzapoppin" Ridge, and a Christmas Day request to aid in the reduction of enemy fortifications on Hill 600A. DeChant summed it up: "In spite of the short campaign and lack of major air opposition, the air show at Bougainville had proved to be a competent, well-rounded affair that was satisfactory in itself and an excellent harbinger of deadlier precision teamwork in the future phases of the Pacific campaigning."

A CEMETERY IN BOUGAINVILLE. Throughout World War II
many Americans fought and died in the most remote portions
of the earth. A chain of cemeteries, similar to the one shown
(above), traces the path of combat through the Pacific to

Japan. In this jungle clearing on Bougainville an Army chaplain conducts final services over freshly-shoveled graves. Needless to say, the ceremony did not lack dignity for want of flowers or mourning clothes. Expressions of living set the mood.

CENTRAL PACIFIC OFFENSIVE. For more than 18 months Allied forces in the Central Pacific had been on the defensive, but now, in the fall of 1943, plans to take the offensive were launched. First of these operations, designed to get forces closer and closer to the Philippines and Japan, was the attack in the Gilbert Islands against Tarawa and Makin. This strike was made on November 20, with the Marines hitting the beach at Tarawa, and a reinforced regimental combat team of the 27th Infantry Division striking Makin. This Army force was under the immediate command of Major General Ralph C. Smith. In just three days Makin was taken, and more than 900 Japs were either killed or captured. UPPER LEFT. Elements of the 2nd Battalion, 165th Infantry, take a look at Butaritari, Makin Atoll, from the USS "Neville" shortly before the landings November 20. LOWER LEFT. An assault wave of the 165th Infantry hitting the beach at Butaritari. Jap machine guns, firing from right flank, strafed and hit the operator of the beached landing craft at right. Smoke is from oil dumps hit by Naval gun fire. UPPER RIGHT. Engineers of the 2nd Battalion, 165th Infantry Combat Team, land with equipment to lay a screen mat for vehicles too heavy to run on sand. Jap sniper fire held them up temporarily, but they were soon at work. LOWER RIGHT. The Japs had emplaced machine guns in the hulks of two old ships off Ah Chonge wharf in Butaritari Lagoon. Here on November 20 Navy planes dive-bomb them in an effort to eliminate them. Makin was taken without too much trouble, but nearby Tarawa was a different story. It was more heavily-defended, and was the scene of some of the war's fiercest and bloodiest fighting.

TARAWA

By Lieutenant General Julian C. Smith

BY the fall months of 1943 the situation for United States forces in the Pacific improved perceptibly: Preparations were underway for an amphibious assault on Bougainville, designed to nullify the importance of the Japanese base at Rabaul and to complete the conquest of the Solomons; the Japanese had been driven from the Aleutians in the North Pacific; and the drive in the Southwest Pacfic had reached the Bismarcks. The time had come to implement further the belief of the Joint Chiefs of Staff that "the Japanese could best be defeated by a series of amphibious attacks across the far reaches of the Pacific." To increase pressure on the enemy, and to secure bases from which subsequent amphibious attacks could be launched, it was decided to seize two atolls in the Gilbert Island group: Tarawa and Makin.

The strategic significance of the Gilberts lay in the fact that they were immediately south and east of important Japanese bases in the Marshalls and Carolines. The proposed pattern of attack against the Japanese in the Central Pacific led from the Gilberts through the Marshalls to the Marianas or to Truk. Capture of the Gilberts was assigned by Admiral Chester W. Nimitz, Commander in Chief, Pacific, to Vice Admiral Raymond A. Spruance, Commander Fifth Fleet. Rear Admiral R. K. Turner had command of the amphibious force involved and Major General Holland M. Smith, USMC, Commanding General, Fifth Amphibious Corps, was in overall command of the troops assigned for the amphibious attack.

The Fifth Amphibious Corps comprised the Second Marine Division, in New Zealand, the 27th Infantry Division, in the Hawaiian area, and the Fourth Marine Division, in the United States, and not available for the Gilberts operation. One reinforced regiment from the 27th Infantry Division was to make the landing on Makin, where the enemy garrison was believed to number one thousand or less. Intelligence reports indicated that of all the islands in Tarawa Atoll, only Betio (Bititu) was strongly held and fortified; in addition, it had a well-developed airfield. The mission of capturing Betio was assigned to the Second Marine Division.

Planning for the Gilberts operation was influenced to a great extent by the fact that, based in the Marshalls, Carolines and Marianas, the enemy had ships, submarines, and aircraft capable of attacking any force landing in the Gilberts within three days of its discovery. In addition, there was a Japanese fleet to be reckoned with, a fleet whose ships, gunpower, and planes equalled those of the United States Pacific fleet, at least in number. Thus it was necessary that the Gilberts be secured as quickly as possible, a fact which precluded preliminary landings on undefended islands adjacent to Betio.

The Japanese had moved into the Gilberts on the heels of their strike at Pearl Harbor and in the late summer of 1942 had begun to fortify Betio and construct an airfield. By November 1943, the strength of the Japanese garrison numbered 4,836, of which approximately 2,700 were first-rate troops. In command of the Betio garrison was Rear Admiral Meichi Shibasaki, whose plan of defense called for destruction of American forces at the water's edge. With coast-defense guns ranging from 80-mm to 8-inch; anti-aircraft guns of from 13mm to 127mm size; anti-boat guns as large as 75mm; and 13-mm and 7.7mm machine guns, Shibasaki was well-prepared to resist.

Shibasaki's main ally, however, was the coral barrier reef, which encircled the entire L-shaped atoll, both on its exterior and interior. To land on Betio meant crossing that reef, which was covered with water, sufficient to permit passage over it by small boats, only at high spring tides; at no other times could boats hope to get across.

When the Second Marine Division was told of its mission of seizing Betio, a study of the reef problem was begun and experiments with amphibian tractors carried out which demonstrated the feasibility of using the tractors as assault personnel carriers in lieu of landing boats; the tractors could crawl over the reef, if necessary.

With one complete combat team (reinforced regiment) held in the Fifth Amphibious Corps reserve, the Second Marine Division based its plans for an assault landing on Betio on using, initially, three battalion landing teams from its remaining two regiments to enter the lagoon and land on the north side of the island, on either side of a long pier which ran out to the reef.

In early November, the Second Marine Division sailed from New Zealand to Efate, in the New Hebrides, for rehearsals and on 13 November, the division left Efate for Tarawa. While the division was en route to the target, Betio was pounded by naval gunfire and aerial bombardment, heavier in intensity per square foot of ground than any previous preparation delivered in the Pacific. Yet this preparation was ineffective, for on the morning of D-day, 20 November 1943, Japanese shore batteries were still operative as the transports unloaded the assault waves of troops into amphibian tractors and boats.

Despite heavy enemy fire from carefully-built emplacements, unscathed by our naval gunfire and aerial bombardment, the first waves (two battalions of the 2d Marines and one from the 8th Marines) got ashore with extremely light casualties. Many of the tractors were hit, however, during the first hours of the landing, and could not be used to carry later waves ashore, as planned. These waves were forced to leave their boats at the reef and wade ashore through nearly five-hundred yards of fire-swept water. Casualties in the later waves were heavy.

At the close of the first day our foothold on Betio was indeed precarious. Two battalions held a shallow beachhead on either side of the pier, while another occupied the northwestern end of the island, separated from the first two. The time was ripe for the Japanese to counterattack and drive the Marines back into the sea. To forestall such a move, the 8th Marines (of which two battalions had already been committed) was ordered to land on the eastern portion of the north side of Betio, but communication difficulties prevented this order from getting through.

Fortunately, the Japanese did not counterattack (possibly because of their own communication and control failures) and thus lost their only real opportunity to dislodge their attackers. We were stronger on the second day, by virtue of the fact that the Corps reserve—the 6th Marines, (Reinforced)—was made available to the Second Marine Division. The best that the Japanese could hope for now was to prolong the engagement and to inflict as many casualties as possible.

On the second day some progress was made toward expanding and consolidating our positions. By mid-afternoon the west end of Betio was cleared of the enemy, which permitted us to land one battalion of the 6th Marines at that point. Troops in the center of the island drove through to the south coast, but the Japanese still held ground between our troops on the west end of the island and those in the center. One particularly active pocket of enemy resistance still held out at the juncture of Red Beach 1, and Red Beach 2, a pocket that was not cleaned out until the last day of the battle.

It was on the third day that the Second Marine Division really gained ground. In the morning of this day, the battalion from the 6th Marines which had landed on the west end of the island the day previous, began a drive down the south coast to the east that carried it to the eastern end of the long airfield. By this time, we had well over half the island, our left flank battalion also having made good progress in reducing some very stubborn pillboxes to its front and flank.

Three days of bitter fighting, during which forward progress was often measured in inches, had served to compress the volatile Japanese into the eastern tail of Betio. The possibility that they might attempt a large-scale counterattack had been foreseen, and such measures as were possible to resist it had been taken. True to form, the Japanese launched three separate counterattacks during the night, each succeeding one in greater strength than its predecessor. The alert Marines held their positions and engaged the enemy in hand-to-hand bayonet and grenade fighting.

The counterattacks broke the back of the enemy resistance and on the fourth day of the battle, a fresh battalion from the 6th Marines drove rapidly down the island's long tail. The remaining Japanese showed little inclination to resist, and less to surrender. Over five hundred of the enemy were killed in this drive, while our casualties were light. In the meantime, the stubborn pocket of resistance remaining in the Beach Red 1—Beach Red 2 area was overcome by an attack from its rear. The battle for Betio was over.

In terms of casualties, Tarawa was a costly operation. Our losses amounted to 3,301 killed, wounded, and missing. The Japanese, on the other hand, lost 4,690 killed, of a force of 4,836, and it must be remembered that the enemy garrison on Betio had all the advantages accruing to the defender. In seventy-six hours, the Second Marine Division had completed the capture of Betio, key island in Tarawa Atoll, and this, coupled with the capture of Makin by a regimental combat team of the 27th Infantry Division, gave the United States control of the entire Gilberts and bases from which an amphibious attack could be launched against the highly strategic Marshalls.

Tarawa was a hard-won but extremely important battle and its real success lay in the purposes it served: It demonstrated clearly the soundness of our doctrines of amphibious assault; it pointed out the inevitable weaknesses in equipment, weaknesses immediately corrected before subsequent amphibious operations in the Central Pacific. The groundwork laid at Tarawa provided a firm foundation for operations in the Marshalls, the Marianas, on Iwo Jima, and at Okinawa.

In Tarawa's fiery cockpit, the disciplined fighting ability and courage of the individual Marine was in keeping with the highest and proudest traditions of the Marine Corps. But in the last analysis, success of individual efforts was only possible because of careful planning made on the basis of exceptionally good intelligence information; because of an unusually full and accurate estimate of the situation; and because the plan for assaulting Tarawa was executed by all commanders and all units with vigor and dispatch. These ingredients added up to a combination against which the Japanese, with all their advantages, could not stand. For us it meant success and victory; for the Japanese absolute defeat.

Julian C. Smith

THE SECOND DIVISION STRIKES AGAIN. By the middle of February, 1943, most Second Division units had left Guadalcanal for New Zealand. Here the Marines enjoyed considerable liberty. Next mission of the Second under its new leader, Maj. Gen. Julian C. Smith, was one for which the text books had not yet been written. The stepped-up operations of the Joint Chiefs of Staff required the taking of a tiny atoll in the Gilberts. In November, 1943, the Second was again on the high seas (above), bound for Tarawa. UPPER RIGHT. Landing craft head for the smoking beachhead where Marines soon pushed ashore against terrible enemy fire and around barbed wire entanglements (lower right).

COMMANDERS WATCH THE BATTLE UNFOLD. UPPER.
Tensely, leaders of the attack on Tarawa observe the action
(below) from the bridge of a U.S. warship. Marine Major
General Julian C. Smith grips his binoculars in the foreground, while Rear Admiral Harry W. Hill faces the camera.

THE BATTLE FOR TARAWA. On November 20th, battalions of the 2nd and 8th Marine Regiments, covered by carrier- planes and a naval bombardment, gained a perilous beachhead on a coral speck named Betio in the Tarawa atoll. The assault waves landed on the lagoon beaches, crossing the coral barrier reef in amphibian tractors and suffered light casualties. Succeeding waves got a hot reception from the emplaced Japs and the beach (upper) soon became clogged with personnel. LOWER. The glaring, hot sun almost fried the exposed attackers.

HELL ON EARTH. Landing on Red Beaches 1, 2 and 3, the Marines of the Second Division soon colored the waters with their blood as the amphibian tractors (upper) were either knocked out by Jap fire, underwater defenses or the fringing coral. Succeeding waves were denied use of the tractors and had to disembark from the Higgins landing boats at the reef and wade ashore against interlacing Japanese machine gun fire and sporadic mortar bursts. Those who reached the beach (lower) took cover behind a sea wall of coconut logs which afforded temporary protection.

"ISSUE STILL IN DOUBT." That was the message that Col. Dave Shoup, radioed to Gen. Smith afloat as the afternoon wore on at Betio on D-Day. The Japanese had recovered from the stunning bombardment and returned to their firing ports in fortifications they had perfected for 15 months against such a landing. The casualties were high and the dead, wounded and whole Marines were broiled on the beach as bullets (upper), zing a few inches over the shelter of the covering sea wall. LOWER. As leaders reorganize their units or form new ones from scattered remnants, small groups of Marines detach themselves from the beach foothold and vault out against the barricaded defenders to knock out pillboxes and emplacements with grenades, TNT blocks, flame throwers and automatic weapons. The ugly business of assault was spearheaded by men of the scout-sniper platoon under Lt. William D. Hawkins who gave his name to the airfield and his deeds to history. Landing on a fortified pier in advance of the assault troops, Hawkins and his men cleared it of enemy troops. Wounded three times, Hawkins was awarded the Medal of Honor, posthumously.

KILLING JAPS. Marines (upper) have just killed a Jap lying in front of a fallen palm tree outside his pillbox on Betio. Moving farther inland, taking what cover was available, Marines (lower) take cover behind a Jap pillbox between the beach and the airstrip. The Jap had some 4,000 men and a triangular airstrip on Betio, constituting a constant threat to our sea lanes. Prior to the operation the Fifth Amphibious Corps (VAC) had been formed at Pearl Harbor with Major General H. M. "Howling Mad" Smith at its head. It included the battle-tried Second Division up from the South Pacific and the untried 27th Army Division. Together they formed the spearhead that was to open the Central Pacific and provide bases for carrying the war to the Jap homeland. The 27th Division landed on Makin, on Butaritari Island. By D plus 2 the island was secured under Major General Ralph C. Smith. The island had been garrisoned by some 300 troops and a similar number of laborers. American losses totaled 56 killed in action. The VAC Reconnaissance Co., later to become famous for hit and run operations, went ashore at Apamama from a submarine.

THE SECOND DAY. In his battle instructions, Gen. Smith said, "You will quickly overrun the Japanese forces; you will decisively defeat and destroy the treacherous enemies of our country." He was right, but it took four days. The first night Col. Shoup, in command ashore, held some 300 yards of shore line. Our troops were from 50 to 150 yards inland in most places. Burning fuel dumps lit up the sky and the naval support fire, whammed home against the Jap portion of the island, made sleep difficult. Beyond the reef Marines huddled, wet and miserable, in their boats, unable to get ashore. Shore party Marines kept ammunition and some food and water moving across the pier under fire. Doctors and corpsmen in a captured pillbox treated the wounded by flashlight. Fire came from the lagoon as Japs occupied the hulk of a wrecked ship and sniped at the rear of our troops. UPPER. With morning and the realization that they were there to stay, the Marines moved forward against more pillboxes and advanced over embankments (lower) around the airfield. Two battalions of the 8th Regiment waded ashore suffering heavy casualties.

TARAWA VIGNETTES. The work of the Navy Corpsmen was outstanding and many were later decorated for their heroism. UPPER LEFT. A stretcher case gets first aid treatment on the beach. One Corpsman slashes open the leg of a utility uniform as the other prepares to apply sulfa powder and a battle dressing. LOWER LEFT. Another wounded Marine is being evacuated from the end of the Betio pier into a rubber boat. Hoisted by willing hands, his left arm in a traction splint, this Marine will be taken out over the reef and then transferred to a landing craft for a run to the nearest transport with a hospital ward. On Pacific operations the mess halls and officers' mess rooms frequently were converted into operating rooms. Cabins served as wards for the wounded. UPPER RIGHT. With much of Betio smoldering before them, these Marines rest up before pushing on. The ammunition boxes in the foreground and the precious canteens of water were most important at this stage. LOWER RIGHT. The refuse on the beach, the camouflaged shelter halves erected as protection against the merciless sun, and the utter desolation make this a scene of chaos. Everywhere the Marines were on Tarawa, combat photographers were on hand. Many had the complete frustration of losing their cameras and film during the trip ashore. The stark reality of Tarawa's casualty figures shocked America as nothing else had up to that time. The combat film, both still and motion picture, gave the home front a brutal indoctrination in what lay ahead across the Pacific. The civilian correspondents were here in force and wrote and suffered with the Marines.

STARS AND STRIPES ON TARAWA. Old Glory goes up on a palm tree (upper) while the smoke of battle hangs heavy over Betio. A British Union Jack also was hoisted over this former British possession. LOWER. Marine Generals Thomas Bourke, Merritt Edson and Julian Smith confer after the battle. Artilleryman Bourke and Chief-of-Staff Edson of Guadalcanal fame were Gen Smith's close associates. Later he said: "The one thing that won this battle was the supreme courage of the Marines . . . who kept coming ashore in spite of their (the enemy's) machine gun fire."

BATTLE'S END. On Tarawa's narrow and littered beach U.S. Marines, some wounded and all exhausted by battle and the suffocating heat, take it easy after being told that the atoll is secured. A few hours earlier, all organized Japanese resistance ceased. Nevertheless individual enemies turned up again that night to make personal war against the victorious Americans. One Jap managed to gain the lip of a shell hole being used as a regimental command post before a sentry dropped him with a bullet. Others, after abortive attempts to infiltrate through Marine lines, retired to their own dugouts and committed suicide rather than surrender. Here on Tarawa the Jap suicides largely abandoned the traditional hara kiri. Instead, they removed their shoes and used their toes to pull the trigger of a rifle whose muzzle was held in their mouths. Dozens of the enemy died this way. Hundreds of others had sacrificed their lives as fruitlessly in frontal assaults earlier in the day in unsuccessful attempts to crack the invaders. Hand-to-hand fighting was commonplace. Story after story drifted across the blackened battlefield of men who killed Japs with their rifle butts or, when the rifle was shattered, with their bare hands. Then, too, there were those other stories . . . stories of the Jap officer who sabered a Marine in the back, of the Marine who was shot in the back as he was in the act of carrying a wounded comrade to safety. ABOVE. A section of the beach on Betio Island, Tarawa Atoll, Gilbert Islands, a resting place for the Marine Corps wounded after the battle. Thus ended the toughest campaign to date.

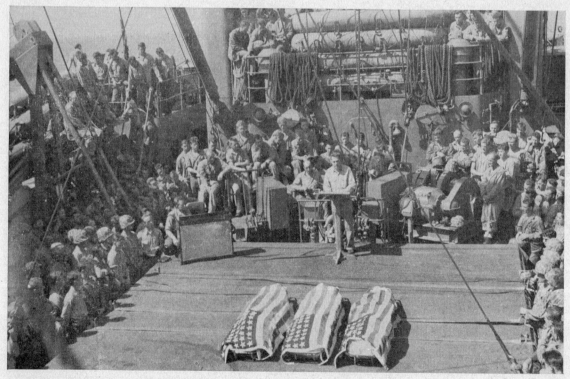

THE HONORED DEAD. UPPER. Scattered along the beach, their faces toward the enemy, Marines lie as they died. A tank also is a casualty. Marines on Tarawa were buried where they lay early in the battle. Later a cemetery was built, and the little white crosses formed their familiar pattern. LOWER. Burial at sea was a solemn rite. These three flag-draped hospital ward baskets contain the bodies of Marines who died of wounds after reaching the transport. Lowered over the side in weighted canvas shrouds, Marines at sea found their final resting place beneath the waves.

THE ENEMY, LIVING AND DEAD. Curled in the grotesque pattern of those who die violently (upper), these Japanese were mowed down by machine-gun fire which caught them in a shallow gully. LOWER. Stripped to shorts and split-toes shoes because of the danger of hidden weapons under their clothing, Japanese prisoners sullenly await removal to a prison camp. Able to repeat English phrases, the Japs frequently were taught to say things such as "Tojo eat dirt. God Bless America. Hurray," and numerous others, by their Marine captors.

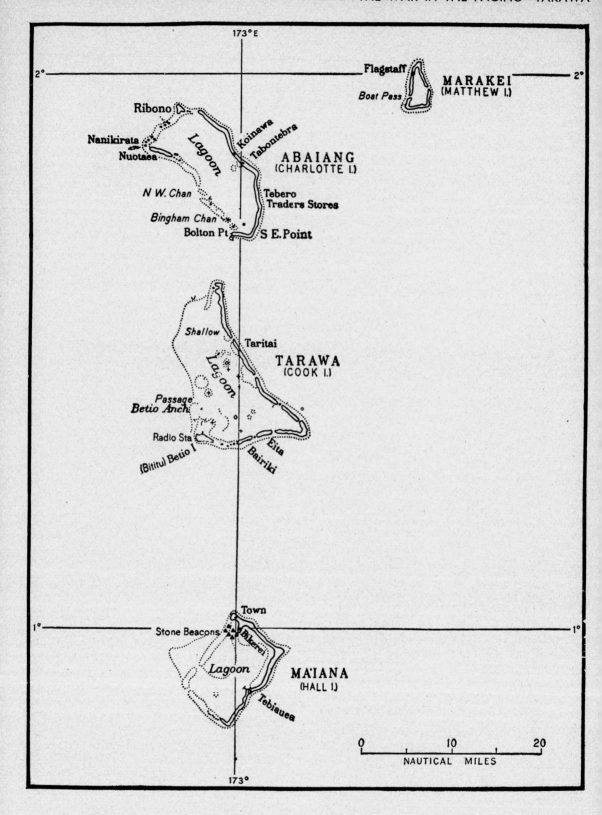

Map of Tarawa and adjacent atolls.

AMPHIBIAN CASUALTIES. The amphibian tractors (above) give silent testimony to the reason why succeeding waves of Marines had to wade across several hundred yards of water. The Japs had many good-sized guns left and they registered on the tractors, blasting the vehicles and killing the personnel. These stalled amphtracs strewn along the coconut seawall were all knocked out of action. As only 175 of these vehicles were available at Tarawa, subsequent engagements saw their number increased with the attachment of amphtrac battalions to Corps troops.

TORN PALMS AND TATTERED TIN. The concrete tetra-hedrons used against boats and tanks (above) were still in these wooden moulds when the Marines landed. UPPER RIGHT. The General Sherman medium tank named "Charlie" knocked out here was one of the best weapons the Marines had ashore. Able to climb the reef and come ashore under its own power, this type tank was used here for the first time in the Pacific war. Two tanks, "Colorado" and "China Gal," were the toast of the embattled Marines. They not only knocked out the smaller Jap tanks, but cruised up and down and around enemy lines knocking out pillboxes. A Marine named Baxter "Cactus" Gann walked beside these two tanks for a period of four hours pointing out enemy positions where-upon he would then hug the ground as the tanks opened up on them. LOWER RIGHT. The debris that was strewn every-where almost defied imagination. Each piece of tin here was a potential hiding place for a cornered Jap. Several months after the operation the President cited the Marines of the Second Division. He named the 2nd, 6th, 8th, 10th and 18th Regiments, along with Division Headquarters and

Special Troops, praising them: "For outstanding performance in combat during the seizure and occupation of the Japanese-held Atoll of Tarawa, Gilbert Islands, November 20th to 24th, 1943. Forced by treacherous coral reefs to disembark from their landing craft hundreds of yards off the beach, the Second Marine Division (Reinforced) became a highly vul-nerable target for devastating Japanese fire. Dauntlessly ad-vancing in spite of rapidly mounting losses, the Marines fought a gallant battle against crushing odds, clearing the limited beachheads of snipers and machine guns, reducing powerfully fortified enemy positions and completely anni-hilating the fanatically determined and strongly entrenched Japanese forces. By the successful occupation of Tarawa the Division has provided our forces with highly strategic and important air and land bases from which to continue future operations against the enemy; by the valiant fighting spirit of these men, their heroic fortitude under punishing fire and their relentless perseverance in waging this epic battle in the Central Pacific, they have upheld the finest traditions of the United States Naval Service."

SILENT GUNS. The initial "neutralization" fire of ships and planes failed to knock out many potent Jap guns. Several opened up on our transports immediately prior to the landing and the ships had to turn tail and pull out of range while the big guns of the fleet angrily silenced the batteries which had given away their positions. UPPER. This 80 mm coastal defense gun was one of eight found on Tarawa. Its used shell casings indicate it was fired several times before being put out of action. LOWER. The Japs had four of these 14 cm guns as part of their defenses. Note holes in the gun shield.

CINCPAC PAYS A VISIT. Admiral Chester A. Nimitz (above), Commander in Chief, Pacific (CINCPAC), inspects an enemy gun in its concrete revetment after the battle. Directly behind him is Gen. Julian Smith. It was Admiral Nimitz who coordinated the air, sea and ground warfare in the Central Pacific from the Gilberts to the final landing on Japan and he was a familiar figure on Makalapa Hill where the Pacific Fleet was headquartered just outside the great Pearl Harbor Navy Yard. Greatly admired by the enlisted men, the Admiral frequently beat them at horseshoes.

THE HONORED DEAD. In many Pacific islands where Marines brought liberation they found strong traces of the civilization they had known at home, a morality brought to the islands by Protestant and Catholic missionaries. As the Marines made possible a return of Christianity they were welcomed and remembered. RIGHT. On Tarawa, a cross stands on the sandy beach, marking the grave of an unknown Marine. Sister Raphael, an Australian nun of the Order of the Sacred Heart, continues her duties among the Gilbertese, remembering the Marines in her prayers. LOWER. Framed by the Pacific sky and the stately palm, this monument to the Marine dead at Tarawa was erected at the western tip of Betio in memory of Second Division Marines who died there. Of Tarawa, Robert Trumbell wrote: "Tarawa fell because every Marine who died had a shot at the Japs before he went down, and more Marines kept coming and coming as the men in front of them died, until finally so many Japs were dead, too, that the Marines were able to get on the beach."

LANDING AT CAPE GLOUCESTER. During September and October of 1943 the First Marine Division moved from Melbourne, Australia, to New Guinea under its new Commanding General, Major General William H. Rupertus. In December the veteran unit boarded ships for its second invasion (upper), and on December 26th moved ashore at Cape Gloucester on the west end of New Britain. Aboard the LST's (lower) and the new Landing Craft, Infantry (LCI's), the Marines spent Christmas Day checking equipment and vehicles prior to the landing.

INTO THE JUNGLE AGAIN.
Marines wrote letters and read pocket books (upper) as their convoy approached New Britain. Down the ramp of this LCI (right), troops go into waist-deep water to wade ashore at Gloucester after the assault troops had landed under a smoke screen from troop carrying destroyers. Actually, the LCI's came on the heels of the small landing craft. There were no transports and only four cruisers. Aviation had performed neutralization missions for days, and all the nearby airfields were inoperative during the early unopposed landings. Operating as part of General MacArthur's Sixth Army, the Division's mission was to secure MacArthur's flank for the Hollandia landing. Gloucester lay at the western end of New Britain, Rabaul at the eastern. General Matsuda, Japanese Commander, had some 8,000 troops to defend the airfield and surrounding area. The 7th Regiment quickly pushed through mucky ground to extend the perimeter and secure Target Hill which dominated the beach. The 1st Regiment's 3rd Battalion moved along the coast toward the airfield to the north and west. The 2nd Battalion landed on the opposite side of Gloucester.

DOUSED IN THE SURF. As the Marines slosh ashore (upper) they sample what life will be like for the next four months during the monsoon season. LOWER. Stumbling ashore through the surf, their weapons held high, the Marines move onto Gloucester's beaches Yellow 1 and 2, and then push on inland. The perpetual rain and mud left many Marines victims of jungle rot and hook worm, ugly annoyances that reduced combat efficiency and lowered morale. The element of surprise was achieved by selecting beachhead sites that were so poor that the Japanese defenders had decided against installing any major installations nearby, guessing that no attacker would try to use them. The Japs reacted quickly by air, sending planes from New Guinea against the D Day landing. Army fighters of the Fifth Air Force turned them away, downing at least 53. The forward companies were well dug in and repulsed several enemy counter-attacks the first night. On December 27th the push for the airfield continued and the 1st Regiment advanced within a mile and a half of the field. The 7th was busy organizing a perimeter defense.

CLOUDED SKIES AND SHADOWS. UPPER LEFT. This Marine is well covered as he slumps in the brush to open his K ration can of meat. Similar in size to a crackerjack box, a K ration also held powdered coffee, lemonade or cocoa, unappetizing but allegedly nourishing biscuits or crackers that looked and tasted like dog biscuits, a chocolate bar, dextrose tablets or fruit bars, and cigarettes. Sometimes a can of cheese or an egg substituted for meat. LOWER LEFT. Marines carry their wounded rearward as troops move out against the enemy. The ease with which the Japs could prepare an ambush on the island made it necessary for the wounded to lie still for long periods while murderous bunkers were flanked, or tanks or amphtracs were brought up for frontal assaults. Members of Marine musical bands usually acted as stretcher bearers, although frequently the walking wounded would help out on the way back to a dressing station. UPPER RIGHT. Its four wheels emplaced in mud, this 105 artillery piece sings a song of death in a small clearing. Far up front, Japs are dying as the "automatic artillery" of the First Division ranges in on their positions in advance of our moving patrols. Ammunition cases and naked shells are piled ready for continued firing. LOWER RIGHT. The mighty mite of the 75 mm. pack howitzer gets a cooling and a cleaning after some continued use. The heat and humidity were everywhere on Gloucester and these crew members are down to their camouflaged utility suit. This garment, all one piece, like coveralls, had large pockets.

TWO KINDS OF JAPANESE. A Marine intelligence officer (upper) studies an enemy situation map with the aid of Sgt. Kitea Yamoda of the U.S. Army, an American of Japanese descent. The Army in the Pacific had a number of these troops as interpreters and intelligence personnel. LOWER. A Marine corporal chats with a Jap captive who seems to be enjoying his prisoner status. The advance to Hill 660 pushed off on Jan. 2, 1944. The next day, at Suicide Creek, Marines ran into prepared positions so well camouflaged as to be invisible, and protected by a "moat" of swift running cold water. Combat Correspondent Bordages recorded the scene: "The jungle exploded in their faces. They hit the deck, trying to deploy in the bullet-lashed brush and strike back. Marines died there, firing blindly, cursing because they couldn't see the men who were killing them. Or not saying anything — just dying. The others could only hug the ground as bullets cut the brush above their heads. They couldn't even help the wounded. You can't describe hell. You can only go through it."

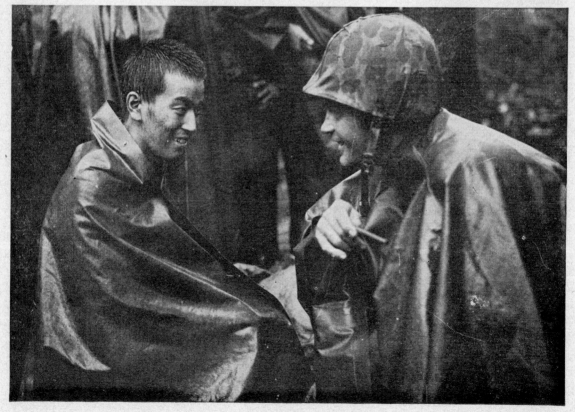

INFORMALITY AND HISTORY. Wherever American troops went they always carried small or medium flags, ready to raise the Stars and Stripes at an appropriate moment. UPPER. Here a platoon hoists Old Glory on a crude staff near the captured Jap airfield, minutes after capturing the strip. Spread on a poncho (lower), this Jap equipment has a ghoulish look with gas masks popped out of their cases. Flat canteens are at the right, bayonets and 25 caliber rifles at the rear. After crossing Suicide Creek the see-saw battle continued for two weeks. Near Hill 660 a ridge was chosen and assigned to the 3rd Battalion of the 5th Marines under Lieut. Col. L. T. Walt. One of the most unorthodox battles of the war resulted. Clawing its way inches at a time, the battalion fought the terrain and the unseen enemy. Finally, by dragging a 37 mm. gun up the ridge and firing cannister shots at the jungle and the Jap, Walt's men reached Jap prepared positions, ousted the enemy and settled down for the night's counter-attack which they repulsed to hold the newly christened "Walt's Ridge." Two days later Hill 660 fell, and by January 20, 1944, the second phase had ended.

THE WAR IN THE CENTRAL PACIFIC

By Lieutenant General Robert C. Richardson

AFTER fighting a defensive war in the Central Pacific for more than 18 months, American forces were ready to take the offensive in the fall of 1943.

The strategy of this offensive consisted of a continuous march westward with the aim of seizing bases and driving the Japanese back to their homeland.

The first of the desired bases were those in the Gilbert Islands—bases which would serve as a stepping stone to the acquisition of the Marshalls. The ultimate destination, of course, was Tokyo by way of Truk, Saipan, Iwo Jima, Okinawa or whatever islands were deemed to be the best route.

In August 1943 I had been designated Commanding General of all Army and Air Forces in the Central Pacific Area. Admiral Nimitz was the Commander-in-Chief of the Pacific Ocean Areas and directed the operations of all Army and Air Forces. He retained also immediate command of the Pacific Fleet, assuming the respective titles of CINCPOA and CINCPAC. On 20 July 1943 he received a directive from the Joint Chiefs of Staff to assume the offensive.

The attack against the Gilberts was launched on 20 November 1943, and consisted of the seizure of Tarawa by the Second Marine Division and the capture of Makin by a reinforced regimental combat team of the 27th Infantry Division, under Major General Ralph C. Smith. This force had been placed under the operational control of the V Amphibious Corps for this operation.

Makin was captured in three days, and about 900 Japanese were killed or captured.

The enemy was given little time to rest. A vast armada assaulted the Marshall Islands 31 January 1944. The upper islands of the atoll, Roi and Namur, were assigned to the Marines, and Kwajalein, the main objective, was the target of the Seventh Infantry Division. Kwajalein was taken with a minimum of American losses, but more than 4,000 Japanese were killed on that island alone. Nearly 10,000 Japanese lost their lives in the seizure of the atoll. The Seventh Infantry Division made 42 amphibious landings in this operation, seizing one island after another following the capture of Kwajalein.

This operation was accomplished with such surprising ease that the Task Force Commander recommended the use of the reserves, which had not been committed, for an immediate assault on Eniwetok Atoll. This decision, approved by Admiral Nimitz, advanced the campaign of the Central Pacific by more than three months. A regiment of the Marines was assigned to the seizure of Engebi and the 106th Infantry of the 27th Infantry Division to Eniwetok. This regiment, commanded by Colonel Russell G. Ayers, lost 61 men killed while destroying 1,094 Japanese.

Operations at Eniwetok had been covered by a bold fleet strike at Truk and the Marianas 17-22 February. The strike at Truk was particularly effective. The Japanese fleet was forced to retire from this advanced base. Nearly all remaining enemy air power in the eastern Central Pacific Area was destroyed. Plans to land on Truk were already in process of formulation. Photographs made during the strike and analysis of intelligence reports convinced the Joint Chiefs of Staff that Truk could be safely by-passed and neutralized by American sea and air power. On 12 March 1944 Truk was dropped as a potential target and Admiral Nimitz was directed to proceed with the capture of the Marianas Islands on or about 15 June 1944. Earlier estimates of the landings to be made in the Marianas had placed the date as 1 November 1944.

Two Marine Amphibious Corps were to conduct the invasion of the Marianas. The V Corps, including the 2nd and 4th Marine Divisions, was to land originally on Saipan. The III Amphibious Corps, comprised of the 3rd Marine Division and the 1st Provisional Marine Brigade, were to land at Guam. The 27th Infantry Division was in floating reserve for both operations, while the 77th Infantry Division, then newly arrived in the Central Pacific, was to be held in strategic reserve in the Hawaiian Islands, for use after D-Day plus 20, if needed.

The landings at Saipan were strongly opposed and on 16 June, the second day of the operation, the 27th Division was committed. From that time until the island was officially declared secure on 9 July, elements of the 27th Division were constantly in the line. At the close of the operation, this division had suffered 3,670 casualties, of whom 1,053 were killed in action. From 9 July until late August the Division was engaged in mopping up.

The bitter struggle on Saipan had resulted in the postponement of the attacks upon Guam and Tinian. Commitment of the 27th Division also necessitated bringing in the 77th Division from Oahu. The landings on Guam eventually took place on 21 July, with the 77th Division going ashore on D-Day, although not in the assault. The island was finally announced secure on 10 August. Approximately 10,000 Japanese had been killed. Casualties in the 77th Division amounted to 270 killed and 876 wounded.

While the fighting had been taking place in the Marianas, two more operations were in preparation. The first of these, directed by the III Amphibious Corps, was aimed at the Palau group. On 15 September members of the 1st Marine Division and the 81st Infantry Division landed on Pelelieu and Angaur respectively. Angaur was garrisoned by about 1,400 Japanese who were subdued by the 81st by 22 September. On the same day, elements of the 81st Division landed unopposed on Ulithi. Meanwhile, opposition encountered by the 1st Marine Division on Pelelieu had been great, and during the first week in October, two regimental combat teams of the 81st Infantry Division were landed to assist in the reduction of that island fortress, manned by about 9,000 Japs. Fighting here ended 8 November.

The second of the two planned autumn operations for 1944 was seizure of Yap on 15 October. For this purpose I organized the XXIV Corps in Hawaii and placed Major General John R. Hodge in command. His troops were loaded for this operation when the Joint Chiefs of Staff, on recommendation of General MacArthur and Admiral Nimitz, changed the target to Leyte in the Philippines. The XXIV Corps landed on Leyte as a part of the Sixth Army on 20 October 1944.

During the summer of 1944, Army headquarters in the Pacific had undergone a major reorganization. USAFICPA now became United States Army Forces in the Pacific Ocean Areas. I still retained command of this headquarters. Three separate base commands were established under USAFPOA. At Fort Shafter on Oahu, the Central Pacific Base Command was established under the command of Major General Henry L. Burgin. The old South Pacific Area was disbanded. In its place appeared the South Pacific Base Command under the command of Major General Frederick Gilbreath. In September, 1944 the island command of newly-conquered Saipan became the Western Pacific Base Command under Major General Sanderford B. Jarman. Operational command in the Central Pacific continued to be held by Admiral Nimitz as CINCPAC-CINCPOA.

Meanwhile, CINCPOA had given me directions to prepare an attack on Formosa. The Tenth Army was activated for this operation, and Lieutenant General Simon B. Buckner was assigned to lead it. Although all plans were made for this attack they were abandoned in favor of a strike in the Ryukyus Islands.

This operation, the last of the war in the Central Pacific, began on 26 March 1945, when elements of the 77th Division seized the Kerama Retto, a small group of islands southwest of Okinawa. On 1 April the Tenth Army landed on Okinawa itself with two corps abreast. The III Amphibious Corps with the 1st and 6th Marine Division landed on the north and the XXIV Corps, comprised of the 7th and 96th Divisions, landed on the right, south. The III Corps turned north and swept rapidly up the island against negligible opposition, reaching the north tip in mid-April. The XXIV Corps met only minor opposition in the south until 4 April when the two assault divisions ran head-on into the Shuri Defense line. Almost two full months later Americans were still pounding their way through the incredibly tangled terrain of a superior Japanese defense system. Shuri fell on 31 May and finally, on 21 June, Okinawa was declared secure. Both the 27th and 77th Army Divisions fought on Okinawa. The latter also captured Ie Shima in a bitter 4-day battle in April, killing 5,000 Japanese. The victory cost the enemy more than 120,000 men, killed and captured. Including naval casualties, American losses in this last battle of the war were over 40,000. Of these 4,675 Army men were killed in the four divisions that participated. Some 18,100 were wounded. General Buckner was among those killed in the final stages of this battle.

During this last desperate battle at Japan's doorstep all Army commands in the Pacific were placed under General MacArthur. Under his direction former Central Pacific units were busily engaged in preparing for the invasion of the Japanese homeland. The Japanese, blasted by the atom bomb, mindful that all the forces of the whole Allied world were massing for this assault, gave up the fight and surrendered unconditionally.

Robert Richardson

STORMING THE ATOLLS. The Japanese were aware of American plans to invade the Marshalls, but did not know where the assault force would strike. They apparently believed that the attack would begin on the eastern chain of atolls, situated closer to the Gilbert Islands which had been taken during November. On January 30, 31, 1944, U.S. aircraft carriers launched swarms of planes that pounded the atoll's defenses. Temporarily blinded by the attack, the Japanese did not discover that a naval force, probably greater than any ever before assembled, was on its way—not to the eastern atolls, but to Kwajalein in the sunset chain. U.S. warships, including new battleships, subjected enemy installations on Kwajalein to prolonged attack unprecedented in history. Within four hours, Japanese airpower was virtually destroyed and 122 wrecked planes littered the ground. Japanese defenses which had been in construction for twenty years, disintegrated in the face of tremendous naval firepower. Beach walls disappeared, concrete tank-obstacles crumbled, and pill boxes were destroyed. The costly assault on Tarawa, where a more sustained bombardment of enemy emplacements might have saved American lives, was not to be repeated. An innovation of the assault was the avoidance of an immediate head-on action with the main defensive elements. Instead of directly attacking Roi and Kwajalein, the enemy strongpoints, the assault was deflected to nearby islets from which troops advanced on the Japanese strongholds under cover of pulverizing artillery barrages. The effect of the bombardment sustained by the Navy stunned the Japanese and lessened the fierceness of their resistance. Roi, the first parcel of prewar Japanese territory to be taken from the enemy, fell to the Marine Fourth Division on February 2. On the following day the Fourth captured Namur. Within a week after the invasion, Seabees had extended the air strips on Roi sufficiently to accommodate the heaviest U.S. bombers. Meanwhile, the 7th Infantry Division encountered stiff resistance on Kwajalein, but by February 5 this, the most powerful Japanese stronghold east of Truk, was in American hands. Amphibious craft (left) transport men and equipment to the battle smouldering shores of Kwajalein.

OPERATION FLINTLOCK. They called the Kwajalein-Roi-Namur assault "Operation Flintlock," and for the defending Japs who received the pre-invasion rain of bombs and shells from the fleet and aircraft it was rough indeed. Kwajalein was literally cut to pieces with the fire preparation for landings. ABOVE. D-Day on the atoll. Infantrymen move in. Smoke is from pre-invasion firepower. UPPER RIGHT. U.S. troops advance inland, leaving blazing Jap installations behind. LOWER RIGHT. On invasion day, these members of the 7th Division routed Japs from this strongly-built, well-camouflaged dugout. The islands of the atoll had been under Japanese mandate for a quarter of a century.

DESTRUCTION. Destruction was the word for Kwajalein. A Naval task force under Vice Admiral R. K. Turner shelled the atoll for 48 hours, and some of the damage inflicted by nearly 15,000 tons of high explosives is evident in these pictures. But of the 8,000 Japs on the series of islands, many survived, and Kwajalein had to be taken foot by foot. ABOVE. Attempting to drive strongly-entrenched Japs into the open, a 7th Division anti-tank gun fires point blank on a pill box. UPPER RIGHT. Part of an infantry company halts while a tank blasts a path into Jap positions on Enubuj. LOWER RIGHT. Stress of battle is dramatic here as an infantry assault force encircles and destroys a Jap pill box.

LET 'EM HAVE IT! While the 7th Division took Kwajalein yard by yard, the Marines were doing the same thing on Roi and Namur. The going was not easy on either front. The advance took courage aplenty. UPPER. On Enubuj, a field artillery howitzer, supporting the 7th Division, blasts away at Japs on the next island. LOWER. It gets more personal in this sort of fighting. Japs are holed in a blockhouse here, and flame throwers of the 7th Division give them the heat treatment on February 4. In right foreground note the business end of an infantryman's M-I rifle and bayonet held in readiness.

MOPPING UP. After the capture of Kwajalein the 7th Infantry Division made 42 amphibious landings, and seized one island after the other. As a result of this and of pre-invasion bombardment, nearly 10,000 Japs joined their ancestors. UPPER. During the conquest of Kwajalein, a 37 mm gun crew of the 7th Division goes up the line of advance. LOWER. Even in battle you get a break sometimes—and these troops had earned this one. There were snipers in the woods, though, and the break was not overly restful. The smoke in the background is from a burning Jap warehouse,

SAME OLD STORY. Applying the lessons of Tarawa, the Fourth landed in all-purpose tractors on the lagoon beaches, which even had a pier, like Tarawa. Some tractors had been reinforced with armor plate and were designated LVTA's (armored). They were expected to take the troops inland, but many of them fired from the water's edge (upper), too close for comfort to the advancing Marines. Hitting the beach at Roi-Namur (lower) may seem tame in retrospect. At the time it was a spectacular tactical stroke, achieved with a maximum of surprise against an enemy who anticipated invasion.

TWIN ATTACKS. As the 23rd Regiment Marines landed on Roi's beaches (upper), another fight was taking place to the south (lower), where the Attu veterans of the Army's Seventh Infantry Division had gone ashore the day before at Kwajalein, 42 miles away. By the fifth day of continued fighting, the larger Kwajalein, main atoll of the chain, was secured. Also cleared of the enemy was nearby Ebeye. In their campaign to the south, the Seventh beat off a few Jap night attacks with the help of flare and searchlight illumination from nearby ships. It was a most competent operation.

FIGHTING ON NAMUR. In many ways, the Kwajalein operation was novel. The two atoll prizes, one about a half mile square, the other about three-quarters, were seized only after artillery was landed the day before on nearby atolls. On D Day, January 31, 1944, the lagoon opening was forced with comparative ease and the two flanking coral dots seized. This allowed ships and boats to enter the lagoon for an attack on the inner beaches of Roi and Namur. Amphtracs soon landed the 25th Marines on three unpronounceable and lightly-held atolls, all within easy artillery range of Roi-Namur. Col. Louis DeHaven's artillery regiment, the 14th Marines, went ashore in spite of a preliminary foul-up in communications and gasoline shortages among the landing craft. By daylight of D 1, the Asst. Div. Commander, Brig. Gen. J. L. Underhill, had set the stage for the main show which pushed ashore at noon (upper) supported by carrier planes. Aided by light tanks with colorful names such as "Hothead" (below), the Marines moved inland on rubble-strewn Namur. The scene that met the troops going ashore on the "red" and "green" beaches was one of almost utter desolation.

MOVING INLAND. The 24th Regiment encountered the toughest resistance on Namur (upper) where each Jap had to be cornered and killed. The vegetation and dense rubble provided excellent last-ditch defenses. Marines had to have eyes to front and rear as by-passed Japs often shot at them. On the beach (lower), shore party crews kept a semblance of order on the sand, moving supplies and equipment inland and keeping lanes open for tanks and other vehicles. In the foreground a communications unit has built a sand bag barricade. The beach had a shelving wall which permitted movement free from enemy small arms fire. The Japs were almost stunned by the weight of the pre-invasion bombardment and had enjoyed little sleep for days. Many had been killed by air and sea bombardment in fire trenches close to the Namur beaches as they stood by to repel a landing. In the unbearably hot sun the stench of death was everywhere. In two hours of cautious advance, both battalions of the 24th reached initial phase lines, but only after by-passing several sniper-infested blockhouses. The right flank battalion moved cautiously ahead while the left paused to reorganize.

SKY HIGH EXPLOSION. As the right flank battalion moved inland, the island suddenly seemed to disintegrate as an enemy storage building of reinforced concrete, packed with torpedo warheads and aerial bombs, blew up (upper) in one of the biggest land explosions seen in the Pacific war. An officer said later: "An ink-black darkness spread over a large part of Namur. Debris continued to fall for a considerable length of time, which seemed unending to those in the area, unprotected from the large chunks of concrete and steel." LOWER. Marines hack through a Jap strongpoint.

CAUSE AND EFFECT. Maj. Gen. Holland M. Smith, the famed "Father of Amphibious Warfare," goes ashore (upper) at Roi-Namur to see how the Fourth carried out the operations plans of the Fifth Amphibious Corps. Leader of many invasions and senior commander of all Pacific Marines, Gen. Smith spoke his mind freely and frankly, dishing out praise and blame as he saw fit. Gen. Smith was at Kwajalein with Army troops, hence wears the Army combat net helmet cover. What he saw (lower) pleased him. His beloved Marines captured the twin atolls in 24 hours, Roi falling the first day as tanks and troops ranged the flat airfield, searching snipers and blasting cornered Japs out of drainage ditches. These Jap troops sprawled near their machine gun died bravely but horribly for their Emperor, a pitiful handful of the 3,472 dead who the Marines buried there. At the end of the first day's fighting on Namur the 24th Marines had pushed to within a few hundred yards of the island's extremity on the left, but had progressed a scant 300 yards on the right. The protracted advance was caused by a series of explosions, one of which completely disorganized a battalion,

ENDING THE BATTLE. A Marine communications lineman helps lace the island with a network of wire (upper) as a defense battalion and Seabees set up shop on the atolls. LOWER. Marines move toward the far end of Namur after a night of heavy casualties during which bullets whizzed overhead, tracers split the darkness with scarlet trails and star shells cast an unearthly light over the blasted island. It rained on and off all night, adding to the misery. To top everything the Jap defenders launched a series of Banzai attacks that see-sawed back and forth from foxhole to bomb crater and back as Marines and Japs fought and died in hand to hand battle. Heroism, which is not measured in hours and days, but in seconds and minutes, resulted in four Medal of Honor awards, three posthumous, for this 24 hours out of a Division's life in battle. Just before the Division had left Camp Pendleton it picked a shoulder insignia, a blocked figure "4." On Roi they found an airfield in almost the identical pattern, three runways converging into a "4." Many of the Marines regarded this as a good luck omen.

THE ENEMY'S TROPIC EMPIRE. UPPER. An aerial view of Guadalcanal Island shows the rugged terrain and dense tropical jungle covering the island. LOWER. An American examines a dummy Jap gun on a captured island. This gun, made of wood and camouflaged to simulate the real thing, is typical of the fake weapons with which the Japs hoped to delude our reconnaissance experts. Airplanes, built of wooden lattice work, were found spotted on airfields or partially hidden in revetments. Fake searchlights were installed to give a false impression of coast defenses.

ROCKETS FOR THUNDERBOLTS. Adaptation of the rocket as a weapon for fighter aircraft enormously increased their versatility and wallop. Through its use, fighters had the striking power of artillery without the prohibitive weight and recoil attendant to the use of guns of a comparable caliber. The rocket rounded out the armament of the fighter, falling between the machine gun and the bomb. Almost anything which would be put under artillery fire if it were within range was considered a good rocket target. The first type used by the AAF was the 4.5" airborne bazooka type, fired from launcher tubes mounted together as an integral cluster of three under each wing, as on this P-47.

THIS LAND IS OURS. Major General Charles H. Corlett, Commander of the 7th Division, and a staff officer survey the newly acquired territory of the United States Army which Tokio regarded as the perimeter of the Japanese Empire. Throughout the nine days the invasion fleet had remained in waters adjacent to the Marshalls, not a single Japanese plane attacked them. The operation was completed without the loss of a single ship.

OPERATION "FLINTLOCK" COMPLETED. Once the Gilbert Island bases (Abemama, Tarawa and Makin) were ready, the campaign in the Marshalls swung into high gear, continuing the pattern of "triphibious" war already established in the Central Pacific. The air elements included 7th Air Force land-based planes, and Navy carrier-based aviation. From December 7, 1943, to March 2, 1944 (D-day for the surprise landing at Kwajalein occurred on the 31st of January, 1944), the 7th Air Force made 2,897 bomber sorties, dropping 2,812 tons of bombs. This coupled with powerful punches by fast carrier task forces and warships, effectually neutralized the Marshalls for the landings. ABOVE. Kwajalein, Headquarters of the 7th Air Force, became an unsinkable aircraft carrier. Planes, including P-61 "Black Widow" night fighters, lined the runways, and every available inch of the world's largest atoll was pressed into American service. For relaxation, men stationed here used inflated mattress covers to ride the pounding Pacific surf.

INVASION OF ENIWETOK. With Roi-Namur and Kwajalein secure, and with Majuro captured by the Fifth Corps Scout Company, the Corps Commander found he had two regimental combat teams available for Eniwetok, the 106th Army and the 22nd Marines. From bases at Kwajalein our planes could continue neutralizing the western chain while the airfields being built at Majuro would soon be sending planes over Mille, Jaluit, Maloelap and Wotje. On February 18, 1944, Marines (upper) landed at Engebi Island, Eniwetok Atoll, and moved inland (lower) despite fanatical opposition.

ON ENGEBI ISLAND. At the northern end of the almost round Eniwetok Atoll, Engebi was one of three islands held in any force. It contained an airstrip, dangerous in enemy hands, because through it the Japs could shuttle planes to the Marshalls and eastern Carolines. Under Col. John T. Walker, the 22nd took the island in less than 24 hours. UPPER LEFT. Marines move forward, carefully alert for the many hidden snipers. LOWER LEFT. Panoramic view of the rubble caused by the Navy's air and surface bombardment. Artillery from nearby Yeiri and Rujiyoru Atolls, occupied by the Corps Reconnaissance Company without opposition on February 17th, also supported the landings. The defenses were good and the new regiment saw some heavy fighting on the small island, but once ashore there was never any question. UPPER RIGHT. It was the familiar story of combing the enemy out of protective terrain and moving steadily forward, letting troops that followed mop up by-passed snipers. LOWER RIGHT. Tanks got ashore early in the battle. Here a tank retriever crosses some of the battered coral, distant palms are almost hidden in the dust and smoke of battle. On Engebi the Marines encountered a new type of "mobile" defense, a series of empty gas drums in line, well emplaced. When a pill box came under fire, its occupants scurried through the drum tunnel to pop up many yards away, firing from the front, flank or rear of the Marines. After a terrible night of infiltration the island was secured. Parry Island's surrender on February 22 ended the campaign in the Marshalls.

TASK FORCE 58. On February 4, 1944, two Marine Liberators left a Solomons base and flew 2,000 miles to make an aerial reconnaissance of Truk. Until that day little was known about this Japanese stronghold which no white man had gazed upon for many years. The Japanese were so amazed at the audacity of the intruders that several minutes elapsed before the U.S. planes met with opposition. In twenty minutes the Marine planes had accomplished their mission and they returned to their base. The photographs they had taken revealed that twenty-five ships were sheltered in the lagoon. This report was conveyed to Admiral Halsey, at Kwajalein, who with Admirals Spruance and Mitscher rushed Task Force 58 into action. On February 14, Army Liberators plastered Ponape, Truk's strategic outpost. This move enabled the task force to proceed unobserved to its destination. At dawn on February 16, swarms of fighters and bombers rose from the decks of the carriers and headed for Truk. A terrific battle, which lasted for several hours, ensued over the island. When it was finished, more than 200 Japanese planes had been accounted for. During the hours after dark, the first carrier night strike ever effected was sent out by Captain William I. Martin. This low level bombing attack directed against the ships in the harbor chalked up thirteen direct hits. When U.S. planes took to the skies to resume the battle on the 17th they remained unchallenged. In all, Task Force 58 blasted the enemy out of the skies, sank twenty-three of his ships, reduced many of his installations, and exploded the theory that the Carolinas' base was invincible. Following the successful raid Admiral Nimitz issued this statement: "The Pacific fleet has returned at Truk the visit made by the Japanese at Pearl Harbor on December 7, 1941, and effected a partial settlement of the debt." Some idea of the terrain of the Japanese base, and the extent of its formidable installations, can be obtained by this official United States Navy photograph (left), taken during the raid. Although much damage was inflicted by Task Force 58, there remained extensive airfields, troop concentrations, and installations that had not been impaired. A flotilla of Japanese vessels are depicted as they huddle under the rain of U.S. Navy bombs. Smoke pours from the foreward hold of one of the larger ships which failed to escape American punishment.

ACTION OFF SAIPAN. Detected by the enemy as it sailed daringly into the range of land based planes, U.S. Naval Task Force 58 grimly fought off Japanese raiders for eleven hours. At the height of the aerial storm it launched its own planes during the morning hours of Washington's Birthday, 1944, to strike at Saipan and Tinian. In the afternoon airfields at Saipan and Guam were hit. Spitting death with precision and accuracy, the ack-ack guns of the force shot down fourteen Japanese torpedo bombers and dive bombers to bring the total score of enemy planes destroyed in the raid to 135. Six U.S. Navy planes were lost. Enemy naval losses totaled five ships sunk or damaged by this same task force which had hammered Truk in the Carolinas only five days before. In this action-studded picture (left), pilots and crew of a U.S. Navy carrier cheer exultantly as guns of their ship send a Japanese plane into a swirling, blazing finale. Smoke from the burning plane and from anti-aircraft shells blend into the leaden background provided by the overcast sky. The boldness with which the strikes were delivered coupled with the maneuverability of the task force badly confused the enemy. After Rear Admiral Marc A. Mitscher's demonstration of U.S. might off Saipan, Premier Tojo summarily dismissed the chiefs of the Japanese Army and Navy general staffs, Field Marshal Sugiyama and Admiral of the Fleet Nogano. The positions held by these men were comparable to those held by General Marshall and Admiral King in the U.S.

STILWELL AND MOUNTBATTEN MEET. ABOVE. Admiral
Lord Louis Mountbatten, Supreme Commander Southeast
Asia Command, confers with Lieutenant General Joseph
Stilwell shortly after Brigadier General Frank Merrill's American infantry units had gone into action. The first assignment
for Americans in Burma was to cut their way through the
trackless jungle, outflanking the Japanese who, at the time,
were holding up the Chinese advance. This maneuver was
an adaptation of Japanese tactics which had proven
devastating against the British at the war's beginning.

ACTION NORTH OF NEW GUINEA. On February 29, U.S. troops landed, unopposed, on Los Negros Island. The Japanese began to battle for the island on the eve of March 3, and within a week U.S. forces had subdued them. On March 15, after a heavy preliminary air and sea bombardment, U.S. troops invaded Manus Island. A day later the airfield was captured, and on March 18, after a fierce tank battle, Lorengau was taken. Most of the Jap defenders were killed. UPPER. Americans ford a stream on Manus Island. LOWER. The invasion of Green Island begins.

JAPANESE INVADE INDIA. During the latter part of March, 1944, the Japanese made a thrust from Burma into India. Their immediate objective was the city of Imphal, situated thirty-five miles east of the border. Although the Japanese succeeded in isolating the city from its ground routes or supply, Allied air superiority made contact by air an easy matter, and an air lift was established. ABOVE. Maj. Gen. Chennault directs operations at his command post.

SLOW ROAD TO CHINA. Troops of the U.S. Army service forces forged their route of supply from Assam in Eastern India, across the Northern Burma border, toward the heart of China. This route was named the Ledo Road. In some places, U.S. Army engineers blasted the road out of hillsides. In others, they cut and hacked the highway through lush green jungles, bridging rivers, streams and chasms. The men who forged the road had to work from sketchy maps more than twenty years old. Despite all obstacles, the road was pushed forward towards its terminus which, in turn, would lead to Tokio. The newly constructed bridge (above) carries the road over a river in India. The use of the Ledo Road entered into United Nations plans for the retaking of Burma and the reopening of a land supply line to China. For many months Chinese troops, who later swarmed across the Salween and headed towards Burma to link up with General Stilwell's men, had been drilling under American supervision.

NEW GUINEA CAMPAIGN. Even as the Bougainville campaign drew to a close, American, New Zealand and Australian troops under General MacArthur were fighting their way up the New Guinea coast toward the Philippines. The terrain was even more rugged than in the Solomons, but they advanced about 800 miles in 11 weeks. Even though the Japs had lost Buna and Sanananda they sent heavy reinforcements to Lae and Salamaua after Allied landings at the latter base. ABOVE. Troops of the 126th Infantry cross the Yangdar River in New Guinea. UPPER RIGHT. A Jap killed by a patrol in New Guinea. LOWER RIGHT. General MacArthur is shown off the New Guinea coast April 20, 1944.

"GREEN DRAGONS" OF NEW GUINEA. Not even American submarines were more feared by the Japs than the U. S. Navy's smallest combat ship, the PT, or Patrol Torpedo boat. Because of their small size and shallow draft, PT boats could be based in the inlets and river mouths that abound within the reefs of tropic island groups. Screened by overhanging foliage the PT squadrons could live in comparative safety during the daytime. Then, at night, they slipped out for sudden attacks on big enemy ships, earning for themselves the name "Green Dragon" from the apprehensive Japanese. UPPER. PT boat, silhouetted against the sunset, begins a night patrol near Lae, New Guinea. LOWER. A PT boat returns to its base, Morobe, New Guinea, with some natives as passengers.

LOADING THE STINGERS. Although PT boats are most famous for their torpedo attacks, they can also repell planes with anti-aircraft machine guns and assail submerged submarines with depth bombs. By the end of the war some of them were equipped also with rockets, and others could lay mines in enemy waters. In addition, PTs have been called upon to assist in commando raids, rescues of downed airmen, harbor surveys, escort trips, and in the laying of smoke screens. In fact, there are very vew jobs which a ship can do that PTs have not been asked to do, and done well. From 70 to 80 feet long, PTs generally carried a crew of ten or eleven men. They were driven by three or more powerful motors, and depended upon their speed (approximately 70 knots) to save them from enemy fire.

A LONG JUMP. After Allied forces had conquered the Japs at Salamaua, Lae, Nadzab, and Saidor, and after Rabaul had been isolated in March, General MacArthur decided to jump to Hollandia, thus by-passing the Japanese 18th Army at Wewak. The Japs were taken almost completely by surprise when landings were made on April 22, 1944, at Tanahmerah, Hollandia, and Aitape, by the 41st Division. ABOVE. Troops of the 163rd Infantry Regiment getting ready for the invasion. UPPER RIGHT. First wave of 162nd Infantry penetrating the jungle at the edge of White Beach, Hollandia, on D-Day. LOWER RIGHT. Infantrymen moving toward the Hollandia airstrip, their first objective.

UP THE COAST. In less than a month after establishing its base at Hollandia, the 163rd Infantry jumped up the coast and took Arare, some 175 miles nearer Japan. Following this action, elements of the 41st Division moved over to Wakde Island on May 21 and took the Jap air base there. ABOVE. First and second waves of invasion forces on Wakde are pinned down at water's edge. Ten days later they went ashore on Biak, and on July 2 took Noemfoor, west of Biak. UPPER RIGHT. A patrol of the 162nd Infantry advances toward the Biak airstrip. LOWER RIGHT. Members of the 158th Infantry advance on Noemfoor. For strategic purposes the landings practically ended the New Guinea campaign.

THE WAR IN THE CBI

By Major General Frank D. Merrill

KEEPING China in the war was the mission of American forces in the China-Burma-India Theater. This was accomplished by aerial operations, by supply, by training Chinese armies—and by some of the roughest and toughest fighting any men ever did anywhere.

China had been at war with the Japanese since 1937 and was drained of resources. Cut off from supply by sea, she was fed by a thin trickle over the tortuous Burma Road. When the Japanese armies overran Burma, the road was cut and closed on April 29, 1942.

General (then Lieutenant General) Joseph W. Stilwell, appointed Commander of the CBI Theater early in 1942, was ordered to implement an American promise to break the blockade of China. His orders were to act as Chief of Staff to Generalissimo Chiang Kai-shek, to improve the combat efficiency of the Chinese army, and to expand the existing air route to China. At first the air ferry route over 500 miles of the Himalayan Hump had troubled days, but it kept our air forces in China operating. Late in 1942 construction of an overland route from Assam was begun by United States Army Engineers, aided by Indian labor.

China's position was critical, and her fall would have been a bitter blow to Allied hopes. Accordingly, at Casablanca, in January, 1943, the Combined Chiefs of Staff ordered that plans be made to re-establish surface communications to that country and to increase the Hump tonnage, even though the facilities and resources of the Allies were heavily taxed elsewhere.

Four months later, at the Trident Conference in Washington, top priority was given to the Air Transport Command to increase its aerial load to 10,000 tons a month by early fall of 1943, and President Roosevelt had ordered that Major General Claire L. Chennault, Commander of the China-based 14th U.S. Air Force, should receive a fixed priority on Hump tonnage in the attempt to carry out his plan to destroy the Japanese air force in China.

In June, 1943, the Southeast Asia Command was created, uniting British, Chinese, and Americans in India and Burma under an Allied Commander. Later, Admiral, the Lord Louis Mountbatten was named to this post, with General Stilwell as his deputy. The decision to undertake an offensive in North Burma in the winter of 1943 was reaffirmed. It was further decided to build a pipeline from Calcutta to Assam and another paralleling the Ledo Road (from Assam to China), as well as to enlarge the capacity of the Hump route

and to plan the bombing of Japan with China-based B-29's. Soon all Royal Air Force and U.S. Army Air Force combat strength on the Burma front, including the U.S. 10th Air Force, was formed into the Eastern Air Command under Major General George E. Stratemeyer.

At Cairo in November, 1943, the Combined Chiefs of Staff, with President Roosevelt, Prime Minister Churchill, and Generalissimo Chiang Kai-shek, decided to continue the land operations already begun in Burma. Preliminaries began in October, when the Chinese 38th Division, trained by Americans at Ramgarh, India, was deployed across the Hukawng Valley ahead of the advancing Ledo Road. They at once engaged the Japanese 18th Division, veterans of Singapore.

In February, 1944, these Chinese forces under General Stilwell were joined by a specially trained American infantry unit of regimental size under my command. Made up of volunteers from veteran combat or jungle-trained units, this special force fought under the most difficult conditions of terrain and climate. At the end of our battles we stood triumphant on the airfield at Myitkyina, the key to North Burma.

Together with the full 22d and 38th, plus some elements of the 14th, 30th, and 50th Chinese Divisions, and the always splendid co-operation of Major General Howard Davidson's 10th Air Force, we defeated two Japanese Divisions (18th, 53d) which had heavy reinforcements from other divisions in Burma. Our marches and battles left our men, popularly known as "Maurauders," riddled by sickness and casualties, and after Myitkyina the unit was considered to have been expended. The survivors plus replacements, and the 124th Cavalry from the States, were formed into the 5332nd Brigade (Provisional), "Mars Task Force."

From March to August 1944, columns of British and Indian troops under the late Major General Orde C. Wingate operated behind the Japanese lines, blocking the Japanese line of communication to North Burma. One brigade entered Burma by the grueling overland route, while the other two were flown in by a special air unit under Colonel Philip C. Cochran, U.S.A.A.F. Meanwhile, a Chinese Expeditionary Force, commanded by Marshal Wei Li-huang, ferried the Salween River at five points in an effort to dislodge the Japanese 56th Division.

But Allied control of north Burma and southwestern Yunnan was not assured until Marshal Wei's troops met Stilwell's men in January, 1945, at the China-Burma border.

In the spring of 1944, the Japanese 15th Army struck at Imphal in India in an attempt to push the Allies off balance and forstall their invasion of Burma. Imphal was cut off by April, and the Bengal-Assam railroad to Stilwell's base threatened, but British and Indian troops flown to the scene were able to turn the invaders back with heavy losses by the end of June.

The Burma campaign was the most ambitious operation yet to be dependent on airborne supply. From the first advance into the Hukawng Valley by the Chinese until the fall of Myitkyina, 11 months later, between 25,000 and 100,000 troops were either wholly or partially dependent on air supply, and it never failed.

The Burma campaign continued at a slower pace during the monsoons of 1944 with American, Chinese, and British troops under Lieutenant General Dan I. Sultan disposed across the upper Irrawaddy River just south of Myitkyina. When the monsoon ended, these forces moved southward astride the Irrawaddy, capturing Shwegu in early November, and clearing the trace of the land route to China.

Working on the heels of the advancing combat forces, occasionally themselves under fire, Army Engineers commanded by Brigadier General Louis A. Pick, pushed the Ledo Road forward. On January 28, 1945, the first convoy of American trucks from India crossed the Burma-China frontier and the road, named the "Stilwell Road" by Generalissimo Chiang Kai-shek, was open.

British forces pressed their campaign in western Burma and the Japanese retreat to the south and east was in full swing by the end of January, 1945. On May 2 British forces entered Rangoon, all but ending the Burma Campaign. Some enemy forces managed to withdraw to the east, but thousands were cut off along the Sittang River and killed as they tried to cross. Admiral Mountbatten reported that the fighting to that time had cost the Japanese some 300,000 casualties, of which 97,000 were counted dead.

American service forces had worked veritable miracles during this campaign. In addition to the Hump and Stilwell Road operations, they doubled the capacity of the Bengal-Assam Railroad. Port battalions at Calcutta, working under difficult conditions, established unloading records unequalled by any other military port in the world.

In southeastern China, however, we suffered reverses. In May, 1944, elements of five Japanese divisions drove southward from the Hankow area into Hunan Province. The Japanese objectives were a string of American airfields reaching from Changsha to Liuchow. In late August, 1944, two Japanese divisions launched a complementary drive west from Canton. The twin drives converged on the American air bases of Kweilin and Liuchow, both capable of staging B-29's to Japan. As Chiang Kai-shek's China was being cut in two parts the United States pressed for command of the disintegrating Chinese armies or any strategic reserves. However, the effort ended in General Stilwell's recall from China and the American command was split into the India-Burma (Lieutenant General Sultan) and the China Theaters (Lieutenant General Albert C. Wedemeyer) on 24 October 1944, with resultant reorganization of command. The high tide of the Japanese conquest in China was on December 6, 1944 when they reached Tushan.

Japan was sorely feeling the impact of our blows across the Pacific, and, in the spring of 1945, was withdrawing large forces from the interior of South and Central China to defend the China coast. Our B-29's were moved to more easily supplied bases in the Marianas, and the Chinese troops, many of them American trained, pressed at the heels of the Japanese as they sullenly retreated. When Russia entered the war against Japan on August 9, she promptly swept into Manchuria, Korea, and Sakhalin Island. Further Allied advances in China, planned by Lt. General Wedemeyer, were halted by Japan's surrender.

The battles of CBI were fought against great odds at the end of the longest and thinnest supply line in the global war. Much of the Burma and China action took place in terrain untouched by civilization, through jungles and mountains, in the face of stifling heat and the monsoon, and amid the innumerable diseases of the tropics. It speaks well of the fighting abiilty, the technical skill and stamina of American troops that they were able to accomplish so much with so little.

Frank D. Merrill

OPERATIONS IN BURMA. By the summer of 1943, though she was doing everything in her power to hang on, China's condition was desperate. Japan's rush into Burma had isolated China except for the thin line of air supply over the 500 miles of the Himalayan Hump between Assam, India, and the Yunnan plateau. It became apparent to Allied leaders that if China was to stay in the war she must have supplies—and plans were made to launch an offensive in Burma in the winter of 1943-44. It was also decided to extend the Ledo Road from Assam to the old Burma Road at Mongyu, to build a pipeline from Calcutta to Assam, and another paralleling the Ledo Road. Thus could China be supplied and kept in the war. This Burma offensive got underway in late October when Chinese forces moved into the Hukawng Valley from forward positions in front of the advancing Ledo Road. In February they were joined by a specially trained American infantry combat team under Brigadier General Frank D. Merrill, and the advance began. UPPER LEFT. On February 12 these Marauders cross the Paqusace Pass from Assam, India, into Burma at Borderville. LOWER LEFT. Preparing for a long, hard march, an officer of the 5307th Composite Unit received his issue of "K" rations near Naubum, Burma, April 29. ABOVE. Several of the Marauders barbecue deer meat in Burma.

JUNGLES AND MOUNTAINS. Merrill's Marauders (the 5307th Composite Unit, Provisional) had been gathered in a call for volunteers that went to all United States jungle-trained and veteran infantry units in the Pacific and in the Western Hemisphere. They had to be tough for the job facing them. ABOVE. A soldier of this unit shows a Chinese soldier of the 88th Regiment how to operate an M-I rifle during a rest period during their drive to Mytikyina in April. UPPER RIGHT. After bitter fighting the air base at Myitkyina was seized May 17. Here Lieutenant General Joseph W. Stilwell, commander of the China-Burma-India U.S. theater, and deputy to Admiral, the Lord Louis Mount-batten, who commanded the Southeast Asia Command, looks out across the airstrip there June 1, 1944. This important base was taken only after Merrill's Marauders, supplied from the air, had moved secretly across country and crossed a mountain range 8,000 feet high. Chinese and American forces had almost totally destroyed the Japanese 18th Division, which had captured Singapore. LOWER RIGHT. In spite of such success, however, it was to be a long time before the Ledo-Burma Road, re-named "The Stilwell Road" in honor of General Stilwell, was to be opened, January, 1945. Here an Army vehicle tows a howitzer across the Salween River suspension bridge.

THE MARIANAS CAMPAIGN

By General Holland M. Smith

BY early 1944, the success of United States operations on the outer fringe of the Japanese island defense periphery, ranging from the Aleutians through the Gilberts and Marshalls in the Central Pacific to Bougainville and Hollandia in the South and Southwest Pacific, indicated that the time was at hand for further aggressive thrusts aimed at the inner Japanese island chain — the Ryukus, Bonins, Marianas, Carolines, and Philippines.

It was obvious that the United States needed only to capture certain islands of key importance in this inner chain in order to effect a serious rupture of the enemy's well-protected lines of communication and supply, and to provide further bases for attack on the Empire itself. The expeditious execution of the Marshalls operation in February 1944, following on the heels of the equally successful Bougainville and Gilberts operations, pointed plainly toward the immediate opportunity for exploitation of the advantages secured.

Thus the decision was reached to breach the inner defense line by attacking the Marianas. The mission, as finally assigned, called for us to capture, occupy, and defend Saipan, Tinian, and Guam. The target date for the first of the three operations—Saipan—was set for 15 June 1944. Command for the entire operation was vested in Admiral R. A. Spruance, with amphibious forces under Vice Admiral R. K. Turner. Command of the largest force of expeditionary troops to operate under Marine command in the Pacific thus far was assigned to me. This included both Marine amphibious corps—the Third Amphibious Corps, based at Guadalcanal; and the Fifth Amphibious Corps based in Hawaii.

The expeditionary troops organization for the Marianas comprised three Marine divisions and one Marine brigade, all reinforced; two Army infantry divisions; corps troops; and miscellaneous supporting units. Every assault unit of brigade size or larger that the Fleet Marine Force had, (except the 1st Marine Division, at this time recuperating from the New Britain operation), was included in this immense task organization.

In order to control and command this large tactical organization efficiently, it was necessary to divide the whole group into two separate commands: Northern Troops and Landing Force (comprising V Amphibious Corps units) for the capture of Saipan and Tinian; and Southern Troops and Landing Force (III Amphibious Corps) for the capture of Guam. Superimposed over the two landing forces was Task Force 56, Expeditionary Troops, the headquarters and staff for which was formed by dividing the V Amphibious Corps staff. Involved were more than 700 vessels, ranging from battle-

ships and carriers to transports and tankers; more than 2,000 aircraft; and over 300,000 Marine, Navy, and Army personnel.

The first move in assembling for the jump-off at newly-won Eniwetok put us 2,420 miles west of Pearl Harbor and nearly 400 miles past our new bases in Kwajalein Atoll. From Eniwetok, we prepared to travel 1,000 miles more to Saipan, advancing the United States front line in the Central Pacific to 3,400 miles west of Pearl Harbor and within long-range bomber range of Japan.

Admirably suited to delaying action by the tenacious Japanese, Saipan's 72 squares miles of rugged terrain, crowned by towering Mount Tapotchau, necessitated a wide departure from practices followed in previous operations against the flat coral atolls in the Central Pacific.

While our invasion of the Gilberts and Marshalls alerted the Japanese to the possibility of a subsequent assault on the Marianas, recent operations in the South Pacific also pointed toward an invasion of the Carolines, wherein lay the fortified bases of Truk and Yap. Since the Japanese could guess with no certainty where our next move would be, they began to pour troops, equipment and supplies into the Marianas and western Carolines.

Before the reinforcement of the Marianas could be completed, we struck. The Japanese commander on Saipan, Lieutenant General Saito, had to resist with what he had on hand, which included some 30,000 troops, hoping no doubt that reinforcements would come in the shape of the Japanese fleet.

Saito met us at the beaches at Saipan in approved Japanese fashion, and our hopes of quickly expanding our beachhead were somewhat dampened. Through the first week of fighting our gains were made slowly, but with substantial results. The 2d and 4th Marine Divisions, after landing in assault on 15 June, moved inland to seize the first high ground, and the 27th Infantry Division was fed in on the south of the 4th Marine Division, as our first prime objective—Aslito Airfield—was secured.

Leaving the 27th Infantry Division to clean up Nafutan Point, the two Marine divisions turned to the north to begin the main assault on the approaches of Mount Tapotchau. Progress was slow, but by the beginning of the third week of the battle we had captured Mount Tapotchau and overrun Kagman Peninsula; more than half the island was in our hands. By this time, all 3 divisions were in line.

On 4 July the 2d Marine Division reached the end of its assigned zone of action and temporarily went into a reserve status, leaving the 4th Marine Division and 27th Infantry Division to finish the island. By this time, General Saito had reached the inevitable conclusion that, without surface and air support from the Japanese fleet, he had no hope for success in continuing his thus-far unsuccessful fight. For the early morning hours of 7 July, Saito ordered all available troops, now compressed in the northern part of the island with their backs to the sea, to launch an all-out mass counterattack.

The brunt of his mass counterattack, numbering about 1,500 troops, was borne, as predicted on the day previous, by elements of the 27th Infantry Division, north of Tanapag Harbor on the west side of the island, and resulted in bloody slaughter for both sides, the Japanese penetrating deeply enough to engage a Marine artillery battalion, supporting the 27th Division, in hand-to-hand combat. The Japanese counterattackers were ultimately wiped out to a man, and with them went the last organized resistance on Saipan. On 9 July, 1944, the 4th Marine Division reached the northern end of the island and the battle was over.

Landings on Guam were originally scheduled to take place two days after the Saipan landings, contingent upon the success of the latter. Because the going on Saipan was more difficult than expected, and because the Japanese fleet in the Philippines made an unexpected sortie toward Saipan during the week of the landings, the Guam assault had to be postponed. In what is known as the Battle of the Philippine Sea, or, colloquially as the "Saipan Turkey Shoot," the Japanese fleet was decisively defeated.

On 21 July, Southern Troops and Landing Force (commanded by my friend, then Major General Roy S. Geiger) went ashore on Guam over a reef similar to that bordering Saipan. Fleet Marine Force units in the assault landings were the 3rd Marine Division, which landed between Asan and Adelup Points, and the 1st Provisional Marine Brigade, which landed below Orote Peninsula, near the town of Agat. The Japanese on Guam concentrated upon containing the landing forces in a restricted beachhead with frequent attempts to dislodge and defeat them through counterattacks. It was not until 28 July that the 3rd Marine Division broke out of its pocket.

The 1st Provisional Marine Brigade was allowed more freedom of movement by the enemy and quickly seized commanding ground inland, including the Alifan massif. Then, on 25 July, the Brigade turned on its left to assault Orote Peninsula and ran squarely into some of the hardest fighting on Guam. In the meantime, the 77th Infantry Division landed and took over the southern part of the island preparatory to a general advance to the north beside the 3rd Marine Division, an advance which was begun on 31 July.

The battle for Guam was fought in the beachhead areas, a fact which was proved when the two divisions made their drive north against sporadic resistance and over difficult terrain. However, as the advance reached that part of northern Guam where the island widens for the last time, the Brigade was brought up to the left of the 3rd Marine Division.

With both divisions and the Brigade in line, the pace of attack increased, and on 10 August it was announced that Guam was again ours; all organized resistance had ceased.

Although we held Guam physically after 10 August and rapidly went about our work of converting it into one of the finest bases in the Pacific, there were still several thousand enemy troops in hiding on the island (between 10 August and 15 November, 6,267 Japanese were killed).

With Saipan finished, and Guam under way, only Tinian remained to be taken. The forewarned —and forearmed—Japanese on Tinian had a long period in which to prepare for our landings, but even so we took them by surprise by landing over two of the narrowest beaches ever used in a major assault landing. These beaches were on the north end, opposite Saipan, whereas the Japanese had anticipated our landing either on the west side of the island near Tinian Town, or about half way down the eastern side.

The 4th Marine Division made the landing on Tinian, closely followed by the 2nd Marine Division. The flat to rolling terrain lent itself to our attack, and the two divisions moved without difficulty until the southernmost part of the island was reached. There, the remaining Japanese elected to make their stand, but, beyond causing some casualties and delaying the final outcome, had little success. Tinian was ours on 1 August.

Although Tinian was seized without difficulty, as casualties go, the operation represented a departure from the usual run of amphibious assaults: A surprise landing was effected against an alerted enemy; half our assault force moved to Tinian in a shore-to-shore movement employing already tested ship-to-shore techniques; the original landings were supported not only by the usual intense naval gunfire and air preparations but by shore-based artillery on southern Saipan; a two-division corps was landed against resistance over approximately 180 yards of usable beaches; and finally the assault and capture of Tinian was done by troops who had only 15 days before finished one of the hardest battles in the Pacific.

Proper evaluation of the cost of the Marianas was not possible until subsequent amphibious operations were mounted from our newly-won bases; until B-29s began pounding the industrial cities of Japan, hamstringing their war production; until we finally realized that the tide of the war, turned at Guadalcanal in 1942, was now crashing on the very beaches of the home islands of Japan.

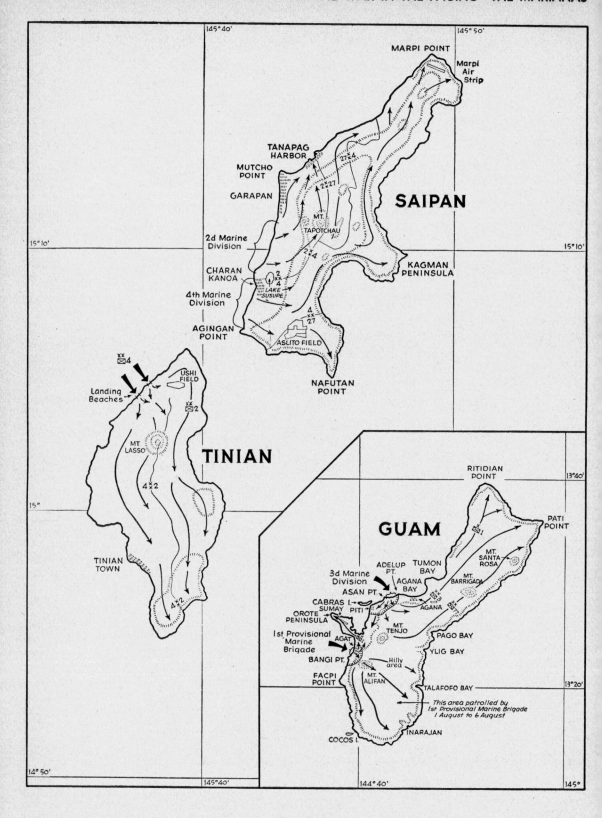

Chart of the invasions of Saipan, Tinian, and Guam.

INVADING THE MARIANAS. Saipan in the Marianas, was the next target for the Fifth Corps. A large land mass, different from the flat atoll islands, Saipan (upper) was dominated by Mount Tapotchau in the island's center. Seaplanes sit on the water near their tender. LOWER. An LCI gunboat stands by while smaller craft move shoreward. Prior to the June 15, 1944 landing, Admiral Marc Mitscher's Task Force 58 for three days gave Saipan, Guam, Tinian, Rota and Pagan a going over. On June 19th, the Fifth Fleet's planes shot down 402 Japs in the "Marianas turkey shoot,"

SAIPAN. Saipan was the first of the Marianas Islands to be hit. It was assaulted June 15, 1944, by the Army and Marines after Truk, the big Jap Naval base, was made almost impotent by American sea and air power. The Saipan strike was made by the 27th Infantry Division under Major General Ralph C. Smith, and two Marine divisions under Lieutenant General Holland M. Smith. Lieutenant General Smith was in overall command. UPPER. U.S. troops heading for the Saipan beaches. LOWER. These GIs are sizzling some Japs ensconced in a pill box on D Day plus three.

FLAMING HELL. Artist Tom Lovell, in his painting, "Battle for Tarawa" (upper), shows Marines wading to the Tarawa beachhead, unprotected and under fire all the way. The landing craft took the Marines only to the end of the pier, where it was unable to continue because of coral reef. A combat photographer caught this picture (lower), of Tarawa's beaches during the thick of the fight. Marine dead, discarded equipment, ruined installations and blasted palms all show the ugliness of war, stripped of any of the fanciful romance and glamor sometimes associated with it.

ATOLL & ISLAND. Fighting on atolls, such as Kwajalein (upper), Marines and Army troops were limited in tactical maneuvers by the small size of the islands, extremely narrow, and only a few feet above sea level at the highest points. The invasion of Guam (lower), was more like Guadalcanal again because both attackers and defenders had plenty of room to move around. On Guam, weapons like this 37 mm field gun proved their worth. Guam had been in our possession for more than 40 years prior to its capitulation. It was the first reconquest of U.S. soil during World War II.

SAIPAN FROM THE AIR. The pier at Charan Kanoa, Saipan (upper), served as the main traffic artery. The blasted sugar mill, center, was the dominating land mark, its ruined sewers giving off nauseating odors. To the rear lies Lake Susupe. On the roads can be seen many of the new amphibious rubber-tired DUKW's (Ducks). These not only crawled over the reef, but came ashore faster than the amphtracs, and once on land could move at high speed on good roads. LOWER. The town of Garapan, which was captured by the Second Division in bitter house to house fighting.

MAKING IT TOUGH FOR NIPS. Installations and enter-
prises that the Japs had laboriously built up for years van-
ished in a hurry on Saipan after the Allied assault there.
UPPER LEFT. This is a general view of Tanapag Harbor,
Saipan, on July 4, 1944. The boiling smoke is coming from
a burning Jap tanker. Note demolished installations in right
foreground. LOWER LEFT. This frightened Jap prisoner is
interrogated during Saipan invasion. The Japs were certain
that the most awful things would happen to them if they fell
into American hands. ABOVE. Lieutenant Colonel William
J. O'Brien, a 27th Division battalion commander, gives instructions for a drive on the main Tanapag seaplane base.

SAIPAN HAD EVERYTHING. The sugar-cane fields of Saipan were burned to stubble by tanks and flame throwers, or leveled by artillery and air and surface bombardment. The sweet smell of the burned or torn cane remained with the Marines the whole time they were on the island. And with the cane there were millions of flies. The buzz they made as they rendezvoused was almost ominous. But there were more deadly things on Saipan than flies as the Marines found out (upper left) as they pushed across open cane fields supported by rockets to their front but in plain sight of well-hidden defense positions in the elevations ahead. LOWER LEFT. Rockets support the advance of this platoon, moving inland. UPPER RIGHT. The only way to take ground is either to walk or crawl over it, killing any enemy who stands in your way. These Marines, their packs long since dropped in platoon dumps, move across the rubble of cane on Saipan. LOWER RIGHT. The big island, thirteen miles long and five wide at its greatest bulge, also had dense vegetation and junglelike areas where Japs could hide and fire at passing troops. To the Marines going in, the Navy-prepared description of island life was frightening. They were warned to beware of "sharks, barracuda, sea snakes, anemones, razor-sharp coral, polluted waters, poison fish, and giant clams that shut on a man like a bear trap." Ashore there was leprosy, typhus, filariasis, yaws, typhoid, dengue fever, dysentery, saber grass, insects, snakes and giant lizards. "Eat nothing growing on the island, don't drink its waters and don't approach the inhabitants." The insects, dengue and dysentery turned out to be real enough, but the rest of the dangers fortunately failed to show.

SUPPORTING WEAPONS ON SAIPAN. Shortly after midnight of D + I the Army's 27th Division came ashore and passed through the Fourth Marine Division on the right flank to take up positions against Aslito airfield. With the Army also came large artillery pieces of the XXIV Corps, and the big guns of the Fifth Corps Artillery. Saipan thus had the largest artillery collection up to that time in the Pacific war, for each division had its own artillery regiment. UPPER LEFT. Bazookas were used with excellent results on Saipan, against enemy tanks and fortifications. These Marines are knocking out a road block on the winding highway in the middle of this picture. Combat writer-photographer Bob Cooke wrote on his caption that the bazooka team had just "struck the block, wiping out the machine gun nest." LOWER LEFT. Because it was easy to move, didn't take any time to emplace, and packed a terrific punch, the 37 mm. cannon was a favorite infantry weapon on Saipan. An officer with binoculars watches results of the crew's fire. UPPER RIGHT. Army equipment marked with a large white star was a new sign to many Marines on Saipan who had not previously fought alongside Army troops. This amphtrac plows along a Saipan road, covering crew and terrain with a fine film of powdered dust. The movement of vehicles on the beach roads was so heavy that at times the dust was six inches deep, necessitating the wearing of dust protectors which had been issued before leaving for the operation. Shore party and motor transport personnel suffered particularly. LOWER RIGHT. A Marine howitzer, well hidden beneath a camouflage net, fires on call.

DIVISION COMMAND POST. UPPER. At the Fourth Division CP, Maj. Gen. Harry Schmidt receives the latest tactical news from his Chief of Staff, Col. W. W. Rogers, in undershirt. Situation maps were changed as new information came in from the Commanders of the 23rd, 24th and 25th Marine Regiments. Terrain maps, marked with grid squares, were covered with transparent isinglass, and forward positions were marked with crayons, giving Commanders the situation at a glance. LOWER. The map couldn't show how a tank was knocked out of action by suicidal Japanese, but the field telephone brought in daily summaries of dead and wounded as well as materiel losses. The Fourth Marine Division was awarded a Presidential Citation for its action on Saipan which read in part: "(It) blasted the stubborn defenses of the enemy in an undeviating advance over the perilously rugged terrain. Unflinching despite heavy casualties, this gallant group pursued the Japanese relentlessly across the entire length of the island, pressing on against bitter opposition for 25 days to crush all resistance in their zone of action."

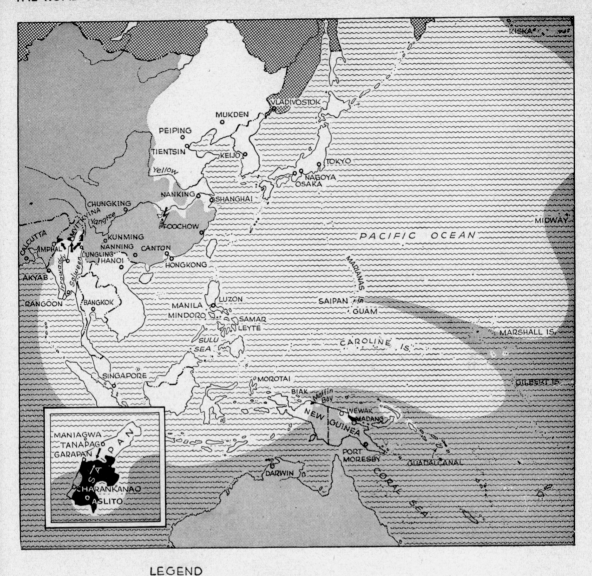

THE ROAD TO TOKIO—1 JULY 1944

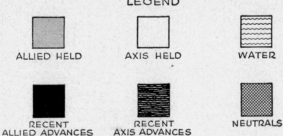

LEGEND

ALLIED HELD

AXIS HELD

WATER

RECENT
ALLIED ADVANCES

RECENT
AXIS ADVANCES

NEUTRALS

BANZAI. In a last desperate attempt to rout American troops
from the island, the Japs launched a vicious, suicidal offensive
on January 6 that proved costly to both sides. During the attack U.S. troops killed more than 1,500 Japs, some of whom

THE ISLAND. Marines had a rare souvenir hunt on Saipan, except for the combat troops who were too tired to carry any extra weight. UPPER. A quaint well is inspected here by two Marines at a Jap shrine a few miles off the beach. LOWER. Natives with their children and remaining possessions were brought out of hiding in the hills by Marine patrols and installed in stockades on the beach, out of harm's way. Told by the Japs that they would be killed by the Americans, many had committed suicide. However, several thousand civilians readily responded to friendly treatment by the GIs.

ASSAULT ON TINIAN. Called a "razzle dazzle" or "back-door" landing, the invasion of nearby Tinian by the Fourth Division on July 24, 1944, was amphibious assault perfected. Landing where they were least expected, the Division put its artillery and infantry regiments ashore with supporting tanks, and by nightfall had secured a beachhead 4,000 yards wide and 2,000 deep. The cost was 15 dead and 150 wounded. UPPER. Their wakes looking like strange tails, these landing craft head for the tiny Tinian beaches, White No. 1 and No. 2. Everything worked as though the operation had been rehearsed several times and the landing craft (lower) maintained a shuttle service, bringing men and supplies ashore. Engineers and Seabees enlarged the roads leading from the beach and the combat troops pushed inland. Previously designated areas were set aside for ammunition and food dumps and supply worked extremely well. Tinian was attacked via a three mile over water journey from Saipan, many of the troops spending one or two nights aboard the LST's and LCI's. A shortage of tractors prevented the Fourth Division's staff from getting ashore on the first day of the invasion.

TINIAN THE NEXT DAY. The Second Marine Division landed some artillery and one battalion of infantry the first day on Tinian. Next day, the 2nd, 6th and 8th Marine Regiments of the Second Division were ashore. UPPER. Holding their rifles high, Marines wade ashore. LOWER. This amphtrac hit a mine but other machines dragged it out of the traffic lanes. All battalion commanders and top members of the Fourth Division staff had made a careful aerial reconnaissance over Tinian prior to the landing, carefully noting terrain features troops would encounter when actually on the ground. Tinian also came under constant pounding by massed battalions of 105 and 155 howitzers from the nearby shores of Saipan. Without air or surface assistance, hammered into his underground hideouts by the ever-constant artillery, short on supplies and lacking good communications, the enemy was not in a very good defensive position. After spending weeks readying the beaches off Tinian Town in the island's middle against assault, the defenders were caught badly off guard by the surprise landing effected on beaches they never suspected could handle two divisions.

OPEN COUNTRY. Marines had a lot of walking to do in the nine days it took them to conquer Tinian, but speed was no longer as vital as it had been on Saipan. The Jap fleet had been defeated decisively, hundreds of first line planes shot down, and Guam successfully invaded. Marine Commanders kept a steady relentless pressure on the enemy and gradually constricted his movement to the south end of the island. Picking up three airfields as they moved, the Fourth on the right, the Second on the left, the two Marine Divisions used tanks (upper left) in support of most infantry advances. The enemy still had to be dug out of numerous hiding places and flame throwers (center left) were a most helpful weapon. Regiments alternately used their battalions in the attack and in reserve in an effort to conserve strength and maintain maximum fighting efficiency. LOWER LEFT. These Marines are moving forward to take the place of a unit which has been leading the advance. UPPER RIGHT. Moving carefully across an airfield, Marines watch out for snipers who frequently lurked in ruined planes, waiting for a shot. These fields were not too badly beat up because we intended using them shortly after their capture. Ruined enemy planes lay everywhere, in revetments, under camouflage, in skeleton hangars or in the burning sun. LOWER RIGHT. Here the troops have covered the field itself and work toward the airport service and supply buildings. In the background a Jap supply dump is burning. Some of the fires from oil, gasoline and munitions lasted for days, sending huge clouds of smoke into the sky.

SECOND DIVISION ADVANCE. On July 28th, the Second Division (upper) advanced over another Jap airfield, passing through the black revetments to the south in a broad sweep. Each day the Marines were assigned specific zones to be covered by each division before nightfall, allowing sufficient time for protecting front lines against possible enemy counter-attacks. **LOWER.** During the pre-invasion observation hardly any Japs or natives were seen above ground; now the Marines found them hidden away in caves and cliffs and underground storage places. These civilians are helped out of their hiding and offered cigarettes. Late in the Tinian campaign the Japs, their backs to the wall, tried to get many of the civilians to commit suicide with them, but without signal success. Marines, as on Saipan, brought up loud speakers, and interpreters spoke in the native language to the people in hiding in caves directly over the jagged beaches 100 yards below. Natives added their voices assuring their fellow civilians that the Americans would not harm them. Thus while many of the Jap soldiers committed hara-kiri or leaped to their deaths, hundreds of civilians left their hiding places and streamed into Marine lines.

HOT WORK. Stripped to his "skivvy" undershirt, the then new Commanding General of the Fourth Marine Division, Gen. Clifton B. Cates, 1948 Commandant (upper), sits (foreground) in his well hidden Command Post engrossed with members of his Staff over an operations map as Marine enlisted men of the operations section stand by. Gen. Cates took command of the Fourth on Saipan after the battle, relieving Gen. Schmidt who became Fifth Corps Commander as Gen. Holland Smith assumed command of the Fleet Marine Force, Pacific. LOWER. A corpsman administers blood plasma on the beach just before this wounded Marine is put aboard an amphtrac for the run to the hospital ships standing off the island. As soon as the airfields on Tinian became operative they were used to evacuate the wounded and bring in supplies. Bad swells made some of the beaches almost unusable for a few days and the supply problem was slightly complicated. Both of the Division rear echelons were on Saipan with the Army's 27th Division, which had gone into garrison duty for the time being, helping mop up many of the Japs who had evaded capture while the island was being taken. Those who were left kept up sniping activities.

ENEMY STILL LIFE. This enemy command post on Tinian (upper) was built of concrete and steel and half covered with earth. Heavy steel plates close over the windows. It was perched on the main Japanese airfield, with an observation tower in the background. LOWER. A view of the dev-astated, rubble-strewn hangar area of a Tinian airfield. Here scouts moved in advance of the main body, alert for any possible enemy snipers. Tinian, like Saipan, later became a major B-29 base for the air war against Japan. Existing enemy airfields were greatly enlarged, and new ones were built.

TINIAN AFTER THE FIGHT. The island was declared secured on August 1, 1944, and the flag officially raised at Fifth Corps headquarters. One of the prizes (upper) was Ushi Point airfield, captured the second day. LOWER. A Marine intelligence officer reads the ironic sign before this Jap plane, "Do not remove any parts." The plane probably had been on exhibition. The battle was not without cost, however. The Fourth lost 290 killed, 1,515 wounded and 24 missing. The Second suffered considerably less, and for the next four months was assigned mopping up operations.

CONCLAVE IN PEARL HARBOR. ABOVE. General Mac-
Arthur, left, President Roosevelt, and Admiral Nimitz discuss
the progress of the war aboard a cruiser in Pearl Harbor,
July, 1944. The President, who had just delivered his 4th term
acceptance speech to the Democratic convention, traveled
to Pearl Harbor from San Diego. His trip served to emphasize
that the Pacific phase of the war had not been forgotten in
favor of Europe. The liberation of the Philippines was on the
program, the President affirmed, and General MacArthur
was assured that he would spearhead the invasion. In Hawaii,
the President talked not only to general and admirals, but
also with pilots who had been fighting the Japanese in the
campaigns throughout the Pacific along with the Marines
and infantrymen who had been wounded in the Marianas.
A few days after President Roosevelt's departure from Hono-
lulu his remarks about the Philippines were translated into action as U.S. planes resumed their assaults against the islands.

RECLAIMING GUAM. In preparation for the invasion, carrier-based planes dropped 720 tons of bombs on Guam on July 19. Under the protection of the fleet and the 7th Air Force, the Third Marine Division, the Seventy-seventh Infantry Division, and the First Provisional Marine Brigade (which included Carlson's Raiders) headed for the sl ores of Guam on July 20. ABOVE. Mine sweepers clear a path for the invasion fleet whose wake carves momentary patterns on the Pacific. This was Operation Forager, and its successful conclusion was to result in the setting up of a B-29 base there.

GOING ASHORE. Because of the length of time that elapsed between the scheduled and the actual D Day landing, Guam got a concentrated going over by the Navy in preparation for the landings and to neutralize enemy airfields there. UPPER LEFT. The former Marine Barracks in the foreground of this picture were almost obliterated and the town of Sumay on the shore was battered and blasted. The long finger of Orote Peninsula and the dry docks also are shown. Later, when Admiral Nimitz moved his Fleet Headquarters forward from Pearl Harbor to Guam, he could see hundreds of large and small ships loading and unloading before him at Orote. This time America was determined to fortify Guam and keep it. LOWER LEFT. The tension of imminent combat keyed up the transport-sore Marines as they headed for shore through the miles of open water that lay between their transports and the beach. As at Saipan, Guam had coral reefs that necessitated transferring troops from the flat-bottomed LCVP's to the tractors or the amphibian trucks. UPPER RIGHT. These troops are waiting to be transferred. LOWER RIGHT. Here Marines wade across the inevitable beaches, wet to their hips and wary of enemy fire. On their left lies a destroyed enemy plane.

RETURN TO GUAM. The aggressive Japanese, with domination of the vast Pacific area in mind, had pounced on Guam the day after they struck at Pearl Harbor. But Allied conquests had, by July, 1944, put us in position for the reconquest of this strategic base. It was softened up by an intensive air and naval bombardment for 18 days—July 3-20. On July 20 the Army and Marines hit the beach. Marine forces consisted of the 3rd Division and the 1st Provisional Brigade, reinforced by elements of the 77th Infantry Division under command of Major General A. D. Bruce. Guam was not easy by any means, but it was not as tough as the bitter fighting on Saipan had been. Only comparatively light resistance was made to the landings, and in 48 hours the Orote Peninsula had been cut off in the west. Main Jap resistance came with night counter-attacks, but these were blunted. A drive was made across the island to the east coast, and the last defenders were blasted out. ABOVE. Troops of the 77th Division wade ashore at White Beach, Guam, on July 25, 1944. UPPER RIGHT. U.S. troops blast a Jap pill box on Orote Peninsula July 26. LOWER RIGHT. Explosive charges burst inside an enemy dugout on the peninsula the same day. In addition to losing the island, this was another costly operation for the Japanese, whose losses in killed exceeded 17,000. U.S. troops sustained more than 7,000 casualties.

FLUSHING OUT THE ENEMY. On Guam, as on Saipan and Tinian, the Japs burrowed deep into hillside caves, cliffs and the underground. Patrols had to either kill, capture or entomb the defenders. Since few surrendered during the battle it was a matter of offering the Japs a chance to come out of hiding and be captured (lower), or of placing a dynamite charge over the mouth of the cave and sealing the unhappy defenders within. These Marines found some enemy defenders in this cave on the Agat road toward Orote Peninsula, and had to close the hole. The normal reaction to give aid to a defeated enemy frequently was impossible because of the peculiar code that gave them glory if they took an enemy with them in death. Consequently, Marines were wary of the enemy because many of their buddies had been victims of booby traps and treacherous deaths while trying to help the wounded or effect a capture of a worn out soldier. UPPER. Japs in the brush ahead of these Marines are firing back, but were eventually wiped out. This picture demonstrates why casualties were unavoidable. In most instances the attacker had to dislodge the defenders from positions that afforded tactical and visual concealment.

BLASTING AND BLEEDING. UPPER. Marine engineers throw some dynamite sticks into a Japanese dugout to the front. Marine on right is alert to see if any enemy try to skip out the back door of the hide-away. LOWER. A bleeding Marine receives medical attention just behind front lines on the Orote Peninsula. An improvised splint has been placed on his leg, and stretcher bearers stand by to evacuate him to the beach where he will be placed aboard an amphtrac and rushed to a hospital ship. Casualties were heavy on the Third Division beachhead, especially on the left flank near Chonito Cliffs where well-emplaced enemy gunners mowed down the Marines as they clawed their way to the top, only to be repulsed time and again. Naval gunfire and artillery covered the area, seeming to blow the top of the hill off, but when the Marines advanced, they repeatedly met determined enemy fire. After three days of this, with the Japs looking right down the throats of Marines on the invasion beaches, a flanking attack flushed out the enemy from a series of coral caves. Moving across Guam's rugged terrain, the Marines found many more groups of caves, all deadly.

BIG AND LITTLE GUNS. The machine gun crew (upper) has selected this window frame in a stone wall of a ruined building and is ready to fire against the enemy. LOWER. The big 155 mm howitzer, its crew stripped down to shorts, fires hot death against Jap installations on Orote Peninsula. While the First Brigade was cleaning out Orote Peninsula, eventually capturing the airfield on July 29th, and the Third Division was fighting inland for the long drive north, two liquor-inspired Banzai charges occurred, one before each Marine area. Combat Correspondent Josephy recalls the night of D + 4: "The wild, swirling fight raged for three hours on the hilltop. Illumination flares made it look like a scene out of hell. The eerie screams of the charging Japs, the smell of "sake" and blood, and the ferocity of the hand to hand fights in fox holes contributed to the terror. The Marines fought grimly back-to-back in their holes, little islands of resistance, trying to stem the rushing tide. Several times it seemed that our whole front might be torn open." The thin lines held firm, but more than 2,000 Japs filtered through them to rear areas where all personnel grabbed weapons to either kill or be killed.

NIGHT DEATH. While the Third Division was fighting for its very life against the "sake"-charged Japs, the First Brigade had a night Banzai. Artillery (above) saved the situation. Noise gave away the Jap assembly area and artillery was zeroed in on the ground immediately forward of the Marine lines. When the Japs, screaming and yelling, ran from their swamp jumping-off point, the field telephone up front told the artillery to the rear to let go. An officer described the moment when the shells landed: "Arms and legs flew like snowflakes. Japs ran amuck. They screamed in terror until they died."

MARINES RETURN. Raising the American flag over the ruins of the old Marine barracks on Guam (upper) was a thrilling occasion for the unshaven and dirty victors of the three-week campaign. Brig. Gen. Lemuel C. Shepherd, Jr., commanding the Brigade, had led the fighting in the area. Ashore for the ceremony were Gen. Holland Smith and Admiral Ray Spruance, Commander of the overall Marines' attack. **LOWER.** A close-up view of Sumay shows the widespread destruction. It was necessary to build several native villages to replace the ones destroyed during the landing and the attack. Complete with church, school and towering American flag poles, the thatch covered native buildings soon rose on both sides of the island as the Seabees helped rehabilitate the Guamanians. These American Nationals suffered the ravages of war and occupation as no other Americans. Not only were the Guamanians built new homes, but clothing, food and medical care were made available to them by the Island Command, headquartered at Agana, the capital. Before the bombardment, Agana had been a proud city of cement-walled homes with a beautiful cathedral. Now it was but a mass of rubble.

DESTRUCTION AND RECONSTRUCTION. UPPER. Firing as it heads in toward land, a PT boat shows a brilliant burst of flame as it supports an amphibious landing. **LOWER.** A Sea Bulldozer rests briefly during its road-building after the recapture of Guam. Moving in with the early stages of assault, the Seabees lost no time in starting the work of reconstruction which was to give us a system of far flung island bases from which to operate.

SURIBACHI. The outstanding picture of World War II, the flag raising on Mt. Suribachi, became a symbol of deathless courage to a nation. The painting (above), by Lt. Col. J. J. Capolino, USMC, is copied from the Associated Press photo by Joe Rosenthal. This was actually the second flag raising by men of Co. E, 2nd Battalion, 28th Marines, on Feb. 23, 1945. Three hours before, a smaller flag had been raised by Lt. H. G. Schrier, Sgt. E. I. Thomas and Sgt. H. O. Hansen. They led a 40 man patrol up the mountain, carrying a small flag given them by Lt. Col. Chandler W. Johnson, the Battalion Commander. Sgt. Lou Lowery, a combat photographer for "Leatherneck" magazine, recorded the original flag raising, quickly throwing himself aside as a grenade landed nearby. His camera was broken, but his film was undamaged. Later, Col. Johnson sent some men to the top with a much larger flag, one that would be visible for miles. With this patrol the tired Rosenthal hiked to the top, "to click the shutter at the right time," as he explained it. The picture, completely unposed but more dramatic than the original because of the larger group and flag, shows six men. Of these, only three left the island. Sgt. Hansen, Sgt. Mike Strank and PFC Franklin Sousley died in subsequent fighting. Pharmacist's Mate John H. Bradley and PFC's Rene A Gagnon and Ira H. Hayes survived.

GUAM SECURED. On July 28, after two and a half years of Japanese domination, Old Glory rose to renew old acquaintances on Guam and to restore American rule. By August 9, U.S. forces had quelled all organized resistance on the island. With the fields on Saipan and Tinian already in American hands, the capture of Orote strip, and the landing there of the first plane (lower) on July 30, made certain the parade of B-29s to Japan. Guam, with its vast flat areas, would hold hundreds of planes. UPPER. Orote strip as it looked from the air before it was reconditioned. The field was soon restored by the ubiquitous Seabees. At one time there were several thousand Seabee troops stationed on Guam. Together with Army engineers they built the fields, raised the various headquarters areas, laced the big island with a network of splendid roads, assembled quonset huts, and constructed huge naval supply installations and whole military cities. The bases on Saipan, Tinian and Guam were a tribute to the labor and technical "know-how" of the "can do" Seabees and their efficient counterparts in the Army. The campaign which would unlock the door to the Philippines, Japan, and the coast of China had now been completed.

ANOTHER ISLAND . . . ANOTHER LANDING. Giant strides across the Pacific carried our forces to the Palau Islands by summer's end, 1944. This central Pacific bastion of the Japs, situated 300 miles west of the Philippines, was stormed by the First Marine Division on September 14, 1944. When the photograph (right) was taken on D Day not a Marine had yet landed. Upon reaching the beach the Leathernecks were met with fierce artillery and mortar barrages which failed to stop them. Two days later, the Army's Eighty-first Infantry Division surged ashore at Angaur with others going ashore at Morotai. General Mac-Arthur, accompanying his men in the latter operation, told them: "You have done well. You now dominate the last stronghold which barred you from the Philippines. The enemy, as usual, was not in the right places at the right time."

PELELIU AND ANGAUR. While the re-conquest of Guam had been taking place in July and August, 1944, two more operations were in preparation—Peleliu and Angaur in the Palaus, two important stepping stones on the road to the Philippines. Marines hit Peleliu on September 15, and two days later the 81st Infantry Division landed on Angaur. UPPER LEFT. Covered by a screen of smoke from artillery fire, GIs of the 81st Division head for the Angaur beach in landing barges September 17. LOWER LEFT. Three days after the assault, elements of the 81st Division on Angaur watch carefully as an explosive charge is set to blow up a Jap-held cave. ABOVE. Troops blast across Angaur.

A FIVE-DAY JOB. Angaur, garrisoned by about 1,400 Japanese, fell to the 81st Division after four or five days of hard fighting. UPPER. The day after invasion, when there were still plenty of Japs around, portions of the 81st Division advance down a railroad track on the island. Ahead of the main body, with rifles ready for instant action, a small reconnaissance group probes the terrain. LOWER. In the face of enemy snipers, a demolition squad on Angaur prepares to blow up a tank put out of commission by a Jap 75 on September 21. They were clearing the road for other tanks.

BLOODY GULCH. In Angaur's "Bloody Gulch" the 81st Division ran into extremely stiff resistance. UPPER. They take cover along the tracks of a dinky railroad, bring up machine guns, and blast out the resisting Japs. LOWER. With the strongpoint removed, infantrymen prepare to continue the advance on September 21. No more trouble will be caused by the Jap lying on the railroad track. He's dead. Though mopping up operations went on for some time, not much organized Jap resistance was encountered on Angaur after September 23. By now, the 81st had also taken Ulithi.

ON TO PELELIU. The First Marine Division encountered great resistance on Peleliu, and during the first week in October two regimental combat teams of the 81st Division were landed there to assist them. This island was defended by nearly 10,000 Japanese, and it fell hard. ABOVE. Members of the 81st struggle up a steep slope on Peleliu. UPPER RIGHT. Men take cover and aim from behind a half-track on Peleliu. LOWER RIGHT. Members of the 81st and First Marine Divisions carry a wounded comrade on a litter. A Marine with his Doberman Pinscher watches from the right. It was a tough fight, but the Japanese were forced to give up the island by November 8, 1944.

THE SECOND DAY. The left flank battalion of the 1st Marines was taking a beating. One company had only 78 left when dawn came on D + 1. It had knocked out five reinforced concrete pillboxes, topped by five feet of coral, four pillboxes, and numerous enemy infantrymen. The low ridge named Bloody Nose was described on the scene by Combat Correspondent George McMillan: "Along the center of the ridge, the rocky spine was heaved up in a contorted mass of decayed coral, strewn with rubble. Crags, ridges and gulches were thrown together in a confusing maze. There were no roads, scarcely any trails. The pockmarked surface offered no secure footing even in the few level places. It was impossible to dig in; the best the men could do was pile a little coral or wood debris around their positions. The jagged rock slashed shoes and clothes, and tore their bodies every time they hit the deck for safety." UPPER. Tanks move up a valley road ahead of the infantry. LOWER. Two 105 howitzers fire against a Peleliu ridge position. Eight days later, with 60 per cent casualties, Marines were relieved, a sergeant commenting: "We ain't a regiment. We're just survivors."

NECESSITY AND INVENTION. Because Peleliu was never in any sense a conventional campaign, Marines developed new methods of getting at the almost impregnable Japanese. UPPER. A block and tackle and lots of sweat and heave-ho move this pack howitzer into position on the side of a captured ridge. These Marine engineers will soon settle the gun into its firing pit and in a short time the 75 mm cannon will be firing almost point-blank at caves in what was named "Death Valley" just across the ridge. LOWER. A flame throwing amphtrac, its gunner hiding behind a steel shield, squirts liquid, burning gasoline against a Jap cave on the slope of one of the many ridges. Operating over terrain never conceived possible by their manufacturers, the amphtracs went everywhere and did everything, suffering extremely high casualties in men and machines. As on other Pacific beachheads, the heat was intense. To all the other discomforts the Marines suffered were added cracked and blistered lips and skin. A soothing white paste was used for relief. This soon smudged with coral dust, and made the men strange sights not only to each other but also to the sheltered Japs.

BELLY TANK BOMBING. The Marine Corsair plane (upper) has just dumped a belly tank of flaming "Napalm" against a Jap hold-out cave position. This flying was continued through October and November, 1944, as the Second Wing remained with the garrison troops. LOWER. Planes later operated from Angaur, shuttling freight and personnel. This picture was taken from the first plane to make the trip between the two western Caroline bases. In bombing Bloody Nose Ridge, Marine fliers most probably made the shortest bombing hop in history, 15 seconds from field to target.

SECOND AIR WING ON PELELIU. Marine artillery spot-
ters in their tiny cub planes landed on D + 2. They performed scout and artillery observation functions. On September 24th the airbase (upper) became operational under
Maj. Gen. James T. Moore, Second Wing Commanding Officer. In the background lies Bloody Nose Ridge. Here artillery, ships and planes had blasted away the vegetation, leaving the scarred coral visible. LOWER. A Commando transport taxies past a Corsair fighter on the strip. The Marine
fliers furnished air support and neutralized nearby islands.

NGESEBUS ISLAND. When the Fifth Marines came to the western end of Peleliu, they found Japs looking across at them from Ngesebus Island. The 3rd Battalion, on Sept. 27th, crossed a shallow reef, landing with the close air support of Marine Fighter Squadron 114. UPPER. The enemy had placed obstacles but the Marines came ashore. Ngesebus and nearby Kongauru were soon in Marine hands and another fighter strip available. By Sept. 30th, the Fifth Marines ended Jap resistance on the eastern side, leaving only the dangerous Bloody Nose Ridge and the surrounding Umurbrogal Mountain area in possession of the enemy. LOWER. Intelligence personnel gained valuable information on Peleliu. The fortifications here were better constructed and more dangerous than those found several months before in the Marianas action. These Marines study the layout of a Jap mortar position. Pictures and specifications of enemy fortifications and weapons were sent back to Pearl Harbor where they were gone over by Navy, Marine and Army intelligence personnel. The knowledge gained in this manner helped in the capture of similar enemy installations in future operations.

UNDERGROUND EXISTENCE. Not until Iwo Jima did the Marines find anything to compare with the labyrinth of defense caves which the Japanese constructed on Peleliu. UPPER. This picture was taken from the inside of a Jap cave, looking out. It is easy to see how air and surface bombardment caused little more than annoyance. LOWER. Here the enemy had established an underground hospital. Major Frank Hough, Public Relations Officer for the operation, reported: "The caves had to be seen to be believed. In size they ranged from little one-man crevices in the rock to vast subterranean chambers up to 500 feet in length. Caves are common to this geological formation, and most of these here were natural. One was found to have nine staggered levels and so many entrances that it was all but impossible to count them, let alone seal them up. Blast walls covering the entrances were a common feature. Their naturally tortuous course, with certain improvements on nature, protected the occupant from concussion, direct fire and often even flame throwers. Some had doors of steel armor plate, set in reinforced concrete."

THE WAR IN THE SOUTHWEST PACIFIC

By Lieutenant General Robert L. Eichelberger

LATE in 1941 the Japanese launched one of the greatest offensives in world history. On December 7th, they committed the outrage at Pearl Harbor; a few hours later they struck the Philippines; on February 15th, Singapore fell; within that month, all of the Netherlands East Indies had fallen to the conqueror. Their attack then shifted to Rabaul, New Britain, from which Japan planned a two-pronged drive. One offshoot was to strike for control of southeastern New Guinea, the other through the Solomon Islands to slash the all-important supply line from America to Australia. Neither was destined to succeed, because of the sacrifice of thousands of American soldiers, sailors, marines and airmen.

The Japanese defeat in the battles of Midway and the Coral Sea was of tremendous importance; yet the Japanese were able to land troops in Eastern New Guinea, and by the late summer of 1942 had driven the Australians over the Owen-Stanley Range, and were knocking at the doors of Port Moresby. Cut off from food, the Japanese were later pushed back over the Owen-Stanley Range, and by 20 November the battle of the beachheads in the Buna-Gona area had begun. On December 1 the Buna Sector was placed under my command, and by 2 January 1943 the I Corps, using American and Australian troops, gained the first major ground victory against the Japanese. The victory at Sanananda soon followed.

The enemy had built up Rabaul as a base for future operations, and from the beginning of 1943 to April, 1944, our efforts were aimed at the neutralization of this dangerous base. The Sixth Army seized Woodlark and Kiriwina Islands in June, 1943, and right on the heels of this action Allied forces (mostly Australian) landed near Salamaua on Huon Gulf, near Lae, at Nadzab, and Saidor. By 10 February 1944 the Huon penninsula had been secured.

Meantime, other offensives had been mounted against Rabaul. Western New Britain had been secured with a landing at Arawe, while the Marine 1st Division had landed on Cape Gloucester. The 1st Cavalry Division had been entrenched on the Admiralty Islands two months ahead of schedule. By 20 March Rabaul was bottled up and General MacArthur was able to drive up the New Guinea coast toward the Philippines.

A long jump was made to Hollandia, a great enemy base in Dutch New Guinea, thus by-passing the Japanese 18th Army at Wewak. Being beyond range of our Army Air Force fighters, the Pacific Fleet made necessary carrier-based air support available, and on 22 April the I Corps under my command landed in the Hollandia area, while the 163rd Infantry of the 32nd Division landed at Aitape, 125 miles to the east.

The Japanese were taken completely by surprise. The isolated 18th Army decided to make one last offensive, and attacked Aitape on 10 July. In three weeks of savage fighting they tried vainly to dislodge the defending U. S. XI Corps, which had been reinforced by the 43rd Infantry Division.

Meanwhile, we had taken some more jumps up the coast, and were several hundred miles nearer our destination. On 17 May the 163rd Infantry landed at Toem-Sarmi, 175 miles northwest of Hollandia, and the next day, Wakde Island and its Japanese air base was seized. On 27 May the 41st Division went ashore on Biak Island, 200 miles northwest of Wakde. A tenacious defense prevented capture of airfields as soon as had been hoped, but reinforcements were sent in under I Corps and by 21 June the airfields had been secured. The Seventh Fleet and the Fifth Air Force prevented enemy attempts to reinforce his troops there.

On 2 July, 100 miles west of Biak, the 158th Infantry and the 503rd Parachute Regiment landed on Noemfoor Island, and on 30 July the 6th Division took Sansapor on the Vogelkop, 200 miles west of Noemfoor. These actions virtually completed the New Guinea operations.

A 350-mile westward jump in September by the XI Corps carried us to Morotai Island, midway between New Guinea and the Philippines, and plans had been made to land in Mindanao in the Philippines. Reconnaissance, following Navy Air attacks, now disclosed serious weaknesses in the Japanese positions in the Philippines, and plans to strike at Yap were changed in favor of an immediate move on Leyte.

The invasion of Leyte began on 17 October, when the 6th Ranger Battalion began clearing islands at the entrance to Leyte Gulf. On the 20th the Sixth Army poured ashore. Three days later the Japanese Navy launched a three-pronged attack aimed at Leyte Gulf, but Admiral Kinkaid's Seventh Fleet, aided by indecision on the part of the Japanese commander, won a major victory off Leyte Gulf. Despite this setback the enemy poured reinforcements into Leyte through the western side of the island. The 112th Cavalry and the 32nd Infantry Division swung into action in the northwest section of the island in November, and the 11th Airborne Division on the south flank. On 7 December an amphibious landing by the 77th Division in Ormoc Bay prevented further enemy reinforcements. On Christmas Day the battle for Leyte was turned over to the Eighth Army which had been formed under my command in September. After heavy fighting the enemy in western Leyte was defeated.

The Sixth Army then began preparing to invade Luzon and on 9 January landed at Lingayen Gulf. Units landing were the I Corps, containing the 6th and 43rd Infantry Divisions, and the XIV Corps, consisting of the 37th and 40th Infantry Divisions.

The Eighth Army on 29 January landed the XI Corps, containing the 38th Infantry Division and the 34th Infantry Regiment of the 24th Division on the Zambales coast north of Bataan where it eventually came under Sixth Army command. On the 31st the 11th Airborne Division (less the 511th Parachute Regiment, which dropped inland on 3 February) landed under Eighth Army at Nasugbu in southwestern Luzon and drove 65 miles to Paranque in south Manila. A week later it was transferred to Sixth Army.

The XIV Corps, using the 1st Cavalry Division, the 11th Airborne Division, and the 37th Infantry Division, secured Manila and then turned its attention to southern Luzon, which was cleared by 1 May. The XI Corps moved into mountains north of the XIV and cleared that area by June. Earlier, the XI Corps had cleared Bataan Peninsula. On 16 February the 503rd Parachute Regiment dropped on Corregidor, while a battalion of the 34th Infantry made an amphibious assault on the same island. The XI Corps then undertook to clear smaller islands in Manila Bay and opened that port in April.

The I Corps, meanwhile, moved into mountainous country in northern Luzon, and Japanese defenses in central Luzon, around Clark Field, were cleared by units under the XI and XIV Corps. On 1 July the Luzon campaign was turned over to the Eighth Army. The Eighth Army started a long series of amphibious operations in the central and southern Philippines on 15 January. In late February its Americal Division and the 1st Philippine Infantry seized the northwest tip of Samar and islands in San Bernardino Strait. On the 28th the 186th Infantry of the 41st Division landed in Palawan, where new airfields brought within striking distance Japanese installations in the Indies and Indo-China.

The Eighth Army continued its rapid reduction of the southern Islands when the 41st Division began clearing the Zamboanga Peninsula of Mindanao on 10 March. It quickly extended its advances down the Sulu Archipelago toward Borneo, thereby securing airbases to cover an Australian invasion of the latter island.

On 17 April the Eighth Army landed the X Corps on Moro Gulf in central Mindanao. The 24th Division quickly seized Parang and Cotabato, and drove eastward. Ten days later it had seized Digos, on the dreaded Gulf of Davao. A few days later Davao City was captured, and a superior Japanese force defeated. In the meantime the 31st Division moved eastward to Kabakan, and then drove north through central Mindanao. Another task force landed in Macajalar Bay on 10 May, drove southward, and joined up with the 31st Division in the vicinity of Impulatao, former Japanese Army Headquarters. The Japanese force was pushed from all strategic positions and the campaign was brought to an end on Mindanao.

The 40th Infantry Division landed on Panay on 18 March and quickly captured Iloilo. It then landed a force on northern Negros on the 29th where it was reinforced by the 503rd Parachute Regiment on 8 April. Final Japanese resistance was overcome in the mountains of central Negros.

The Americal Division landed on Cebu on 26 March and overcame heavy Japanese resistance. Other landings were made by the Americal Division on southwestern Negros and Bohol. The southern Philippine campaign was declared officially closed on 1 July 1945.

In April, 1945, central Pacific forces had landed on Okinawa. General MacArthur was already in command of all United States Army Forces in the Pacific with the exception of units at Okinawa, and in July these also came under his command.

Plans for the invasion in Japan were proceeding rapidly with the Sixth Army directed to make the initial landing on the southern Island of Kyushu. The Eighth Army was selected to make the main blow into the heart of Japan by landing in Sagami Bay and advancing northward to capture Tokyo, Yokohama, and the Kanto plain. The First Army was to land southeast of Tokyo to protect the right flank of the Eighth Army. Fortunately, the invasion of Japan never took place. On 6 August an atomic bomb was dropped on Hiroshima; on the 9th Russia declared war on Japan; on the 10th the enemy accepted the Potsdam surrender terms.

The Eighth Army was directed to land by air and water on the Island of Honshu. On 30 August, I landed by air with the advance elements of the 11th Airborne Division on Atsugi Airfield near Yokohama. Two hours later General MacArthur's plane landed, and the occupation of Japan had begun. On 2 September, aboard the "U.S.S. Missouri" in Tokyo Bay, the Japanese signed the formal surrender documents. World War II was over.

Robt. L. Eichelberger

DAWN ASSAULT ON LEYTE. When the U.S. forces were ousted from the Philippines General Douglas MacArthur said, "I shall return." Exactly two years and six months later he did. At dawn, on October 20, a huge U.S. naval force approached the eastern coast of Leyte Island situated in the central Philippines, just 300 miles north of Morotai. LEFT. A small portion of the armada just prior to the major amphibious operation. Thus at one stroke the Jap forces in the Philippines were split in two. Landings were quickly effected under cover of a violent naval and aerial barrage. Troops and heavy armor pushed inland against initially light resistance, rapidly gained control of the coastal road, and seized the town of Tacloban. Yet the campaign was to last two months before the Nips finally capitulated. The price for Leyte: 11,217 American casualties as contrasted to 113,231 for the Japanese.

BACK AT LAST. The assaults at Angaur and Peleliu had coincided with General MacArthur's 350-mile jump to Moro- tai. Next plans called for landings at the great naval base at Yap, at Mindanao, and at Talaud and Sangihe Islands. However, on September 12, Admiral Halsey, striking at the central Philippines, found serious weaknesses in Jap defenses there, and recommended that the target be changed to Leyte. Admiral Nimitz and General MacArthur agreed with this idea, and plans to assault Leyte were put in operation. On October 19 two assault forces that stretched across the vast Pacific horizon approached the central Philippines. Troops and materiel with which we were to seize Leyte were loaded in 53 assault transports, 54 assault cargo ships, 151 landing ships (tank), 72 landing craft (in- fantry), 16 rocket ships, and over 400 other assorted am- phibious craft. In addition, there were 18 aircraft carriers, six battleships, and their screen of cruisers and destroyers. ABOVE. Loaded to the gunwales, one of the LSTs approaches Leyte. Out to sea, a mighty carrier task force under Ad- miral Halsey, which had helped prepare the way for the landings by air bombardment, was standing watch for pos- sible Japanese naval opposition. UPPER RIGHT. Going in for the landing October 20. LOWER RIGHT. Natives of Dulag village greet the first American soldiers to land.

MOVING INLAND. With surprisingly light opposition from the Japanese 16th Division, American troops pushed inland. In about 10 days a line from Dulag to Carigara was held. Could it be that the Japs were not determined to hold the island? Events proved they were very much determined to hold on. UPPER. Even the first few days were unpleasant. Here on October 20 troops are pinned down by Jap mortar fire on Red Beach. LOWER. President Osmena of the Philippines and General MacArthur are shown en route to inspect the beachhead on the same day.

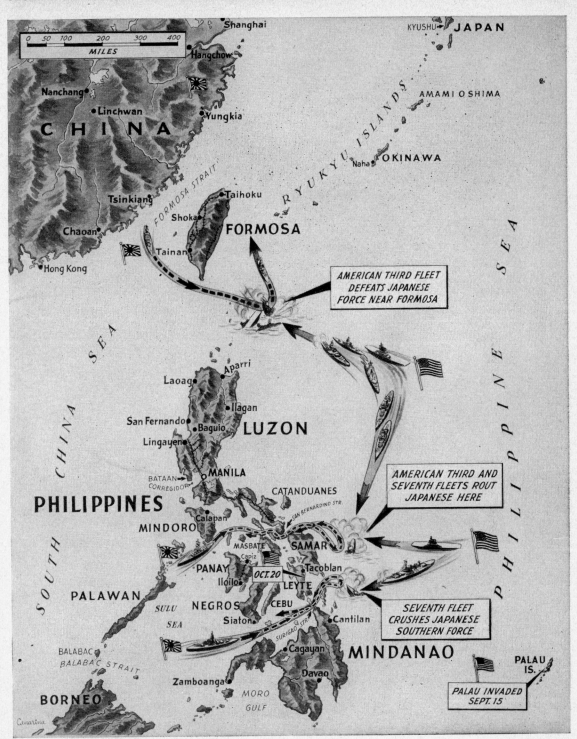

AMERICAN THIRD FLEET
DEFEATS JAPANESE
FORCE NEAR FORMOSA

AMERICAN THIRD AND
SEVENTH FLEETS ROUT
JAPANESE HERE

SEVENTH FLEET
CRUSHES JAPANESE
SOUTHERN FORCE

PALAU INVADED
SEPT. 15

NAVAL DISASTER FOR THE JAPS. When American forces invaded the Philippines, the Japanese Imperial Fleet steamed forth in strength to slug it out with the U.S. Third and Seventh Fleets. It may have been the last of its kind, this epic struggle of iron-clad warships. At its conclusion the results were catastrophic for the Japs as those of their ships still floating at the end were a shambles of buckled plates and gore-spattered decks. Japanese sea power was broken.

DISASTER FOR JAP CONVOY AT ORMOC BAY, LEYTE.
The end at Leyte came when the Japanese discovered it
was just as difficult as back in New Guinea to reinforce
a besieged garrison. On November 10, high hills around
Ormoc Bay concealed FEAF B-25s until they roared over
the bay at masthead height, accompanied by P-38s and
P-47s which shot down 16 out of 20 intercepting enemy
planes. The Mitchells sank three of the convoy's transports and six escorting ships, damaging several others.
Flak was intense, one pilot reporting, "It was the roughest
mission I ever hope to see." Next day Navy carrier planes
smashed up another Ormoc-bound convoy, and on December 7 and 11, 5th Air Force fighter-bombers destroyed two
more substantial convoys, both near Ormoc Bay. Shown
(above) is a Jap destroyer broken in two by hits amidships.
This was in the first operation on November 10, the same
day that U.S. forces captured the port of Ormoc itself,

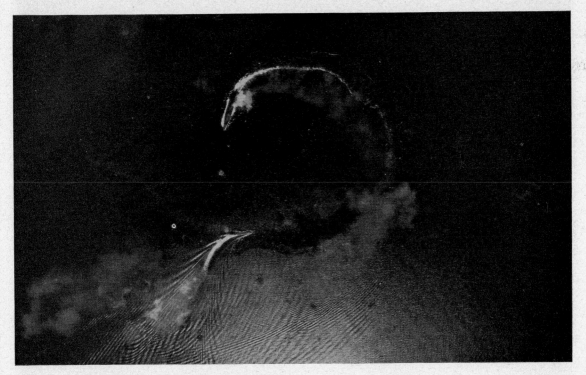

MISSION THWARTED. Out of a total of 7 Japanese battleships, 2 carrier-battleships, 4 carriers, 17 cruisers and 23 destroyers which approached the Philippines in October, 1944, American Naval Forces sank 3 battleships, all 4 carriers, 10 cruisers and 5 destroyers in the Battle for Leyte Gulf. U.S. Navy losses amounted to 1 light carrier, 2 escort carriers, 2 destroyers and 1 PT boat. UPPER. Hard pressed by fliers of the United States Navy's Pacific Fleet, this great Japanese battleship-aircraft carrier vainly tries to duck bomb and torpedo hits. Just a few hours before, the Japanese Southern Force, trying to sneak up on the Leyte landings via Surigao Strait, had been trapped by our Seventh Fleet, and only meager remnants of it managed to get away. LOWER. The wake of a fleeing Japanese ship etches a gigantic question mark in the waters of Tablas Strait as it vainly dodges the aerial attack of carrier planes from Admiral Halsey's Third Fleet. As in all World War II naval battles, carrier planes were indispensable to victory.

THE CHALLENGE. The invasion of Leyte presented a challenge that neither the Jap Army nor Navy could afford to ignore—and they decided to do battle with both forces. On the ground, Field Marshal Terauchi relieved Lieutenant General Kuroda of command in the Philippines, replaced him with General Yamashita, who had conquered Singapore and Bataan. Yamashita was one of the best-known Jap generals. Shortly after he took over he sent this message to General Makina, commander of the 16th Division, then fighting a delaying action against General Krueger's U.S. Sixth Army: "The Army has received the following order from his Majesty, the Emperor: 'Enemy ground forces will be destroyed'." The tempo increased after this, and shortly afterward, the Japanese Navy steamed forth to do battle also. UPPER LEFT. Past splintered trees and fires caused by heavy bombardment, troops of the 12th Cavalry move inland on Leyte. LOWER LEFT. Elements of the 7th Cavalry Regiment cross a tank trap during their advance on San Jose. UPPER RIGHT. Troops of the 2nd Battalion, 34th Infantry, in town of Pawing. LOWER RIGHT. Members of the 24th Division move up to occupy a hill near Pawing.

NO PLACE TO HIDE. ABOVE. American carrier planes wrought this scene of destruction in Manila Harbor on November 19, 1944. Skimming devastatingly over the seaport the planes unleashed both bombs and torpedoes. The vessel in the foreground is scuttled, one to the left is blazing

furiously, while a third, in the center, is floundering precariously from a near-hit. The scene ashore was soon to become a facsimile. The Philippines' capital and most beautiful city, in subsequent ground and aerial pounding, was razed. In this raid 118 Jap planes were also destroyed.

MORE INVASIONS. By November 1 Allied troops occupied all of northeastern and southern Leyte. But by now the Japs had decided to do or die, and they managed to send in reinforcements. Many of their transports were sunk, but some troops landed. More American troops poured in, too. Ormoc, principal Jap installation on the island, was taken by the 77th Infantry Division on December 11. Cogon, Valencia, and Kananga fell. An amphibious jump to Palompon was made Christmas Day, and organized resistance there ended. Meanwhile, elements of the 24th Infantry Division and the 503rd Parachute Infantry Regiment invaded Mindoro on December 15, and within 24 hours American planes and PT boats were operating off the southern coast of Luzon. Leyte and Mindoro were but preliminaries for the assault to come—the invasion of Luzon. In the first week of January a new American assault force slipped through Surigao Strait, heading for Lingayen Gulf and the invasion. Elaborate plans and feints were made to confuse the Japs. On January 9 our Sixth Army hit the beaches in the Gulf. ABOVE. Elements of the 43rd Infantry Division load up for the Luzon assault. UPPER RIGHT. Troops of the 77th Division unload on a beach of northwest Leyte. LOWER RIGHT. Yank infantrymen and Filipino guerrillas are pinned down temporarily by Japanese machine-gun fire at Bambam, Luzon.

GI'S CROSS THE PASIG RIVER. U.S. Army forces smashed into Manila on February 5, 1944, but the Japs put up a fanatical resistance within the city. The enemy destroyed all bridges across the Pasig River, but the Yanks swarmed across in assault craft. ABOVE. Here they are depicted crossing the stream in hot pursuit of a wily foe.

NEARING THE HOME ISLANDS. UPPER. At Iwo Jima a U.S. tanker is hit by enemy action and goes up in flames as the battle rages ashore. LOWER. A Baka bomb which was captured intact on Okinawa. These tiny suicide planes were released from their parent plane and piloted in to hit their targets. Loaded with explosives they were certain death for their fanatical pilots, since they were either shot down or reached their objective.

ROCKETS IN FLIGHT. One of the oldest of modern weapons, and one of the most spectacular, rockets came into their own in this war. Because of the lack of recoil in their launching, they give fire power to smaller vessels far in excess of what could be obtained from guns which require more stable mounts. ABOVE. Rockets streak from a U.S. Navy support ship with bow pointed shoreward during the early stages of the invasion of Brunei Bay, Borneo.

THE LAST STAGE. The elimination of snipers was usually the final phase in the conquest of a town or city. In Manila, however, the Japs were particularly tenacious, and after infantry and armored columns had freed most of the city, artillery barrages had to flatten the last remnants of resistance. ABOVE. Troops stealthily hunt for Jap snipers.

FIGHT FOR LUZON. American landings had caught all major Jap combat units in motion, and they were forced into a piecemeal commitment of troops. U.S. forces landed on the west coast of Luzon near Subic Bay, on January 29, and drove east to cut off the Bataan Peninsula. The 11th Airborne Division made an unopposed amphibious landing at Nasugbu south of Manila January 31. Three days later a parachute regiment jumped to Tagaytay ridge dominating the Cavite area, and that night troops of the 1st Cavalry Division raced to Grace Park in northeastern Manila, which fell on February 23 after bitter fighting. Portions of the 38th Division landed at Mariveles on the tip of Bataan February

15. Corregidor, under Allied bombardment since January 23, was invaded February 16. Two long trains of Army C-47 transports brought the veteran 503rd Parachute Regiment to the "Rock." Against scattered small arms fire these troops landed near the lighthouse and golf course of the little island. UPPER LEFT. On February 3, advance troops take cover as Jap troops fire from hidden positions in a forest near Olongapo, Luzon. LOWER LEFT. A member of the 503rd Parachute Infantry Regiment, of Noemfoor and Markham fame, scouts out an area on Corregidor February 17. Gas is being used to burn out Japs. ABOVE. While 'chutes are scattered over the landscape, more infantrymen drift down.

FIGHT FOR MANILA. The tough struggle for Manila lasted from February 8 to 24. Until the battle actually began, it appeared that it would not be too difficult to capture the city. But the Japs withdrew to the southern section, and they had to be blasted out street by street, house by house, yard by yard. UPPER. Elements of the 48th Infantry, manning a 37mm gun, fire at Japanese machine gun positions from a street in Manila's vast Chinatown. LOWER. From a vantage point atop Elana Apartments, members of the 37th Division fire on the enemy in the Intramuros section.

THE WALLED CITY. Some of the hardest Manila fighting occurred in the Intramuros section, around the port, and in the old walled section. UPPER. From a window of a building across the Pasig River near Jones Bridge, a member of the 37th Division shoots at Japs in the walled city. LOWER.

U.S. troops cross from the freed north bank of the Pasig River and storm ashore toward the walled city, which at that time was a hotbed of Jap resistance. The 37th Infantry, 1st Cavalry and 11th Airborne Divisions bore the brunt of the battle to take the Philippine capital.

SHOT TO PIECES. By the time American troops had over-
powered the Japanese defending Manila, this once-
beautiful city was shot to pieces. These pictures furnish
graphic proof of what war can do to streets and buildings.
UPPER LEFT. This street—Avenida Rizal—was a shambles
on February 18 as U.S. troops moved along its ruins, heading for the front. LOWER LEFT. American GIs who spearheaded the attack through the center of Manila, and who
were relieved after 16 days of fighting from building to
building, pass through the Pace (Peace) section. ABOVE.
A view of the Intramuros section gives aspect of the damage
as some of our troops move into it February 23, 1945.

INVADING PANAY. In late February the 41st Division, Eighth Army, had landed on Palawan Island. Corregidor had been taken, and Japs killed there totaled 4,215, as compared to 136 American dead. The port of Manila was in operation. In early March elements of the 41st Division had landed on Mindanao, and a little later landings were made on Panay, Cebu and Negros. ABOVE. On March 18 troops of the 185th Infantry, 40th Division, hit the beach on Panay. UPPER RIGHT. This picture of the 185th Division advance on Panay was made by Lieutenant Robert Fields March 18 shortly before he was killed. LOWER RIGHT. 40th Division troops move up on Panay.

SLOW PROGRESS. Driving north in March from the central plain of Luzon the Sixth Army met fanatical resistance from the Japs in the mountain ranges between Baguio and Balete Pass. Progress was slow. In one area U.S. troops advanced only two miles in three weeks—but Balete Pass fell to the 25th Division and the 37th Division on May 15. UPPER. Here on April 1 troops of the 128th Regiment, 32nd Division, are dug in on top of Hill 604 to fire at Jap positions on the next ridge. LOWER. In a thicket atop Hill 511 on the Villa Verde Trail other GIs are dug in.

GREAT ACTIVITY. April and May, 1945, were months of great activity on the part of the American forces in the Philippines. Elements of the Eighth Army went ashore on central Mindanao north of Cotabato. The 24th Division took Davo City on May 4 after house to house fighting. The 31st Division drove up the Pulangi Valley to Kibawe. On Luzon, the city of Baguio had fallen. UPPER. Men of the 43rd Division move up near San Juan, Luzon, to clear road of Japs who ambushed a convoy. LOWER. Troops of 37th Division advance toward Baguio on April 14.

GAINS EXTENDED. By May 1, the Allies were gaining ground extensively, That day an amphibious force of Australian and Netherland East Indies troops landed on oil-rich Tarakan Island, off the northeast coast of Borneo. Another American landing was made in mid-May in Mindanao, this time at Agusan, in the guerrilla-held north. Earlier, Americans had landed on Carabao. UPPER. Covered by their buddies, troops of the 151st Infantry Regiment advance on Carabao. LOWER. Infantrymen of 151st Regimental Combat Team blasting Japs on Carabao.

BLASTING 'EM OUT. On Carabao, as in nearly all other invasion spots in the Pacific, the Japs had to be blasted and burned out of their caves, dugouts and holes. UPPER. Suspecting Jap snipers, American soldiers machine gun the entrance to a cave. Smoke rising from cave mouth comes from an explosion of a white phosphorus shell previously thrown in by these members of the 151st Infantry Regiment. LOWER. In the midst of smoke from phosphorus grenades thrown into tunnel mouths, infantrymen of Company B, 1st Battalion, 151st Regiment, cross a ravine in northeast Carabao.

GUERRILLA AID. Nearly everywhere in the Philippines, the American liberators received valuable information and help from the Filipino people. On practically every front native guerrillas came to the aid of U.S. troops, and fought with great skill and bravery. One of the places where they served exceedingly well was at Balete Pass, gateway to the Cagayan Valley. ABOVE. In April, veteran artillerymen of the 90th Field Artillery, 25th Division, lay down a murderous barrage on Japanese positions in the Pass. UPPER RIGHT. On the lookout for snipers, a 33rd Division patrol moves up through the remains of a market place in Baguio. LOWER RIGHT. Troops cross the Pauili River on May 2.

CLOSING IN. By the middle of June, the Japanese position was critical. What was left of the Jap 14th Army had been trapped in the Cagayan Valley. Ilagan, capital of Isabela Province, fell on June 19, and Jap forces in northern Luzon were split in two the next day when Filipino guerrillas crossed the Cagayan River. ABOVE. A patrol of the 149th Infantry advances through the last tunnel along a trail to the Wawa Dam in the Marikina Watersheds on Luzon. UPPER RIGHT. Tanks of the 37th Division blast a path for infantry northward toward Lantap June 11. LOWER RIGHT. Troops of the 148th Infantry Regiment, with tanks of the 775th Tank Battalion, advance into Lantap June 12.

THE LAST ROUTE. The last route from which the Japs could escape from Luzon was closed June 21 when American and Filipino troops seized Aparri. A few days later the 11th Airborne Division, moving south, and the 37th Division, moving north, met and split the Jap troops into three parts. UPPER. In mid-June, fighting was bitter. Here, on the 13th, infantrymen of the 37th Division crouch to escape heavy enemy fire. Half tracks, some with multiple 50's of the 209th Anti-Aircraft Battalion, join tanks in returning the fire. Tanks are firing 105s and .50 caliber machine guns. LOWER. Soldiers carry ammunition over a bamboo foot bridge 15 miles south of Aparri on June 27. The steel bridge at right had been blown up by retreating Japs. By July 5 the situation was such that General MacArthur could announce that the Philippines were liberated, and that the campaign had virtually ended. Japs who had been isolated in Luzon continued to resist to the end of the war, but the organized fighting had ended. The Emperor's order had been put in reverse. The Japanese ground forces—not those of the Allies — had been destroyed. Altogether, the Japs lost about 400,000 of their better troops in the Philippines campaign.

YAMASHITA SURRENDERS. General Yamashita, "Tiger of Malaya," conqueror of Singapore, and the Japanese hero of Bataan, was defiant to the last, but the moment came when he had to sign on the dotted line. Here, on September 2, 1945, at Kiangan, in northern Luzon, he surrenders to the 32nd Division. Left to right are: Major General Robert S. Beightler, commanding general of U.S. Forces in Luzon; Major General Leo Donovan; Brigadier General Robert B. McBride, Jr.; Colonel Ernest A. Barlow; and the Japanese general. General MacArthur had declared that he would return to the Philippines, and by now no one knew better than Yamashita that MacArthur's word had been kept.

THE ROAD IS OPENED. The long-awaited opening of the Ledo Road came in January, 1945—and no longer would China have to be supplied from the air alone. It was a crooked road, but it ended the long isolation of our ally. It was put to good use in a hurry. ABOVE. Mountain-climbing U.S. medium tanks, manned by Americans and Chinese, use the Burma Road for the first time after Jap control had been broken. UPPER RIGHT. On January 26, 1945, first convoy over the Ledo-Burma road takes sharp turns between Bhamo and Nankham. LOWER RIGHT. This sign, being read by an American and a Chinese, at the China-Burma border at Wanting tells its own story in both languages.

"PICK'S PIKE." No matter what else its name, to the men under Brigadier General Lewis A. Pick, who directed a great deal of the work, this great new road was "Pick's Pike." It was fitting that General Pick led the first convoy from India to China into Kumming. UPPER LEFT. With the picturesque Mitu Valley in the background, this first convoy rounds a few curves on the Burma Road. LOWER LEFT. The General, at the head of the column, enters Kumming on February 4. ABOVE. While thousands of happy Chinese line the streets and cheer, this first convoy, loaded with the goods of war, parades through Kumming. This group of trucks was only the forerunner of others to come.

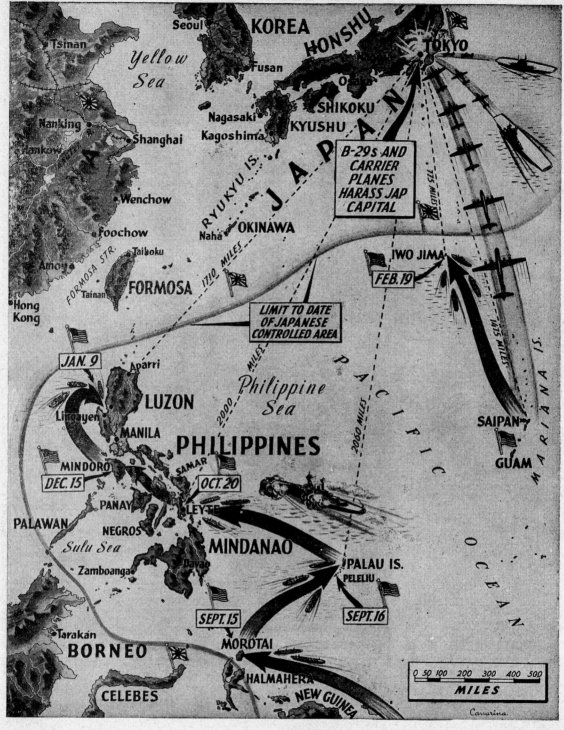

ISLAND HOPPING TO TOKIO. General Douglas Mac-Arthur's long, arduous campaign of island hopping now fruitioned in the dramatic invasion of Iwo Jima, situated 775 miles south of Tokio itself. From the Palaus in September, 1944, the U.S. armed forces had moved without faltering to Leyte, Mindoro, Luzon, and now to Iwo Jima. This campaign, probably the toughest of the Pacific, was the semi-final. Only Okinawa remained prior to the Japs' unconditional surrender.

EN ROUTE TO IWO JIMA. Marine Lt. Gen. Holland M. Smith (upper), Expeditionary Troops Commander of the 60,000 Marines soon to land on Iwo, briefs war correspondents aboard the Task Force Command Ship. The men in the back of the ward room taking notes are veterans of numerous Marine Pacific landings. Many had landed on one beachhead after another in the Central Pacific, beginning at Tarawa. In the front row are the top Navy Commanders. Seated in the middle is Navy Secretary James V. Forrestal who went ashore with Gen. Smith and remained to see the flag raised over Suribachi. On his right is Vice Admiral Richmond K. Turner, Amphibious Force Commander for the operation. To his left is Rear Admiral Harry Hill, an Amphibious Group Commander. Also out from Washington was Rear Admiral Louis Denfeld, far left with glasses, who became Chief of Naval Operations when Fleet Admiral Chester W. Nimitz retired in 1947. RIGHT. For the troops, the stop off Saipan provided an opportunity for relaxation. These Fifth Division Marines, going into combat for the first time, enjoy a plunge while awaiting sailing orders. It was a long dive—and a longer climb.

USS "NEW YORK" POUNDS BASTION. For two days prior to the Marines' invasion of Iwo Jima, battleships of the U.S. Pacific Fleet rained the island with shells. ABOVE. The USS "New York" is depicted pouring shells out of her 14-inch guns on enemy positions. At the end of the 48-hour bombardment, the "New York" moved in to fire at point blank range.

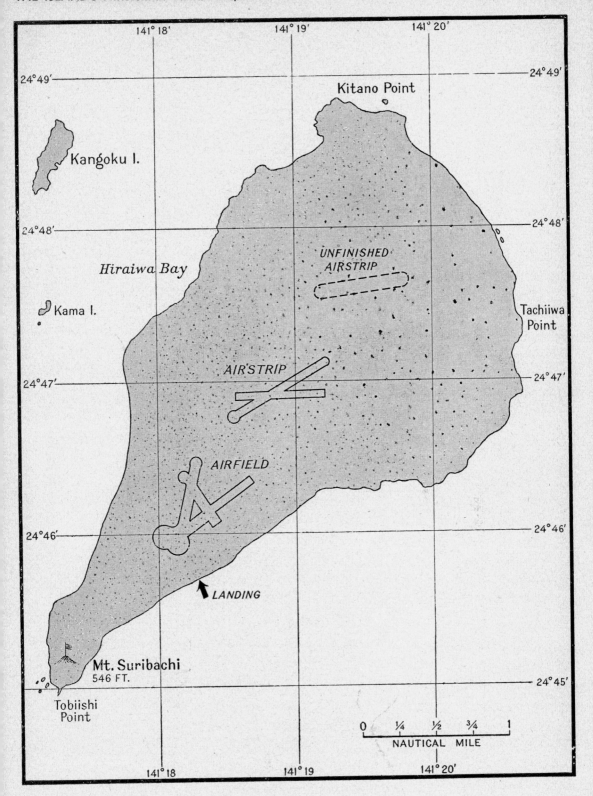

Map of the island of Iwo Jima, showing landing points.

GOING IN AT IWO. On February 19, 1945, the troops of
the Fourth and Fifth Marine Divisions were boated and heading for the low beaches of Iwo. UPPER LEFT. The warships
were almost sitting on the beaches, or so it seemed to the
Marines going in on the landing craft. Suribachi's dim shape
loomed large on the left end of the island. Much of the shore
was hidden in smoke and clouds of powdered volcanic
ashes churned up by shellfire. LOWER LEFT. As Marines
moved toward the beaches in waves, surface and air bombardment continued. However, the heavy shelling came far
from knocking out the 22,000 Japanese in their well-
prepared positions. ABOVE. Amphtracs pass a control boat.

THE FIFTH DIVISION. Under murderous fire, the Fifth Division troops (upper) worm their way up the slanting beach. The intensive training they had received at Camp Pendleton and at Camp Tarawa on Hawaii proved invaluable here. There were many veterans of earlier Pacific landings in this new Division, including raiders and parachutists. The advance was slow, tortuous. LOWER. On Red Beach One, the 27th Marines under Col. Tommy Wornham await the order to cross the ridge against the withering fire from all sides. On his left were troops of Col. Harry Liversedge.

IWO WAS NECESSARY. Iwo lies about 600 miles from Tokyo and about the same distance from Saipan. Intercepting devices from Iwo could detect flights of B-29s bound for Japan and alert defense aviation long before the bombers arrived. Planes staged through Iwo could make kamikaze suicide attacks against the B-29 fields on Saipan and Tinian. With Iwo in Allied hands, fighter protection and emergency landing fields could be provided for the B-29s. UPPER. Marines on beachheads had little time to think of this overall picture. LOWER. Instead, they watch the enemy.

KURIBAYASHI'S PLAN. The Fifth Amphibious Corps, comprising the Third, Fourth and Fifth Marine Divisions, plus Corps troops, all under the command of Maj. Gen. Harry Schmidt, had its plans for the assault and capture of Iwo. Lt. Gen. Kuribayashi, Japanese Commander of Iwo, also had plans. He realized that it would be impossible, without his own fleet and planes, to prevent a landing on the beaches. He figured, however, that he could wipe out the Marines after they got ashore by using his strong array of artillery, rockets, mortars and automatic weapons. He came close to succeeding. The 72 days of aerial bombing by the Seventh Air Force did surprisingly little damage. Even the three-day pounding given the island by the Fleet (minus many of its most powerful units on a strike against Japan or in preparation for Okinawa) was relatively ineffective. RIGHT. Our wreckage on Iwo's beaches piled higher than during any previous Pacific invasion. First aid stations were set up amidst the debris to care for the wounded. UPPER. Vehicles, tanks, amphtracs and trucks were primary targets and the Marine dead lay where they fell as death continued to rain down on the beaches.

FIGHTING ON OKINAWA. The closer the Marines came to the Japanese home islands, the tougher the fighting. ABOVE. A flame thrower burns out fanatical defenders from caves on a ridge. The 95-day Okinawa operation was a rugged, brutal, deadly struggle. The Presidential Unit Citation of the Sixth Marine Division tells the story: "For extraordinary heroism in action against enemy Japanese forces during the assault and capture of Okinawa, April 1, to July 21, 1945. Seizing Yontan Airfield in its initial operation, the Sixth Marine Division, Reinforced, smashed through organized resistance to capture Ishikawa Isthmus, the town of Nago, and heavily fortified Motobu Peninsula in 13 days. Later committed to the southern front, units of the Division withstood overwhelming artillery and mortar barrages, repulsed furious counter-attacks and staunchly pushed over the rocky terrain to reduce almost impregnable defenses and capture Sugar Loaf Hill. Turning southeast, they took the capital city of Naha and executed surprise shore-to-shore landings on Oruku Peninsula, securing the area with its prized Naha Airfield and Harbor after nine days of fierce fighting. Reentering the lines in the south, Sixth Division Marines sought out enemy forces entrenched in a series of rocky ridges extending to the southern tip of the island, advancing relentlessly and rendering decisive support until the last remnants of enemy opposition were exterminated and the island secured. By their valor and tenacity, the officers and men of the Sixth Marine Division, Reinforced, contributed materially to the conquest of Okinawa, and their gallantry in overcoming a fanatical enemy in the face of extraordinary danger and difficulty adds new luster to Marine Corps history, and to the traditions of the United States Naval Service." This citation might well have been applicable to the First Marine Division, or to certain of the Army divisions which likewise fought bravely and well on Okinawa. The saga of the Sixth typified a hard battle spurred by the heroism of the footsoldier.

UTTER DESOLATION. Somehow seeming ever more terrible against the green hills surrounding it, the city of Nagasaki presents a scene of complete destruction in these two photographs taken after the atomic bomb hit had wiped out the city. Only a twisted mass of rubble, now unrecognizable, remains of what was a prosperous city. When the Americans occupied Japan, they made detailed studies of the results of the bomb hits here and in Hiroshima.

BATTLE OF THE CAVES. The Japs, fighting savagely, had to be routed from the rocks and crannies of Iwo Jima by flames, grenades, and machine-gun fire. ABOVE. One Marine poises himself at the mouth of a Jap-infested cave while another stands by ready to cover him up with a tommy-gun.

MOBILE ARTILLERY. Rocket firing trucks (lower left) could place a pulverizing tonnage of high explosive shells in a relatively small area. These fired eight tons in three minutes. Then they could be driven to new positions before the Japs had time to bring counter-battery fire from their artillery. UPPER LEFT. The Staff of the Fourth Division comes ashore with Gen. Cates, center, pointing. Headquarters troops carried carbines or pistols plus the assorted office equipment, maps, boards and other gear needed for beachhead operation of a division CP. ABOVE. This culvert, littered with the debris of artillery shell cases and battered equipment, serves as a command post for the 23rd Marines.

FLAMING DEATH. On the right flank, the Fourth Division caught hell. A number of combat correspondents summed up their experiences thus: "With flame throwers and demolitions, we blasted the enemy out of his pillboxes, many of which were connected with tunnels and trenches. On a 100-yard stretch we fought through the cross fire of 50 pillboxes and 10 blockhouses, only to find that some of the Japs had sneaked back through those we had already passed, and were now firing on us from the rear. The fighting became hotter as we moved toward the airfield. Each shellhole was a potential hiding place for a sniper, and we jumped into one only after throwing a grenade in first. Nothing any of us had ever known could compare with the utter anguish, frustration and constant inner battle to maintain some semblance of sanity, clarity of mind, and power of speech." UPPER LEFT. First the flame thrower, covered by rifle fire, then the charge around or over the pillbox. That was the way it went. LOWER LEFT. Blasting at the base of Suribachi the third day, flame throwers burn a path for the assault. ABOVE. This pattern is formed by tracers lighting the sky.

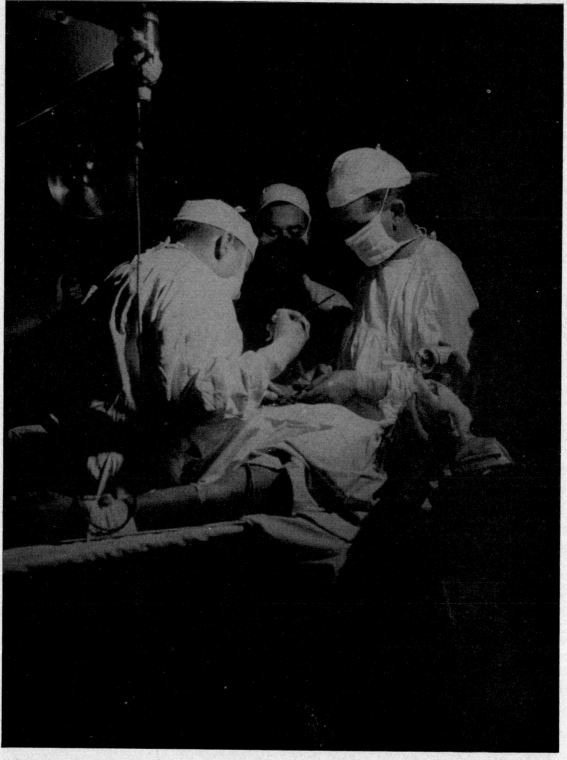

BLOOD FROM HOME. Whole blood was used extensively for the first time at Iwo Jima. Some Marines were treated with blood actually given back in the States after the invasion had begun and flown out as priority air cargo. ABOVE. Navy surgeons operate on a stomach wound in an emergency evacuation hospital, formerly a converted Jap dugout. A corpsman administers the ether. Correspondent Keith Wheeler, wounded on Iwo, described his evacuation, "The stretcher was jerked up and the bearers slogged through sand and surf, half running, sobbing in the effort . . ."

GOD WITH US. Chaplains accompanied the Marines throughout the battle, generally working out of field hospitals or aid stations, comforting the wounded and the dying. Some were attached to command posts of battalions, regiments and divisions. Protestant, Catholic and Jewish, they rendered great service before, during and after operations. Generally, each division had three chaplains at headquarters, one of each faith. Each regiment had one Catholic and one Protestant chaplain. They lived with the officers but were close to the men. The chaplains, like the medicos and corpsmen, were loved by the Marines and soon took on the fierce pride of their charges. In rear areas they frequently had such additional duties as running libraries, managing recreation, censoring mail and other jobs. UPPER. Father Tommy Driscoll of the Fourth says Mass on Iwo. His Marines had been in four campaigns within 13 months. LOWER. Father Joe Hammond of the Fourth distributes Holy Communion within 100 yards of the first airfield.

LETHAL WEAPONS. UPPER. Here is the first picture ever released of the U.S. Marine mobile rocketeer units at work. The photograph was taken on Iwo Jima. The value of this weapon is self-evident. Its projectiles soared over hills to blast the Japanese on the other side. Mobility was also a great asset. Before enemy artillery could find the range of rocketeers, the units were off to another sector. LOWER. This picture shows one of the many kinds of booby traps rigged up by the retreating Japanese troops. Sharp-eyed ordnancemen were not so easily fooled.

NICE GOING, BOBBY. Lt. Gen. Holland Smith paternally pats his friend and former Chief of Staff, Maj. Gen. Graves B (Bobby) Erskine, of the Third Division (right) after the formal flag raising on Iwo. Erskine's 21st Marines had landed D + 2 and were attached to the Fourth until D + 5 when the 9th Marines were ordered in and Erskine took the central high ground of the island, pushing hard against the second airfield. It was a 28-man patrol from Co. A of the 21st Marines that reached the northern shore to send back a can of water to Gen. Erskine with a message: "Forwarded for approval, not for consumption." Of the original 200 men who had made up Co. A, three were left. A sergeant remarked that "the Third's fight into the sulphuric crags and gullies of the center of the island was uphill and desperate." Supported by the 12th Marines' artillery all the way, Erskine's Division, less the 3rd Marines, fought hard, sometimes only moving a few hundred yards a day. UPPER. These men are part of the patrol that placed the first small flag on Suribachi's top, using a piece of Jap pipe for a staff. In later fighting, many of this group were killed, almost all wounded.

THE ENEMY DEAD. The Japanese on Iwo Jima fought bravely, brilliantly, stubbornly and futilely. UPPER. One of the enemy dead, buried temporarily where he fell. LOWER. Another Jap soldier lies to the right of a pillbox. These men had taken a "Courageous Battle Vow," promising: "Above all else we shall dedicate ourselves and our entire strength to the defense of this island. We shall grasp bombs, charge the enemy tanks and destroy them. We shall infiltrate into the midst of the enemy and annihilate them. With every salvo, we will, without fail, kill the enemy."

THE ENEMY LIVING. From places like this blockhouse (lower), battered by rocket fire, Japanese fighting men like these (upper) crawled, walked or stumbled into Marine hands as prisoners. Gen. Erskine, trying to save lives, wrote a note to Col. Ikeda Masuo, commanding the last pocket of resistance. It was delivered deep into enemy territory by two prisoners who carried a walkie-talkie and communicated with Erskine's CP. Erskine's note said: "Our forces now have complete control and freedom of movement on the island of Iwo Jima except in the small area now held by the valiant Japanese troops just south of Kitana Point. The fearlessness and indomitable fighting spirit which has been displayed by the Japanese troops warrants the admiration of all fighting men. You have handled your troops in a superb manner but we have no desire to completely annihilate brave troops who have been forced into a hopeless position. I suggest that you cease resistance at once and march, with your command, through my lines to a place of safety." The enemy refused to answer the ultimatum and had to be dug out, causing more Marine casualties.

THE LORD IS MY SHEPHERD. The Fourth Marine Division cemetery (upper) is under construction by the Seabees. The Fifth (lower), sitting at the foot of Suribachi, is crowded with Marines, tight lipped and dry throated as they search for their buddies. Men found brothers, tent mates, relatives and life-long friends buried beneath the tiny mounds. The Fifth lost 104 officers and 2,378 men, with 250 officers and 5,968 men wounded. The Fourth lost 1,806 dead and 7,292 wounded. Third Division and Fifth Corps casualties raised the total to 5,349 dead, 16,090 wounded.

ETERNAL REST GRANT UNTO THEM. These words behind the altar of the 28th Marines (above) serve as a reminder to those who survived to pray for their buddies. Rabbi R. B. Gittelsohn, Jewish Chaplain of the Fifth, said in dedication prayer directed to men of all faiths: "All that we can even hope to do is follow their example. To show the same selfless courage in peace that they did in war. To swear that by the grace of God and the stubborn strength and power of human will, their sons and ours shall never suffer these pains again. We promise that . . ."

WHY IWO JIMA? Although the casualty figure was shocking to the people at home, the big bomber (upper), first to land on Iwo Jima, was the answer to the question, "Why Iwo Jima?" On March 3, 1945, the crippled bomber landed on Iwo, en route home from Japan. It was the first of more than 2,800 to land safely. Without Iwo's landing fields they would have crashed into the ocean with their 10-man crews. With Iwo in American hands they received fighter cover over the target and back, saving hundreds of additional planes and thousands of lives which might have been lost against enemy fighters over Japan. RIGHT. The officers and men of Maj. Gen. Curtis LeMay's Twentieth Air Force dedicate a B-29 to the Third Marine Division in appreciation for its part in the capture of Iwo. Maj. Gen. Graves B. Erskine of the Third, right, participated in the ceremonies with Maj. Eliot Tobin, pilot of the Third Marine Division B-29. Maj. Tobin, who landed on Iwo with two motors shot out in a raid over Kobe, Japan, made 25 bombing missions over Japan. Other B-29's were named for the Fourth and Fifth Marine Divisions for their share in the seizure of the viciously fought-over island fortress.

SUPERFORT WARFARE IN THE PACIFIC

By Major General Curtis E. LeMay

IN January 1944 General Arnold, as Commanding General of the Army Air Forces, made his first public report on the progress of the air war. Of the plans already made for operations in the Pacific and against the Japanese homeland General Arnold could say little, but he dropped a hint. To the statement that "Offense is the essence of air power" he added: "Neither Japanese shipping nor Japanese industry will survive the bombing in store for them." The history of our air war in the Pacific is above all the history of the aircraft that carried our main attack to the Japanese homeland and proved the principle of the strategic concept.

Because of the early termination of the war, only a small part of the large force of B-29s destined for ultimate attack on the Japanese home islands was ever employed in combat operations, but it is a significant fact that a single B-29 flew the last important bombardment mission of World War II, to drop a single atomic bomb on Nagasaki.

In November 1939 General Arnold, as Chief of the Air Corps, had requested permission of the War Department to initiate action which would lead to the experimental development of a four-engine bomber of approximately 70,000 pounds weight and possessing characteristics superior to those of the B17 and the B-24. One of the specific requirements for performance was "Tactical radius at design altitude (40,000 feet), capable of carrying 2,000 lb. bombs, 5333 mile range." The requested authority was granted in December, and on January 1940 five leading aircraft manufacturing companies were consulted in reference to design and manufacture. The first XB-29 model, built at a cost of $3,392,396.60, was put through 22 test flights between September 21 and December 28, 1942. But the bold decision to order mass production of B-29s had been made by General Arnold some 16 months before the first test flight, and when that flight was made, 1664 B-29s were already on order.

The first strategic employment of the B-29 was from bases in India and China, after it was decided, late in 1943, by the Joint Chiefs of Staff (on the recommendation of General Arnold) to make first use of the full production of B-29s in the China-Burma-India Theater, instead of the European Theater of Operations.

Hand-picked, well-trained, battle wise veterans formed the cadres for the four groups of the 58th Bombardment Wing, organized in June 1943, at Marietta, Ga. This bombardment wing was the nucleus for the XX Bomber Command, which, operating in the China-Burma-India Theater after April 1944, under the command of Brigadier General Kenneth B. Wolfe, was the first organization to use B-29s operationally.

The XXI Bomber Command and the bombardment wings that used B-29s in the Marianas were staffed and trained by the Second Air Force. Headquarters of the XXI was activated March 8, 1944 at Salina, Kansas, and training began in this command about the time that the XX Bomber Command moved into the CBI theater for preliminary operations.

The Army Air Forces had decided upon an unusual plan for direction of its strategic air operations against Japan. The Twentieth Air Force was designated as the global striking force. Operational control of the force was deposited with the Joint Chiefs of Staff, in Washington, D. C., and General Arnold, as Commanding General of the Army Air Forces and the Twentieth Air Force, was named as executive agent of the Joint Chiefs of Staff.

In the theater, over-all direction from Washington was translated into action by the commanding generals of the XX Bomber Command in the CBI and (later) of the XXI Bomber Command in the Marianas. Direction by the Joint Chiefs of Staff made possible the construction and defense under the responsibility of various theater commanders of the widely scattered bases necessary for use by a plane of such great range as the B-29, and an Air Force as truly global as the Twentieth.

The XX Bomber Command had operated since June 1944, from individual group bases in India and through advanced staging bases in China which were never established as permanent bases. The organization of the XXI Bomber Command, which was to consist of five VHB wings instead of one, did not permit the use of a similar system of bases. The limited land mass available in the Marianas necessitated the establishment of wing bases, and the concentration of more than 12,000 combat and service personnel and 180 B-29s on a single base.

In January 1945 I was transferred from command of the XX Bomber Command in the China-Burma-India Theater, to command of the XXI Bomber Command in the Marianas, and Headquarters was transferred to Guam.

The Joint Chiefs of Staff, in Washington, had set up two major target priorities for the XXI Bomber Command: (1) aircraft industry, and (2) port and urban areas. In the early missions, the B-29 forces of 60 to 90 aircraft had been attacking at from 25,000-30,000 feet. But using these tactics in the face of the operational problems which confronted the B-29s over and en route to Japan did not produce the desired results. By February 1945 the striking force was increased to 200 planes, which on February 25 dropped more than 600 tons of bombs on the urban section of Tokyo. This was the beginning of larger-force raids, which led to the 800 plane climax a few months later.

In March 1945 the decision was made to stage bombing attacks on Tokyo with incendiaries at low level at night. Seldom in previous operations, night or day, had our B-29s bombed from altitudes of less than 24,000 feet, but on the night of March 9, Tokyo was attacked by 279 B-29s at a mean bombing altitude of 7,050 feet. The Japanese defenses were confused, and only 14 B-29s were lost to all causes. Some 15.8 square miles of the heart of Tokyo were burned out in what was the most destructive air attack in history. Other devastating night incendiary attacks on other cities followed in quick succession.

Bomb load per aircraft increased from an average of 2.6 tons per aircraft in November 1944 to an average of 7.4 tons per aircraft in July 1945. During the entire period of operations the XXI Bomber Command flew nearly 90,000,000 miles to and from the Japanese homeland, with an accident loss rate of slightly more than one aircraft for every 1,000,000 miles flown.

In April 1945 the four XX Bomber Command groups were transferred from the China-Burma-India Theater to new airfields on Tinian, to become part of the XXI Bomber Command. Personnel of the disbanded XX Bomber Command Headquarters were later moved to Okinawa as the nucleus for a new Very Heavy Bombardment Air Force—the transferred Eighth Air Force. Headquarters of the Twentieth Air Force remained, for the time being, in Washington, D. C.

In April Iwo Jima became available as an air base for emergency use. Wrested from the Japs in March 1945 in some of the bloodiest fighting of the war, tiny Iwo, situated between the Marianas and Tokyo about 600 miles north of the B-29s' home-base on Saipan, soon became an emergency haven to Superfortresses that ran out of fuel or were too badly shot up to get home. The VII Fighter Command was based here after March, and the April 7th Superfortress mission to Tokyo and Nagoya was given fighter escort.

Assured of its new technique by the success of the March fire raids, the XXI Bomber Command opened up a 4½-month incendiary campaign which burned out the heart of Japan's industrial centers. One by one, the principal cities of Japan received their bath of fire.

In the summer of 1945 certain organization and command changes were made in strategic operation in the Pacific. On July 5, Headquarters of the United States Army Strategic Air Force of the Pacific was formed under command of General Carl Spaatz, who had directed the successful overall air operations in Europe. General Spaatz arrived at the Headquarters on Guam and assumed command on July 16. The new air organization was planned for the coordination of operations of the Marianas-based B-29s and future operations of the Eighth Air Force. The latter, fresh from victory in Europe and still commanded by Lieutenant General James H. Doolittle, was to be based on Okinawa as the second B-29 arm in the Pacific.

On July 16 the XXI Bomber Command in the Marianas officially became known as the Twentieth Air Force.

On August 2, I became Chief of Staff to General Spaatz in USASTAF, and command of the Twentieth Air Force passed to Lieutenant General Nathan F. Twining.

Even though B-29 operations had not been developed to the maximum potential, by July 1945 the Japanese were already hopelessly defeated. Use of the Eighth Air Force, which would have flown shorter distances and therefore could have carried a greater weight of bombs than the Twentieth Air Force, would have wrought destruction and devastation beyond any useful purpose. Fortunately for the Japanese, the war was not to be prolonged.

On August 5, the "Enola Gay," piloted by Colonel Paul Tibbetts, Jr., dropped the first atomic bomb. The important industrial city of Hiroshima was almost completely leveled in a few seconds. Smoke shot up 40,000 feet from the wreckage of four square miles of destroyed area. More than 100,000 persons were killed.

Three days later Nagasaki was target for atomic attack, with the "Great Artiste," piloted by Major Charles W. Sweeney, dropping an improved and more powerful atomic bomb. Nagasaki was blasted into ruins. Japan's surrender followed shortly.

The 1945 application of American air power, so destructive and concentrated as to destroy 65 Japanese cities in five months, forced an enemy's surrender without land invasion for the first time in military history. Because of the performance of the Twentieth Air Force from March to August 1945 no United States soldier, sailor or marine had to land on bloody beachheads or fight through strongly-prepared ground defenses to ensure victory in the Japanese home islands.

The Twentieth Air Force, which proved the strategic concept of modern air attack, proved also that American inventive genius, American industry and American manhood can rise to the needs of any occasion. It is a lesson to remember.

But a corollary to the lesson is that our scientific and industrial workers must be given the chance to develop the weapons we need with which to defend the United States, and our Air Force must be given the men to train in the handling and use of these weapons—if they should be needed.

Curtis E. LeMay

IWO JIMA—UNSINKABLE AIRCRAFT CARRIER. UPPER. The busiest place on humming Iwo Jima was the flight line at Central Field after a night mission to Japan. Here indefatigable ground crews administered whatever repairs the Boeing B-29s needed to keep them constantly in flyable condition. LOWER. These Mustangs on a fighter sweep against objectives in Japan, keep their shepherding Superfortress well in sight all the way from Iwo to the target area and back. The B-29s had all-weather navigation equipment, far too heavy for the P-51s to carry.

ISLAND SECURE. The small isle was declared secured on March 26, 1945, D + 25. Ten days later a few hundred Japs hurled themselves against the second airfield, killing aviation personnel in their bunks. Running against the 5th Pioneer Battalion and the Negro Marines of the 8th Field Depot, the Japs were stopped, cut down and professionally disposed of. Two weeks after that, an ammo dump near the Island Command CP exploded, going off in a night-long fireworks display, leveling every tent and building in the area. For weeks and months soldiers and Japs killed each other on this "secured" scrap heap. It was always that way when the Jap could go underground or fade into the jungles. UPPER. Suribachi at night, with construction going on as bulldozers cut a road to the volcano's top. Twin beacons warn pilots of the danger. RIGHT. First Sgt. Louis Dake has his grim little joke. In the Corps almost 20 years, Dake represents "the old Marine Corps" with service at Guam, China and the Philippines in yesteryear. It was a combination of the old time regulars and the vigorous eager-to-learn reserves that made it possible for the Corps to secure the Pacific chain.

THE OKINAWA CAMPAIGN

By Major General Lemuel C. Shepherd, Jr.

AT 0830 in the morning of 1 April 1945, on Easter Sunday, assault elements of the United States Tenth Army, comprising the Third Marine Amphibious Corps, XXIV Corps, Tactical Air Force, and other units, commenced landing on the western beaches of Okinawa to begin the final great amphibious operation of World War II, an 82-day campaign that was marked by some of the bitterest fighting in the Pacific War.

Rampart of the Ryukyu Islands and key to the inner Japanese defense system, Okinawa's strategic importance lay in its proximity to Kyushu and Honshu, its excellent airfield sites, and its anchorages, from which elements of the Pacific Fleet could deny East China Sea shipping lanes to the Japanese.

Responsibility for Okinawa's defense rested with Lieutenant General Mitsuru Ushijima, commanding the Japanese 32d Army. In order to husband his forces carefully, Ushijima decided against opposing the landing, which he believed would come between late March and early June, and ordered his troops to prepare extensive underground positions in the southern half of the island.

In the absence of any organized resistance to their front, Marines of the Third Amphibious Corps quickly gained their initial objectives and pressed inland. The Sixth Marine Division, on the left secured vital Yontan Airfield by noon on the first day, and moved on in the next three days to throw a block across the Ishikawa Isthmus. On the Corps' right, the First Marine Division met only scattered resistance, and by the fourth day had reached the east coast and cleared Katchin Peninsula.

With all Army restrictions on the advance removed, Major General Roy S. Geiger, USMC, Third Amphibious Corps Commander, directed the Sixth Marine Division to advance north up Ishikawa Isthmus to the base of Motobu Peninsula, which was reached on 7 April.

In view of the threat of dangerous "Kamikaze" attacks, the Second Marine Division was now ordered back to Saipan. Originally, it had been planned to use this division to support the Third Amphibious Corps if the landings were opposed.

The enemy situation on Okinawa was reasonably clear. Intelligence reports indicated that, in addition to Ushijima's main force in southern Okinawa, a sizable force existed in Motobu Peninsula. After dispatching one regiment to secure the remainder of northern Okinawa, the Sixth Marine Division sent another regiment to locate the enemy on the peninsula. By 13 April, the enemy position was fixed at Mount Yaetake, which was taken in a series of sharp clashes as the 4th Marines made the

main attack from the southeast while the 29th advanced on the enemy's rear. On 17 April the trap closed with the Japanese lashing out in a desperate, if futile, counterattack to regain the summit. The ensuing battle was brief but climactic; the Japanese were completely overwhelmed.

With the seizure of the remainder of northern Okinawa by the 22d Marines, the conquest of the Third Amphibious Corps zone was completed. To the south, however, the battle for Okinawa was progressing on a larger and more difficult scale as the XXIV Corps' advance against Ushijima's main defensive positions, which ran in depth from Naha on the west coast across the high, steeply scarped Shuri hill mass in the center to Yonabaru on the east coast, ground to a halt in late April.

The Third Amphibious Corps now prepared to take over the western half of the southern front as Tenth Army took over direction of the attack. The First Marine Division, after patrolling central Okinawa, was moved south to replace the 27th Infantry Division, which in turn entrucked to the north to relieve the Sixth Marine Division so that the latter could be used on the Third Amphibious Corps front.

During the first week in May, the First Marine Division, initially attached to XXIV Corps, was busily engaged as the 1st Marines cleared the enemy from the Jichaku area, north of the Asa River, and the 5th Marines reduced a troublesome pocket south of Awacha.

Believing that Tenth Army would not attempt an amphibious landing in southern Okinawa, Ushijima ordered an all-out attack for 4 May, to be preceded by counter-landings on XXIV Corps' flanks. Both failed miserably.

On 8 May, the Sixth Marine Division moved the 22d Marines in on the right of the First Marine Division as the Third Amphibious Corps took control of the attack in its zone. Two days later, in a pre-dawn attack, the 22d Marines executed a surprise crossing of the Asa River, seized a foothold on the south side, and during the next three days advanced to the heights overlooking Okinawa's capital city—Naha.

It was in this area that a triangular system of hills was uncovered on 12 May, beginning one of the bitterest battles of the long campaign—the battle for Sugar Loaf Hill. Foremost in importance of the three hills comprising the western anchor of the Shuri line, Sugar Loaf not only dominated the other two—Half Moon and Horseshoe—but all the rolling broken ground in the Sixth Marine Division's left front. The fight for Sugar Loaf lasted for six days before it finally fell on 18 May.

In the meantime, the first Marine Division moved slowly but steadily on Third Amphibious Corps' left front against Dakeshi Ridge, bitterly-defended by the enemy. After steady pounding for three days, Dakeshi Ridge fell to the 7th Marines on 12 May.

Next step for the First Marine Division was to cross the open valley from Dakeshi to Wana Ridge and the wide open ground of Wana Draw, which led into the heart of the enemy's Shuri position. By 22 May the 7th Marines had fought its way to the top of Wana Ridge, and the 5th Marines had captured Hill 57 in the mouth of Wana Draw. Then the rains came.

With the fall of Sugar Loaf on the west, and the advance of the 7th Infantry Division into Yonabaru on the east coast, Tenth Army's plan for enveloping Shuri had well-nigh materialized. As expected, Ushijima ordered a withdrawal of most of his forces from the Shuri area. This movement coincided with heavy rains and low visibility prevalent during the early part of the last week in May. During the last nine days, over thirteen inches of rain fell.

On 29 May, the 1st Battalion, 5th Marines, probed its way through the shell of enemy rear-guard resistance to seize desolated Shuri Castle, one time seat of Okinawa's early rulers, and lately the site of the Japanese 32d Army's headquarters. The First Marine Division now moved rapidly to clear western Shuri, while the 5th Marines advanced to the Kokuba River.

After capturing Sugar Loaf Hill, the Sixth Marine Division sent the 4th Marines across the Asato River into the outskirts of Naha, where the Japanese put up a stubborn resistance. During the last week in May, the division, with the 22d and 29th Marines abreast, drove southeast into the Schichina hills to secure the high ground above the Kokuba River valley.

With the remaining Japanese compressed into the extreme southern portion of Okinawa, except for a strong force on Orokus, the Third Amphibious Corps sent the First Marine Division across the Kokuba toward Itoman and Kunishi, while the Sixth Marine Division made a surprise landing, on 4 June, on the northwestern beaches of Oroku Peninsula against the rear of carefully-prepared enemy positions. The battle for Oroku lasted ten days, as the 4th and 29th Marines struck hammer-like blows aganist the anvil provided by the 22d Marines, which had crossed the base of the peninsula to execute a holding attack.

In the meantime, the 7th Marines had reached Itoman, opening beaches for badly-needed waterborne supply. By 12 June, they had begun the bitter battle for Kunishi Ridge, where the Japanese lashed back in desperate fury. It took two regiments, the 1st and 7th Marines, four days to capture Kunishi Ridge. With the latter secured, the First Marine Division swung the 5th Marines far to the right, and then back, to attack Hills 79 and 81 from the west. Here, as before, Japanese resistance was furious.

After clearing Oroku, the Sixth Marine Division again moved south, this time with the 22d Marines in the lead, and on 17 June secured Mezado Ridge after a pre-dawn attack. Next day the 4th Marines took over the assault and drove south to Ibaru Ridge, captured on 19 June. Pausing only momentarily, the 4th Marines then advanced to Kiyamu-Gusuku Ridge. With the fall of this ridge, Japanese resistance collapsed and the enemy began to surrender in unprecedented numbers.

Over in the First Marine Division zone, the 8th Marines (from the Second Marine Division, recalled from Saipan to seize the islands of Ilheya and Aguni) relieved the 7th Marines and drove quickly to the south coast. In the meantime the 5th Marines continued its attacks against Hills 79 and 81 and on 21 June completed their capture.

The 82-day struggle for Okinawa ended on 21 June, after taking a heavy toll in casualties from both Marine divisions; Japanese casualties, however, were infinitely greater. Through the long campaign, success may be attributed in no small measure to the excellent close-air support and fighter coverage provided by Tactical Air Force, commanded by Major General Francis P. Mulcahy, USMC.

By the time organized resistance had ceased, this force had four Marine and two Army fighter groups on Okinawa and the adjacent island of Ie Shima. Altogether, Tactical Air Force planes had brought down some 600 enemy planes and had flown over 38,000 sorties.

On Okinawa, the First and Sixth Marine Divisions, Third Amphibious Corps, had met the best troops that Ushijima had, on ground of his own choosing, organized to his own satisfaction, and had decisively defeated them on every occasion. While careful training, good planning, and excellent coordination of all supporting arms were all vital ingredients in the Third Amphibious Corps formula for the defeat of the Japanese, it remains that final victory was possible only because of the high courage and disciplined fighting ability of the individual Marine, who carried the battle home to the enemy on his own terms and vanquished him in keeping with the highest standards of Marine Corps traditions.

Lemuel Shepherd Jr

LAND ON RYUKYU ISLANDS. On April 1, 1945, GIs and Marines of the U.S. Tenth Army stormed the southwest shore of Okinawa following landings on the smaller islands to the west. The ships depicted on the map (above) show the direction of the two operations and aircraft carrier support. The inset shows the relation of the Ryukyus to Japan.

KNOCKING AT TOKIO'S DOOR. The guns of Admiral R. A. Spruance's Fifth Fleet cut loose on Jap installations on Okinawa on Easter Sunday, April 1, as the Twenty-fourth Army Corps and the Marine Third Amphibious Corps landed ashore against negligible opposition. Landing on the west coast of Okinawa, which is 362 statute miles from the home islands, the troops quickly worked inland to seize Yontan and Katena airfields. It was the largest amphibious operation carried out in the Pacific to date; more than 1,400 ships were in the armada; carrier and land-based planes as well as Superfortresses participated. The Twenty-fourth Army Corps was under the command of Maj. Gen. John R. Hodge and the Marines were led by Maj. Gen. Roy S. Geiger. For some inexplicable reason, the Japanese abandoned their strong coastal defenses and retired inland where they later fought with the ferocity characteristic of the "do-or-die" fanaticism exhibited in earlier fighting.

EASTER SUNDAY, 1945. Marines and soldiers of the Tenth Army walked ashore at Okinawa on L (Landing) Day, April 1, 1945. It seemed like an "April Fool" trick, a trap. The 70-mile long island, only 385 miles from Japan, was ominously quiet as the troops (upper) waded in, walking upright against no opposition. Capitalizing on their good fortune, the Third Corps on the right and the XXIV Army Corps on the left pushed inland. Three hours later Yontan airfield was captured, including some operational enemy planes. LOWER. The Navy kept rushing troops ashore.

PLANES AND TOMBS. LEFT. Overhead the planes of the Fleet and Air Force flew support and patrol missions. LOWER. Even the suspected gun positions, blasted in pre-invasion bombardment, turned out to be ghostly tombs, as silent and as empty of the enemy as the rest of the island's middle. A half hour after landing, a Marine CP was set up in front of this tomb. Later, tombs became a much different proposition, full of defending Japs, as fighting returned to "normalcy." But while it lasted it was wonderful. By the third day a reconnaissance company reached the eastern shore. By the fifth, the First Division covered the territory which it had been allotted three weeks to take under the original plans. The island had been cut in two in little more than half a week, the north and south separated. Supply became a problem as lines were rapidly extended. The island's road net was not sufficient to handle the traffic of large and small vehicles carrying men, supplies, food, ammunition and weapons. The Sixth Division moved into Motobu Peninsula and ran into cave fighting and bad terrain. By April 21st, fighting ceased and this area also was secure.

A BROADSIDE FOR THE JAPS. The camera's high speed shutter captures the flight of these 16-inch shells as they start their long trajectories to targets on Okinawa. The bursts of fire set up tremendous recoil aboard the battlewagon. This action of the Fifth Fleet under the command of Admiral

Spruance, contributed immeasurably to the success of the
largest amphibious operation of the Pacific war. The joint
expeditionary force which attacked and occupied Okinawa
consisted of 1,213 ships carrying 451,866 ground troops.
The latter comprised the Marine III Corps and Army's XXIV.

AVIATION HELPS OUT. On Okinawa the capture of two airfields, Yontan by the Third Corps and Kadena by the XXIV Army Corps, made ground-based aviation support possible almost immediately. As the Third Corps wheeled left to secure the entire northern half, the XXIV turned south, soon smashing head-on against the well-fortified and fiercely defended enemy defense area. ABOVE. A flame thrower-BAR team cautiously stalks the enemy in a misty valley. The forward man carries fuel tanks for his weapon strapped to his back. The BAR man is alert for possible counter-attack. UPPER LEFT. General of the Army Henry "Hap" Arnold, right, visits the Pacific theatre after V-E Day. With him, on Yontan airfield, is Marine Maj. Gen. Louis Woods, Tactical Air Force Commander on Okinawa. This picture was taken after Gen. Woods had relieved Maj. Gen. F. P. "Pat" Mulcahy on June 11th. The latter headed TAF's combined Army, Navy and Marine air staff. The Second Marine Air Wing began operations on Okinawa April 4th. LOWER LEFT. With an improvised sign, these pilots add a touch of humor to their air raid shelter.

FLAME THROWERS IN ACTION. We had prepared well for Okinawa. Abundant supplies for practically all possible needs were shipped out. The operation sea, land and air force units included 548,000 men, and part of the British Navy operating under Admiral Spruance's top command. There were 318 combat vessels and 1,139 auxiliary craft, exclusive of the small personnel landing craft. ABOVE. Among the most effective weapons used was the reliable flame thrower. Here two First Division Marines flush out some Japs in hiding. UPPER RIGHT. Tanks moved wherever the terrain would permit, spewing flames against positions which held up infantry advances. A Marine behind the tank casually watches the results of this version of a scorched earth policy. LOWER RIGHT. A flame expert crouches low as he squeezes off seconds of hot death. A Jap sniper refused to come out of the tomb in which he had taken refuge. Somebody else's tomb thus served as his final resting place as the flames sucked the oxygen out of the air, choking the Jap, and at the same time roasting him to a horrible cinder. Flame thrower and tank made a fearsome combination, but a necessary one, for the job of ferreting out Japs.

DEATH VALLEY. ABOVE. Marines advance over the waste of a battlefield, littered with enemy dead, as they ferret out hiding places of survivors who might menace their rear. The rugged, natural caves provided the Japs with ideal positions in which to hide. The enemy, aware of the importance of Okinawa, put up stubborn resistance during this campaign.

SIGNING THE PEACE WITH JAPAN—2 SEPTEMBER 1945

OCCUPATION OF JAPAN. Because of the atom bomb, anticipated casualties from a landing on the enemy homeland never materialized. The Third and Fifth Corps, ready for the planned assault on Japan, were among the first troops assigned occupation duty; the Third going to China with the First and Sixth Divisions, the Fifth Corps to Japan with the Second and Fifth. UPPER. Marines of the reactivated 4th Regiment, land at the Yokosuka naval base. The 4th's original complement was lost in the Philippines. LOWER. Marine Fifth Division tanks burn Jap planes at Sasebo.

FIGHTING TO THE SOUTH. As the Marines completed their duties to the north it became increasingly evident that they were needed down south against the main line of Japanese resistance. By the end of April the First Division had been attached to the XXIV Corps and was pushing against strong defending positions. The Army had its Seventh and 96th Divisions in line on the left; the Marine First was on the right. Early in May the Sixth was brought into the line on the far right, and on May 10th the four divisions jumped off abreast in attack after a withering artillery preparation supported by aircraft from the captured fields on the island. There was very little intelligence available on which to base estimates, but American commanders had no doubts about the strength of the defensive positions or the tenacity of the defenders. The casualties attested to that. UPPER. Marines fire against Jap defenders on the outskirts of Naha, key city and largest port of Okinawa. LOWER. Crouched low and moving fast over rocky ground, stretcher bearers rush a wounded Marine to the rear after a corpsman bandaged his face wounds.

BAZOOKA BOYS. RIGHT. Marines inch their way toward Naha supported by a bazooka team. The rocket firing weapon was used primarily against enemy fortifications and artillery. However, it was also effective against clusters of enemy troops. Marines on the far right peer through the stunted trees to see what lies ahead. LOWER. Sixth Division Marines pass under a Japanese Torii Gate at Onayama, on the outskirts of Naha. The long distances on the island made motor transport extremely valuable in conserving energies of the troops during the 83-day battle for Okinawa. Combat correspondent Elvis Lane relates that in one sector the casualties among the corpsmen had reached alarming numbers. The Sixth Division Marines made an agreement that, if wounded, they would return to the medical station some 200 yards to the rear without help. "We refuse to let any more corpsmen risk their lives for us," a Marine, wounded in the chest, told the Navy doctor working on him. Lane reports the dialogue: "Hey, Mac, did you keep our agreement?" the wounded Marine asked a buddy in the station. "Yeah, I made it," said the man whose foot had been blown off.

TAKING NAHA. Sixth Division Marines (left) forced the back door of Naha, avoiding the heavily defended main roads, and crashed through the partly blasted houses with tanks and other vehicles. The fire-gutted city (lower) was the scene of some of the most vicious fighting of the war. The debris served as excellent defense positions for enemy soldiers who had to be rooted out of every hiding place. Sgt. Herman Kogan said it was not unusual to be greeted outside the blackened city with the question, "Hell, you still living?" To which he added, "This was less a testimonial of your endurance or special skill in staying alive than in your luck. You could get it walking along a road over which hundreds of trucks had rumbled without harm. You could get it after you escaped a few times. Men died, not in great concentrations as on Iwo or at Anzio, but they died and their deaths were very close because you knew them personally. There was a sharp pain in your side when you heard about 'Pappy' or 'Ski' being cut to pieces by machine gun bullets. It was even sharper when you saw them go down, their arm flopping crazily as they fell."

MOVING INTO NAHA. Taking advantage of cover (upper), Marine flush Jap snipers from buildings during their advance through Naha. LOWER. Another Marine patrol is on the alert for snipers. During this period the Japanese had not yet begun to surrender in large numbers and had to be cornered one by one. With the island secured behind them, the Marines had ample time to advance carefully in the south. Artillery was used in greater volume than at any other time during the Pacific war. To the massed battalions of artillery was added naval and air bombardment.

THE DEATH OF A GENERAL. The Commander of the Tenth Army (upper), Lt. Gen. Simon Bolivar Buckner, with camera, watches action from a ridge with Maj. Gen. Shepherd whose Sixth Division Marines are storming Naha. Gen. Buckner frequently visited the divisions under his command to see how the action was progressing. Subsequently, on June 18, 1945, while observing the jump-off of the fresh 8th Marines from the Second Division, he was killed by an artillery burst. It was at a time when the enemy artillery had "been reduced close to the vanishing point." The single explosion that got the General did not touch those around him. He died before he could be evacuated. Gen. Geiger took over temporarily, later being relieved by Lt. Gen. Joseph Stillwell at the end of the campaign. LEFT. The body of the General is carried to a plane at the aerial evacuation center behind the front lines. Navy Doctor Henry J. Koch, carrying the stretcher at extreme left, worked under fire trying to save the General's life after the shrapnel felled him. It was an ironic death for the campaign was almost over and the fatal shell was one of the last sputters of the enemy.

THE WOUNDED. The Marines and Army suffered heavy casualties during the long Okinawa campaign. Losses due to kamikaze attacks on the supporting Fleet also were great. The strategy of the enemy was to try to knock out the Fleet with suicide planes on one-way missions. The Japs figured the Fleet, if crippled by heavy losses, would be unable either to support the operation, or transport in the vast quantities of necessary supplies. As in other operations, the losses radioed back to Tokyo greatly exaggerated the actual damage inflicted by the kamikaze planes. UPPER. Tanks were sometimes used to bring out the wounded because enemy fire prevented stretcher party activities. This Marine is being carried rearward to a spot where Navy surgeons and corpsmen will patch him up. RIGHT. Amid primitive surroundings, two Navy medicos, assisted by a corpsman, operate on a stomach wound. A canvas overhead in the Jap cave makes certain that no rock or dirt will be shaken onto the patient by a nearby explosion.

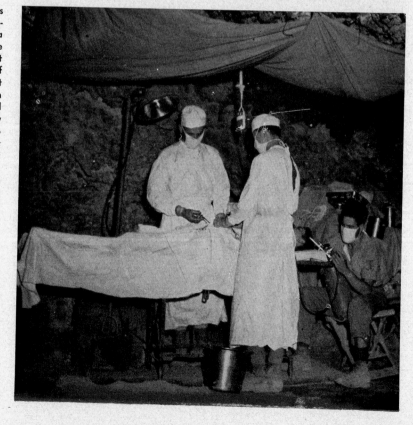

NAHA, RUINED CITY. The Japanese defense in depth was based on the Naha-Shuri-Yonabaru line. The Marines had the right flank on which stood the island's capital, Naha. Before Naha lay such difficult terrain as Charlie Hill, taken by one company with 35 killed and 68 wounded out of 256, and Sugar Loaf Hill. A Marine wrote of Charlie Hill: "On each of three shelves were weapons of all types; seven knee mortars, thirteen Nambus (machine guns), two 20 mm guns, two 46 mm guns, one heavy field piece mounted on a railroad track, dozens of plastic mines and hand grenades, 17 small and three large ammunition dumps, satchels filled with dynamite." These spots breached, the Marines moved ahead (left) with tanks. Jap soldiers opened fire from a house and drew shells in return. LOWER. The tiny grasshopper observation planes, frequently drawing small arms and antiaircraft fire, flew over Naha, calling for artillery fire in areas where they observed Japanese activity. The city stretched out below is almost leveled. Stone and concrete buildings can be seen still standing and in the harbor to the rear, ships are on the bottom, sunk by the American planes.

NO MORE NAHA. Once the home of 60,000 Okinawa natives, Naha was the largest city captured by the Corps in the war. UPPER. A Marine pauses for a view of the ruined city. LOWER. Another stands in the wreckage of a theatre building in Naha, dwarfed by the hole in the side wall. Navy surface support of the troops ashore eliminated much potential enemy air interference. The task force planes, picket ships and other units knocked down great numbers of the red meat ball planes. Our carrier force, alone, destroyed 2,336 Jap planes in 90 days, losing 557 U.S. planes.

SHURI CASTLE. The First Marine Division fought for Shuri for a long, bitter week, beginning May 15, 1945. Mired in mud and tired from the long fighting, the troops in front of Shuri made slow progress. The enemy tried to evacuate the area but came under air observation and was bombed and shelled with high casualties. First Division Marines (upper) are driving the last few defenders out of the ruined Jap barracks on the outskirts of Shuri. LOWER. A patrol of the 5th Marines who pushed their way into Shuri Castle in the final stages of the battle.

SNIPERS AT SHURI. Two Marines (right) cover a Jap sniper in the spires of the Christian church at Shuri while a patrol sneaks in from the rear of the ruins. First Division Marines (lower) move across the debris-strewn area of Shuri Castle. The same church is in the background. Maj. Gen. Pedro del Valle, commanding the First Division, finally was able to reduce Wana Draw and Ridge after Shuri Castle fell. The First then pushed on to Oroku Peninsula and Kunishi Ridge to the south. Life during this phase was described by Sgt. Murray Lewis, a combat correspondent: "In a foxhole lay a Marine. He wore no poncho because it would have impeded him if he had to advance. He was soaked to the skin and the soft mud had been packed into clay over his face and clothing. He had spent a sleepless night, drenched in the water pouring steadily from the gray skies, and his eyes were red-rimmed with weariness. All through the night the Japs had kept up an intermittent artillery and mortar barrage into the area and for each dragging minute of that night he had heard the deadly shells hitting the earth around him."

FATHER AND SON. Marine Colonel Francis I. Fenton (upper) kneels at his son's burial. Private First Class Mike Fenton was killed during a Japanese counter-attack on the road to Shuri. LEFT. Ernie Pyle, loved by all fighting men, sits on an Okinawa hill with some of the Marines with whom he came ashore. The landing had delighted him. He wrote about souvenirs, the mascots, the kindness shown the island people, the surprising lack of Japs. He had said that Marines were the friendliest people, always trying to do things for you. His death in mid-April on the tiny nearby island of Ie Shima was tragic. He had made the landings with some friends of the Army's crack 77th Division and was killed by a sniper. Capt. Johnnie Popham recalled how Ernie slept on the floor with the men at the war correspondents' shack, helped them in general duty details, chatted with them at every chance, and scratched his name with a pen on his clothing roll. "The low, hollow rumble of naval gunfire from Ie Shima was like a funeral dirge to our ears," he said, upon hearing of Ernie's death.

RAISING THE FLAG. Lt. Col. R. P. Ross, Jr., plants the American flag (upper left) on a parapet of Shuri Castle. This same flag was the first to be raised over Cape Gloucester and Peleliu. LOWER LEFT. Some Japanese planes knocked out on the ground are bulldozed to one side to make way for the American planes that came to Okinawa in large numbers, including several squadrons of fighters and bombers from the Second Marine Air Wing. UPPER RIGHT. A Marine, helmet in hand, stands silent in the presence of death. Marine dead were buried in two large cemeteries on Okinawa Shima. The Sixth Division Cemetery (center) lies facing the East China Sea. It was dedicated on July 4, 1945, 95 days after the original landing. A Third Corps chaplain at the dedication said: "This is not a bivouac of the dead. It is a colony of heaven. And some part of us all is buried here." LOWER RIGHT. Jewish, Protestant and Catholic chaplains read burial services as the bugler blows final taps for the First Marine dead. Total Tenth Army casualties were 7,283 dead and 31,398 wounded.

IT'S ALL OVER. UPPER. On Hill 89, captured by troops of the Seventh Infantry Division, Soldiers and Marines celebrate the final victory as the American flag is raised to signal the end of organized resistance. The signpost reads: "Within this hill is sealed the command post where Lieutenant General Ushijima, Commander of the Japanese Army, surrounded by his senior officers, made his final stand. This hill was seized by troops of the Seventh Infantry Division on June 21, 1945, thus ending the battle of Okinawa." The fighting Seventh was one of four Army divisions under Lt. Gen. John R. Hodges, XXIV Corps Commander on Okinawa. LOWER. The Flag goes up on Okinawa as Marine Lt. Gen. Geiger salutes at right. Gen. Geiger was at Guadalcanal in command of Allied aviation at Henderson Field. He marched the long road up the Solomons to the Marianas and finally to the very outskirts of Japan. He later relieved Lt. Gen. Smith as Commander, Fleet Marine Force, Pacific. A few months after the war's end he died, as much a casualty of war as was the President, Ernie Pyle, Gen. Buckner and young Mike Fenton. Under Generals Smith and Geiger a smooth relationship had been forged with the Army and the Navy. Both men were professionals of the highest type, both positive and outspoken on occasion, proud of Marine traditions and certain of Corps tactics. Both at times disagreed with their superiors, sometimes violently. Both were loved and admired by officers and enlisted men alike for they had that necessary quality of leadership; a compassion for the other fellow and a willingness to understand his problems and troubles while overburdened with their own.

GENERALS AND PRIVATES. Gen. Stillwell (upper) and other ranking officers discuss the final phase of the Okinawa battle outside the captured headquarters of the Jap Commanding General. LOWER. Marine Private First Class Harry Kizirian from Providence, R. I., grins because it's good to be alive after 12 continuous days in the front lines on Okinawa. This war, like no other one in history, was reported for the people back home, and although the generals and admirals were more often mentioned in the communiques, it was the privates and the seamen who were of most interest to the people. In Kizirian's dirty dungaree pocket repose some letters from his girl; in the extra helmet some souvenirs. It was the "Joe Blows," the "GI's" who the Marine combat correspondents wrote about. And later the Army and the Navy had their own correspondents to work and live with the men and compose news pieces and take pictures for home town papers. The Russians and the Germans had fighter-writers before Marine Brig. Gen. Robert L. Denig decided to add correspondents to Marine units in 1942. Eventually there were more than 350 officers and enlisted Marines attached to Public Relations to write about the little guy, the enlisted man or the junior officer, who was fighting and winning the war, the fellow with the rifle and machine gun, the squad leader and platoon commander. Marines were often jokingly accused of having one combat correspondent per squad; actually there were seldom more than two to a regiment with four or five at division or wing headquarters along with one or two officers. Because they lived and fought with the men their stories were authentic, and because the folks at home sent back clippings to the Marines when they were written up that necessary quality of morale was strengthened throughout the Corps.

THE LIVING PRAY. With a stark wasteland for a backdrop, these troops solemly stand with bowed heads as services are conducted for those who died in the invasion of Okinawa. Although the campaign for the island was unusually bitter,

casualties for the U.S. were relatively light. Approximately 7,000 GIs and Marines were killed as contrasted to more than 130,000 Japs. In addition, some 30,000 men of the U.S. Tenth Army (Marine III Corps and Army XXIV) were wounded.

TALLY 1,256 "KILLS." The Pacific submarine fleet, three craft of which are shown (right), helped indispensably to cut Japan's sea lifelines and to hasten her blockade and defeat. In the last three months of the Pacific war U.S. underseas raiders accounted for 69 Japanese ships sunk, bringing the total to 1,256 "kills." Vice-Admiral Charles A. Lockwood, Jr., Commander of the Pacific Fleet submarine task force, reported that many other ships were almost certainly sunk, but could not be counted because of the strict standards set up for determining sinkings. In addition, he estimated that more than 300 other Japanese vessels had been damaged.

THE SURRENDER OF JAPAN

By Admiral of the Fleet William F. Halsey, USN

BY JULY, 1945, the United States Fleet had brought to bear in the Pacific tremendous sea-air power. Our carrier planes were blasting air fields, navy yards, industries, and storage facilities throughout the "home islands" of the Japanese Empire. Our battleships, cruisers, and destroyers bombarded the "sacred soil" of Nippon almost at will. Our submarines had ventured into the innermost parts of the Inland Sea and the Sea of Japan and had made those waters as unsafe for Japanese shipping as the waters of the Southwest Pacific and the China Sea.

As a prelude to the main and final objective, the invasion of Japan, the preliminary bombings and bombardments were stepped up. Our secret weapon, the atomic bomb, was used, first against the military targets and industries at Hiroshima, later against the munitions plants and repair yards at Nagasaki. Our ally, Russia, entered the war in Manchuria; China, armed with lend-lease supplies, began new drives against the enemy.

THE JAPS ACCEPT SURRENDER

WHEN the Japanese delivered their message of acceptance of the Potsdam Ultimatum on 14 August, the Third Fleet was ready with plans for occupation, and the unprecedented operation was executed smoothly. The official instrument of surrender was presented to the Japanese representatives by General of the Army MacArthur at Manila on 19 August. This instrument provided for the capitulation of the Imperial General Staff, and the surrender of all ground, sea, and air commanders of the Islands of Japan, the Philippine Islands, and the Southern parts of Korea to the Commander-in-Chief, United States Army Forces, Pacific; the surrender of all land, sea, air, and auxiliary force commanders in the Japanese mandated islands was to be made to the Commander-in-Chief, United States Pacific Fleet.

The first units of the United States Third Fleet, after being delayed for two days by a typhoon, moved into Sagami Bay, southwest of Tokio Bay, on 27 August in the first step of the occupation. On 29 August, Fleet Admiral Nimitz arrived from Guam and boarded his flagship, the battleship "South Dakota." This writer, Commander of the Third Fleet, entered Tokio Bay and anchored off Yokosuka Naval Base in the forenoon of that day. On 30 August, 10,000 Marines and Naval personnel landed on this base and the surrounding fortress islands. The naval base at Tateyama, across the bay from Yokosuka, was occupied on 1 September by Marine forces as the occupation control progressed smoothly and rapidly.

The formal surrender of the Imperial Japanese Government was made aboard the United States battleship "Missouri" in Tokio Bay at 0908 on 2 September 1945. General of the Army MacArthur signed as Supreme Commander for the Allied Powers, and Fleet Admiral Nimitz as representative for the United States.

THE ISLANDS SURRENDER

EVEN before the formal surrender of the Japanese government, the enemy commanders of Marcus Island and of Mille atoll in the Marshall Islands had capitulated to American forces. The largest scale island surrender came shortly after the beginning of the occupation of the main Japanese Islands. The commander of the 31st Japanese Army committed the islands of Truk, Wake, the Palaus, Mortlock, Mille, Ponape, Kusaie, Jaluit, Maleolap, Wotje, Enderby, Mereyon, Rota, and Pagan to the United States. On Truk alone the surrender involved 130,000 Japanese military personnel.

While the naval and air forces of Japan were either destroyed or rendered impotent by our sea-air blockade, her army was still more than four million strong and better trained, and larger than at the time of the initial attack at Pearl Harbor.

Never before in the history of warfare has there been a more convincing example of the effectiveness of sea power than when, despite this undefeated, well armed, and highly efficient army, Japan surrendered her homeland unconditionally to the enemy without even a token resistance.

The devastation wrought by past bombings plus the destruction of the atomic bombs spelled nothing less than extinction for Japan. The bases from which these attacks were launched—Saipan, Iwo Jima, and Okinawa—were to have been the springboards for the mightiest sea-borne invasion yet conceived by man. The "fighting fleets" of the United States which had made possible every invasion victory for America and her allies were ready and waiting. The Japanese had two alternatives: to fight and face destruction, or to surrender. The Imperial Japanese Empire chose to surrender.

W.F. Halsey

NAGOYA DESTROYED. UPPER. This is not a big green-house, but the remnants of the Mitsubishi aircraft engine plant burned to cinders during a low-level night incen-diary attack by 468 B-29s against Nagoya, Japan's No. 1 aircraft manufacturing center. This blazing attack of May 16, 1945, followed a daylight attack of 478 B-29s made on May 14th. Sporadic attacks on Japan's 4th city, which turned out 35 percent of its aircraft, began on March 11th and reached a climax in May. LOWER. Nagoya after the attacks. A total of 15.6 square miles were burned out,

THE NOT-SO-MERRY MONTH OF MAY. Yokohama's first B-29 attack came on May 29. 450 Superforts, escorted by 100 7th Air Force Mustangs from Iwo, dropped 3,800 tons of incendiary bombs. LEFT. Smoke and flames pour out of this Jap port. The P-51s met 140 enemy planes over the target area, with 26 destroyed, 10 probables, and 18 damaged. Three B-29s and three P-51s were lost. Damage to the city was very heavy. Early on May 24, 520 Superforts dropped 4,000 tons of fire bombs on the industrial area of Tokio. The second blow of a one-two punch came near midnight on the 25th, when 450 B-29s dropped 3,500 tons of heavy bombs on central Tokio, bordered on the north by the Imperial Palace (upper right). Enemy opposition, especially by flak, was intense and B-29 losses were highest of any mission to date. Damage from these two raids was devastating. LOWER RIGHT. Nagoya caught it again on May 14, eight weeks after the big March attack. This one was easier, 500 B-29s dropping 3,300 tons of bombs, with only two losses; a holocaust of flame blazed up.

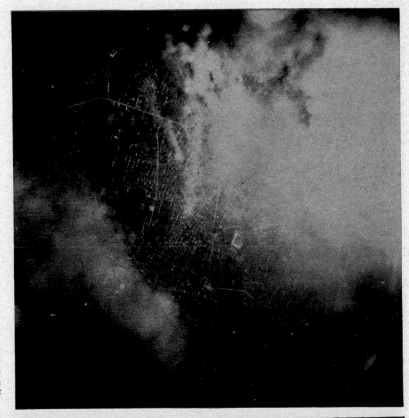

JAPS' NO. 2 CITY A CAULDRON. ABOVE. Smoke boils
skyward from Osaka after B-29 Superfortresses raided the
second largest city and industrial center of Japan. Tons
of incendiaries set the entire waterfront ablaze. Four hundred and fifty B-29s dropped 3,200 tons of fire bombs. The
Superforts were escorted by a fighter group of 150 Army
P-51 Mustangs. The "Forts" flew from airfields on Okinawa.

AUSSIES INVADE BORNEO. Australia's famed Ninth Division made a series of surprise landings on Borneo on June 10, 1945, following heavy bombardments by American air forces and the U.S. Seventh Fleet. Waves of Venturas, attached to the U.S. Thirteenth Air Force Fighter Command, made a shambles of Brunei Town, Borneo. ABOVE. Here the papier mache town is depicted in complete conflagration.

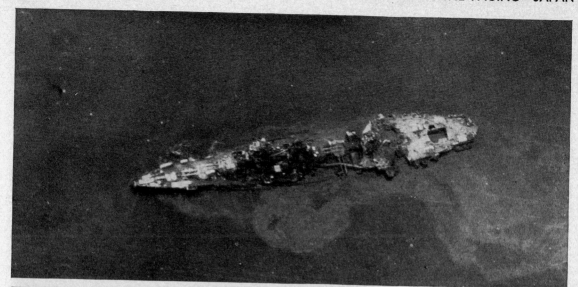

AN INGLORIOUS END FOR THE IMPERIAL JAPANESE NAVY. On July 10, 1945, the planes of the Third Fleet's carriers, at a point 170 miles from Kyushu, Japan, were sent aloft to strike at targets in the Kure-Kobe area. On the 17th of July, our forces were joined by units of the British Fleet and struck at the Japanese naval units in Yokosuka naval base near Tokio. UPPER. The Japanese battleship "Hyuga" rests on the bottom of the Inland Sea near Nasake Shima. She was sunk by planes of the Third Fleet. LOWER. The battleship "Haruna" is heavily bombed by Allied planes as she lies at anchor in Kure harbor. The "Haruna" was later found to be a floating hulk.

" . . . THE SOUND AND THE FURY . . . " When the Third Fleet moved north toward the islands of Japan, it had a specific task ahead of it, the systematic destruction of anything that floated and was Japanese. It was also to bomb and bombard the coastline at various points and destroy certain strategic objectives. The Third Fleet carried out its job with a thoroughness that left Japan completely shaken. UPPER. Obscured by smoke and geysers of water, a Japanese ore ship, caught as it leaves the inlet at the top left of the page, is destroyed by planes from the Third Fleet. LOWER. The battleship "Haruna" fares no better than the ore ship. No effective naval resistance followed.

A-BOMB WIPES OUT HIROSHIMA. ABOVE. A monumental
column of smoke mushrooms into the stratosphere after the
atomic bomb was dropped on Hiroshima, vital army depot
and embarkation point. The lethal smoke climbs 20,000 feet
from a 10,000-foot-wide dust cloud base. The cataclysm
stunned the world, climaxed the war, gave birth to a new era.

WORLD WAR II ENDS. UPPER. President Truman reads the history-making document proclaiming the surrender of the Japanese to his cabinet and key officers, thus bringing the long and bloody Pacific war to a close. Flanking the President at his desk are Admiral William D. Leahy, Secretary of State James F. Byrnes, and former Secretary of State Cordell Hull. LOWER. The President joins in a three-way handshake with Byrnes and Hull. Official V-J Day had to wait for the formal signing of the surrender document. The war would not end technically until proclaimed by the President, or by a joint resolution of Congress. But for those who had fought and suffered through the enervating three years and 250 days following Pearl Harbor, this day was the one to be remembered. On September 2, General of the Army Douglas MacArthur and Fleet Admiral Chester W. Nimitz boarded the USS "Missouri" to complete the final terms of Japan's formal surrender. With the affixing of signatures to the surrender instrument, the fighting was ended. The same day, the President declared September 2 V-J Day. Gen. MacArthur then pursued the momentous task of establishing a military government on the Jap Islands.

TRANSFER AT SEA. As the American Fleet steamed toward Tokio Bay for the surrender ceremony, major combat vessels transferred Marine contingents to the "Ozark" via breeches buoy. RIGHT. For two long days this went on as the vessels continued on their way. Here a member of the "Yorktown's" Marine complement makes the journey in 35 seconds. Not a single man got so much as a wet foot in the largest mass transfer at sea in the history of the Navy. In addition to a provisional Marine regiment, a group of 450 Royal Marine Commandos and Royal Navy Sailors were placed in landing ships. Sailors of the Fleet also were formed into battalions for duty ashore. The plan was for the naval regiment to take over the navy yard after it was secured by a battalion of the 4th Marines, and for the seagoing Marine regiment to relieve the battalion of the 4th at the airfield. In this way the 4th Marines would remain intact for further duty. LOWER. A Third Fleet destroyer holds a steady course 75 feet from the LSV (Landing Ship, Vehicle) "Ozark" as it transfers a man via the bucket seat.

SURRENDER INSTRUCTIONS.
After the Japanese had offered to
surrender, because, as they said,
they were "ever anxious to enhance
the cause of world peace," the
Allied powers sent instructions
for a direct and prompt cessation
of hostilities. They were told to
send emissaries to the Supreme
Commander with full information
of the disposition of Japanese
forces and commanders, and fully
empowered to make any arrangements directed by the Supreme
Commander that would enable him
to receive the formal surrender.
They were informed that General
MacArthur had been named Supreme Commander, and that he
would notify them of the time,
place and other details of the surrender. UPPER. Here on August
28 General MacArthur arrives
at Atsugi Airport near Tokio to
work out final plans for ceremonies in which the Japs were to sign
the peace papers. He is surrounded by reporters. LOWER.
Here are two happy Generals —
Brigadier General Lewis Beebe and
Lieutenant General Jonathan
Wainwright. Both were captured
on Corregidor in 1942, and were
prisoners for three years. The Allies required that all prisoners be
transported to places of safety so
they could be sent home quickly.

U.S. NAVY RETURNS TO TOKIO. Commodore Perry first opened up Japan to the outside world in the mid-19th century; and almost 100 years later the Navy again opened Japan to the outside world. The scenes on this page show the return of the Navy, and by contrast depict accurately how that return was effected. UPPER. Part of the great Third Fleet commanded by Admiral William F. Halsey, Jr., who engineered the first and last naval offensive blows against Japan, is seen in Sagami Wan (Bay). This picture was taken from the USS "Shangri-La," an "Essex"-class carrier, named for the mythical place from which the first Tokio air raiders took off. Actually the raiders took off from the old USS "Hornet." LOWER. In contrast to the power of the Third Fleet is the antiquated tug which bore the Japanese admiral in command of Yokosuka Naval Base out to make arrangements for surrender of the base. The Japanese admiral probably would have preferred a more pretentious ship, but such vessels were resting on the bottom, or were unseaworthy.

INSTRUMENT OF SURRENDER

Signed at __TOKYO BAY, JAPAN__ at __0904 I__

on the ____SECOND____ day of ____SEPTEMBER____, 1945.

重光葵

By Command and in behalf of the Emperor of Japan and the Japanese Government.

梅津美治郎

By Command and in behalf of the Japanese Imperial General Headquarters.

Accepted at __TOKYO BAY, JAPAN__ at __0908 I__

on the ____SECOND____ day of ____SEPTEMBER____, 1945,
for the United States, Republic of China, United Kingdom and the Union of Soviet Socialist Republics, and in the interests of the other United Nations at war with Japan.

Supreme Commander for the Allied Powers

United States Representative

Republic of China Representative

United Kingdom Representative

Union of Soviet Socialist Republics Representative

Commonwealth of Australia Representative

Dominion of Canada Representative

Provisional Government of the French Republic Representative

Kingdom of the Netherlands Representative

Dominion of New Zealand Representative

We, acting by command of and in behalf of the Emperor of Japan, the Japanese Government and the Japanese Imperial General Headquarters, hereby accept the provisions set forth in the declaration issued by the heads of the Governments of the United States, China and Great Britain on 26 July 1945, at Potsdam, and subsequently adhered to by the Union of Soviet Socialist Republics, which four powers are hereafter referred to as the Allied Powers.

We hereby proclaim the unconditional surrender to the Allied Powers of the Japanese Imperial General Headquarters and of all Japanese armed forces and all armed forces under Japanese control wherever situated.

We hereby command all Japanese forces wherever situated and the Japanese people to cease hostilities forthwith, to preserve and save from damage all ships, aircraft, and military and civil property and to comply with all requirements which may be imposed by the Supreme Commander for the Allied Powers or by agencies of the Japanese Government at his direction.

We hereby command the Japanese Imperial General Headquarters to issue at once orders to the Commanders of all Japanese forces and all forces under Japanese control wherever situated to surrender unconditionally themselves and all forces under their control.

We hereby command all civil, military and naval officials to obey and enforce all proclamations, orders and directives deemed by the Supreme Commander for the Allied Powers to be proper to effectuate this surrender and issued by him or under his authority and we direct all such officials to remain at their posts and to continue to perform their non-combatant duties unless specifically relieved by him or under his authority.

We hereby undertake for the Emperor, the Japanese Government and their successors to carry out the provisions of the Potsdam Declaration in good faith, and to issue whatever orders and take whatever action may be required by the Supreme Commander for the Allied Powers or by any other designated representative of the Allied Powers for the purpose of giving effect to that Declaration.

We hereby command the Japanese Imperial Government and the Japanese Imperial General Headquarters at once to liberate all allied prisoners of war and civilian internees now under Japanese control and to provide for their protection, care, maintenance and immediate transportation to places as directed.

The authority of the Emperor and the Japanese Government to rule the state shall be subject to the Supreme Commander for the Allied Powers who will take such steps as he deems proper to effectuate these terms of surrender.

INSTRUMENT OF SURRENDER. The above document, the instrument of surrender, was signed on September 2, 1945, aboard the USS "Missouri," in one of the strangest and most unusual ceremonies in the annals of history. The Japanese Empire, after four years of undeclared warfare against China, formally declared war on the United States and Great Britain on December 7, 1941. By the first of September, 1945, her armies were actually larger than they were in 1941. Her air force was larger. Her main armies had never been defeated. Outlying garrisons had been smashed on many islands; other garrisons had been by-passed. One of her armies in the Philippines had been cut to pieces. But the bulk of her forces had never tasted battle. Yet she was cut off from many of her troops, and the troops remaining in the homeland were cut off, isolated from vital supplies. Her Navy had been completely defeated, and coincidentally with that defeat, her merchant shipping had been sunk. Japan's life line had been severed. Because of superior sea power, frock-coated little men, representing the emperor, climbed aboard the USS "Missouri," bowed low, apologized sibilantly, and carefully, meticulously, signed the instrument of surrender, shown with the signatures of the Japanese and Allied representatives. Never before had a once great nation, with its military strength still almost intact, quit so quickly and completely. It was clear-cut, convincing and emphatic evidence of what an independent Navy can do when pitted against a Navy which is used primarily as an auxiliary to an Army.

THE DOCUMENT IS SIGNED. The "Big Mo"—the battleship "Missouri"—anchored in Tokio Bay, was the scene of impressive ceremonies September 2, 1945. The greatest war in history was brought to a close there when representatives of the Allied Powers and the Japanese signed the official instrument of surrender. ABOVE. This is a general view aboard the USS "Missouri" at the start of the ceremony. General MacArthur and the other signatories are hidden by the crowd on the deck in center. UPPER RIGHT. After having removed his silk hat, the Japanese representative puts his signature on the document. Signing is Namoro Shigomitso, who acted on behalf of the Emperor of Japan and the Japanese government. Lieutenant General Richard K. Sutherland, Army Chief of Staff for the Southwest Pacific Area, stands at the table and sees that the job is well done. LOWER RIGHT. It was a moment of great triumph when General MacArthur signed the document as Supreme Allied Commander. Behind MacArthur are Lieutenant General Jonathan Wainwright and Lieutenant General A. E. Percival, the British commander who had been forced to surrender to the Japanese at Singapore. Immediately after the surrender, General MacArthur issued General Order No. 1 to the Japanese General Staff, with instructions concerning the surrender and disposition of Japanese forces and equipment.

THE PRICE OF AGGRESSION. With her attack on Pearl Harbor, Japan sought to dominate the Orient and possibly the world. After initial successes had brought her to the

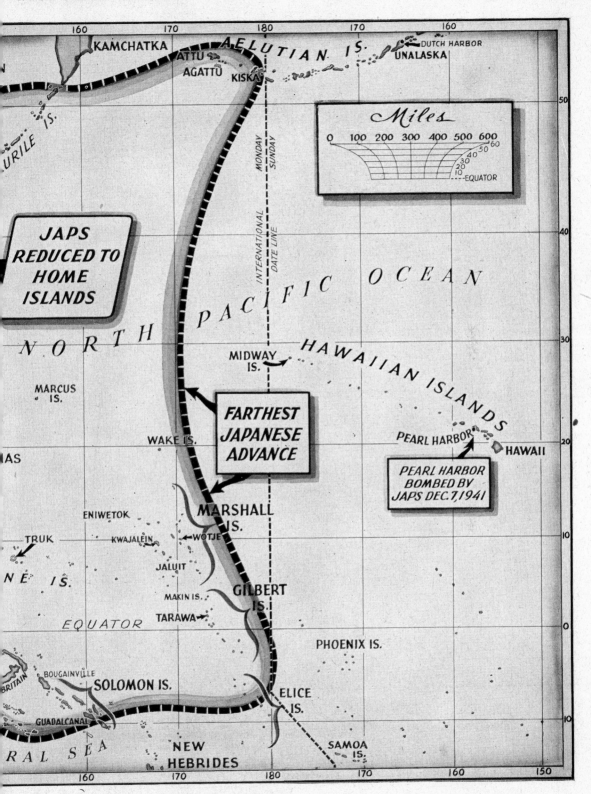

fringes of the enclosed areas depicted (above), she was
forced back by land, sea and air until, with her capitulation,
she was compressed within the confines of her home islands.

WAKE REGAINED. On September 4, 1945, a destroyer escort pulled up alongside Wake Island and Col. Walter L. J. Bayler stepped ashore. The cycle was complete. Bayler, last man off Wake Island before its defenders were forced to surrender, returned in triumph as a member of the official Allied surrender party under Marine Brig. Gen. Lawson, H. M. Sanderson, commanding the Fourth Air Wing. UPPER. The American flag flies again over Wake Island as Gen. Sanderson and a small party salute smartly. To the right front is the Japanese Commander who surrendered the island and his staff. A Navy guard presents arms.

RETURN TO THE ORIENT. Brig. Gen. William T. Clement,
commanding Task Force A for the occupation of Japan,
speaks to the men of the 4th Marine Regiment aboard the
"Ozark." Gen. Clement, former staff officer in the Philippines, had been evacuated from Luzon by submarine before
the fall of Corregidor. Because of its long history in the
Orient, the 4th was given the honor of returning as the
first occupation unit to land in Tokio Bay. Task Force A
was swelled by the addition of a provisional regiment of
Bluejackets and one of Marines from ships of the fleet,
coupled with a battalion from the British Royal Navy.

THE FINAL TRIUMPH. ABOVE. Old Glory is unfurled above
the Nippon Times Building on September 6, 1945. Two days
later the official occupation flag was raised at the U.S.
Embassy compound. At the ceremony General MacArthur
remarked as the flag went up: "General Eichelberger (C.G.
U.S. Eighth Army), have our country's flag unfurled and in
Tokio's sun let it wave in its full glory as a symbol of hope for
the oppressed and as a harbinger of victory for the right."

OCCUPATION UNDERWAY. The same flag that flew over the White House on the day the Japanese attacked Pearl Harbor is about to soar aloft over the American Embassy in Tokio. Members of the First Cavalry Division participated in the ceremony which marked the official U.S. occupation.

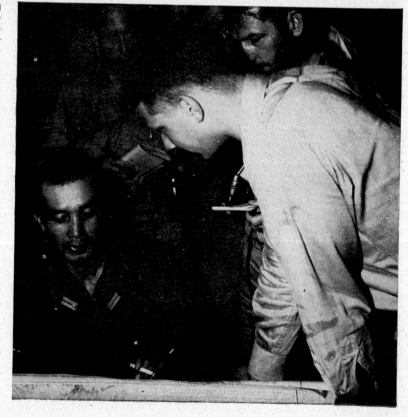

NOW HEAR THIS. Embarking from Guam on short notice, the 4th Marines spent their time aboard ship familiarizing themselves with maps of the Japanese terrain, as well as the habits and customs of the nation they had helped to defeat. UPPER. Lt. Col. Fred D. Beans, commanding the 4th, instructs his men concerning the new duties they would soon undertake on the Japanese mainland. All units going ashore at this time were fully armed and prepared for any and all eventualities. Despite the fact that the Japanese had surrendered, no one wished to take unnecessary chances. Many Marines quickly recalled other Japanese surrenders which too often resulted in the death of their buddies. The 4th, composed of four raider battalions, was a seasoned outfit which had recently conquered much of the land area of Okinawa as part of the Sixth Division. LOWER. Lt. Cmdr. Junichi Kusudo of the Japanese Navy aboard the "Ozark" will soon pilot the vessel through the mine-infested waters of Tokio harbor. He is questioned by war correspondents as the Task Force approaches the end of its long journey. Webley Edwards of the Columbia Broadcasting System, interviews the Jap officer.

OPERATION TOKIO. Marines of Task Force A landed at Yokosuka Navy Yard and at the Air Station. They had received instructions to seal off the peninsula and secure the Zushi area. UPPER. During the early morning hours, Marines slosh through the water holding their M-1s at high port. Thus they completed the cycle of amphibious landings, for which they had become famous, as their shoes sank into the sandy beach of Japan. Not a single shot was fired, and not a man lost his life. The emperor had spoken to his people and they had heeded his word. LOWER. More Marines pour ashore. In the background, newsreel crews and photographers record the landings on Japan. A few miles away the Army's Eleventh Airborne Division was landing at Atsuqi Airfield near the northern end of the peninsula. Marines were the first American troops to land on Japanese soil. Maj. Frank Carney, 2nd Battalion, 4th Marines, commanded the initial landing party. Gen. Clement and Rear Admiral O. C. Badger had gone ashore two days earlier and given the orders: remove personnel, demilitarize and mark coast defenses and AA with white flags, have guides on the beaches and provide motor transport.

YOKOSUKA AND SASEBO. The occupation of Japan called for the Fifth Amphibious Corps to occupy Kyushu and southern Honshu. In carrying out this mission the Second Marine Division was told to set up its CP at Nagasaki, the Fifth Division at the Sasebo Naval Base. In support was the Second Air Wing. The 4th Marines were assigned the Tokio waterfront. Lt. Bevan C. Cass, aide to Gen. Clement, remembers the scene: "There was no resistance and no violence. Only a few Japanese were present, all wearing white armbands as instructed, to indicate they were essential to the maintenance and operation of public utilities. Guards were left at the warehouse and other installations and the troops moved through the navy yard and across the airfield, checking guns to see that the breechblocks had been removed and herding non-essential Japanese before them." UPPER. Marines carry their weapons as they occupy the naval base at Yokosuka. LOWER. Marines coming ashore at Sasebo included the Fifth Division band which plays Marine Corps Hymn. Future verses may include a reference to the occupation duty of the Fifth Corps.

HAPPIER RAYS. UPPER. To the five men on the ground here, it had been a long war. They were among the defenders of Bataan and Corregidor, and had been taken prisoner there in the early days of the war. Here on August 30, 1945, their long captivity comes to an end, and they welcome the first American troops of the 11th Airborne Division after their landing at Atsugi Airport, just outside of Tokio. LOWER. This is another view of the same airport. Planes are hurriedly bringing in the occupation troops. Here elements of the 188th Parachute Infantry Regiment are loaded onto trucks as fast as they unload from the planes. Their task — to secure Yokohama. At long last, Japan was being made to pay in full for her treacheries at Mukden, at Shanghai, at Pearl Harbor and at Bataan. In first offering to surrender she had agreed to accept the terms of the Potsdam Declaration if the sovereignty of the Emperor was not questioned. Secretary of State James F. Byrnes, after consulting with the other Allied powers, informed them that from the moment of surrender the authority of the Emperor and the government to rule the state should be subject to the Supreme Commander of the Allied Powers—General MacArthur.

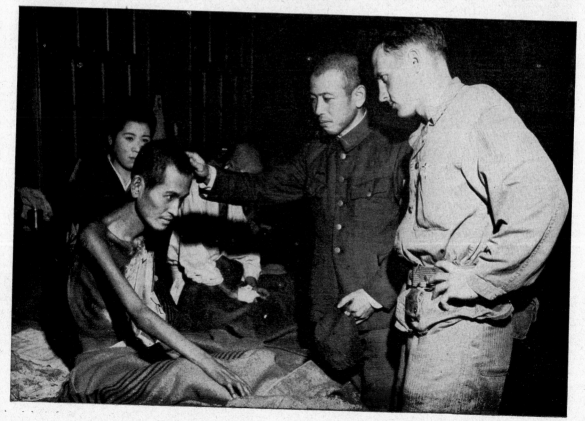

COMEDY AND TRAGEDY. The Marine MP (above) towering over the youthful Japanese policeman is Lt. Joe Ochsie, former New York "Giants" football player. Everywhere, the Americans were conscious of the short stature of the Japanese people. UPPER LEFT. A few light moments as Marines of the Fifth Division puzzle directions while on liberty. The Japanese policeman has a small dictionary and is trying to tell the Marines what they want to know. LOWER LEFT. Dr. Tom Brown of the 27th Marines examines a victim of the Nagasaki atom bombing. Dr. Shigeru Kawada explains the flash burns as a Japanese nurse watches. Dr. Brown said, "Most of the patients in these wards were suffering from flash burns. Though many of them were severely burned they were also suffering from malnutrition. Japanese doctors claimed that due to the atom bomb's rays' effect on the white and red corpuscles, the patients wasted away. I contend that the half-starved condition of the patients was due to the treatment they received while patients and not as the after effects of the radioactivity of the bomb's rays as was claimed." The Fifth Division headquartered at Ainoura Training Station, former home of Navy recruits. The American occupation job included supervising demilitarization of returning Jap soldiers, destroying ammunition and weapons, and turning into scrap any possible future instruments of war.

WELCOME HOME. As the occupation proceeded, search teams hurried to known prisoner of war encampments, eager to restore freedom to captured Americans. The scenes were touching. Marines captured on Corregidor were reunited with the men who carried their old regiment's name into battle. ABOVE. From Yokohama 120 former members of the 4th Marines came to Yokosuka as guests of the "New 4th." After a steak dinner the outfit held a formal guard mount and turned over regimental colors to the liberated Marines of the old 4th. Gen. Clement met many of the Marines he had last seen in 1942 on Luzon. Lt. Col. Jimmy Devereux of Wake Island was the toast of his rescuers. One team caused a national sensation by finding Marine Lt. Col. Greg "Pappy" Boyington alive in a Jap prison in spite of all the baseball bat beatings he had taken. Boyington received a hero's welcome at home and the Congressional Medal from President Truman as Marine ace of aces in the Pacific air. UPPER LEFT. A group of Japanese girls, clad in their traditional kimonos, smile for a Yank photographer. LOWER LEFT. A stray pooch seems to be coming in first at a Fifth Division track meet. The improvised attire of the runners, with their heavy shoes, adds to the general merriment.

THE PEACEFUL OCCUPATION. The Third Amphibious Corps moved quickly from Okinawa to North China. The First Marine Division went to Peiping and Tientsin with Corps headquarters, while the Sixth Division, less the 4th Marines, sailed from Guam and took over duties at Tsingtao. In support, the First Marine Air Wing maintained a number of fields in the area. UPPER. The citizens of Tientsin gave the First Division a warm welcome, repeating a scene familiar to Marines in every Chinese city they passed through. LOWER. Friendly small fry crowd Private Sheldon Lander.

AVIATION OCCUPATION. Supporting the troops ashore in Japan, Marine air squadrons performed transport and supply missions. UPPER. Lt. Tyrone Power of the movies, a transport pilot, sweats out the chow line with his fellow Marines. Power, one of many actors to join the Corps, went through boot training at San Diego and then to officer's training, later winning his wings. LOWER. Comedian Danny Kaye entertains the Marines in Japan with a song. The sign chalked on the stage reads: "Enlisted Men's Country" to distinguish it from "Officers' Country."

JAPANESE DEMOBILIZATION. As American soldiers "sweated out" the elaborate point system by which they became eligible for discharge, the defeated Japs were rapidly disarmed. These Jap soldiers (above) await mustering out in a Tokio street. Under General MacArthur's direction, 4,000,000 expeditionary and 3,000,000 homeland troops were demobilizedin less than two months. By Oct. 16, the job was done.

BANNED. Los Angeles born Iva Toguri, better known as "Tokio Rose," awaits trial in a prison cell in Yokohama. Her broadcasts, aimed at undermining the morale of American GIs, were familiar to thousands who listened to hear American records interspersed between her insidious "chit-chat." She was charged with treason against the U.S., found guilty, and is presently serving her ten-year sentence in prison.

SALUTING THE MIKADO. When the Yanks arrived in Tokio they soon observed that the Japanese had the greatest respect and reverence for their emperor. ABOVE. Japanese

bow, as custom dictates, to the "Imperial Presence" within the Imperial Palace. Many Japanese also bowed in deference to their American conquerors, who were greatly puzzled.

VICTORY DISPLAY. Fireworks set off from the decks of ships anchored in the great American naval base in the Pacific heralded the end of the war. In four years of bloody installments, the Americans repaid the Japanese for their treacherous attack which rendered the Pacific Fleet impotent and threatened the security of the United States. The unconditional surrender of Japan and the American occupation under the direction of General Douglas MacArthur demonstrated clearly that the American people would long remember Pearl Harbor.

IT'S OVER, OVER THERE. During the war 7,300,000 soldiers and 126,859,000 tons of cargo were shipped from U.S. ports. The bulk of the cargo remained where it was, and more than 250,000 men would never return. Total casualties, including wounded, were 1,069,632. Many of the armed forces remained overseas for occupation duty, and conscription was continued after V-J Day. A portion of the thousands who were lucky enough to return home for early discharge are shown cheering as their ship reaches an American port.

INDEX

A

Abemama, 162
Adak, 71
Admiralty Islands, 35, 171, 244
Agana, Guam, 226
Air Force, U.S. Army
  Borneo raids, 355
  China, bases in, 183
  China-Burma-India Theater, 182, 183
  Coordination with other forces, 1, 2
  Dedicate B-29s to Iwo Marines, 310
  Fifth Air Force, 137
  "Hump," The, 182
  Iwo Jima advantages, 293, 310
  Japan, bombing results in, 351, 354
  Kwajalein base, 162
  Midway, Battle of, 32
  New Britain, 137
  "Superfort Warfare in the Pacific," art.,
    311, 312
  Tokio raid under Doolittle, 22, 23
  "War in the CBI," art., 182, 183
  "War in the Solomons," art., 34
  "War in the South Pacific," art., 244
  "Your Navy in Action," art., 1
Air Transport Command, 182
Aitape, New Guinea, 178, 244
Alaska, 2
Alaska Scouts, 71
Aleutian Islands
  Adak, 71
  Alaska Scouts, 71
  Amchitka, 71
  Attu, 70, 71, 73
  Dutch Harbor bombed, 33
  4th Infantry Division, 71, 73
  Holtz Bay, 71
  Kiska, 70
  Kodiak, 72, 73
  7th Infantry Division, 71
  "Tarawa," art., 112
Amchitka, 71
Americal Division
  Bougainville, 35, 102
  Cited for New Georgia operations, 68
  Guadalcanal, 34, 35, 38, 39, 49
  Luzon, 245
  164th Infantry Reg't, 34
  Patch, Alexander M., Gen., 34
  Solomon Islands, 34, 35
  "War in the Solomons," art., 34, 35
American Volunteer Group, see Flying
  Tigers
Andaman Islands, 20, 21
Angaur, 230, 233-235, 240
Aparri, Luzon, 280
Arare, New Guinea, 180
Arawe, New Britain, 244
"Arizona," 4, 6
Army ground forces, see articles, division
  headings, Engineers
Army ships, 65
Arnold, Henry H., Gen., 311, 325
Arundel, 34
Assam, 173, 182, 185
Atomic bomb, 143, 296, 330, 350
Attu, 70, 71, 73
Australia
  Asiatic Fleet remnants reach, 10
  B-17s evacuated from Philippines to, 8
  1st Marine Division, Melbourne, 135
  Liaison with United States, 2
  New Guinea, troops in, 36, 66, 174
  9th Division invades Borneo, 355
  Supply line from America, 244
  Tarakan Island, troops land on, 274
  Threat of invasion checked, 48
  "War in the Solomons," art., 34, 35
  "War in the South Pacific," art., 244
  "Your Navy in Action," art., 2
Ayers, Russell G., Col., 142

B

Baanga, Solomons, 34
Baguio, Luzon, 272, 273
Baka suicide planes, 261
Balete Pass, Luzon, 272, 276
Bambam, Luzon, 258, 259
Barlow, Ernest A., Col., 281

Barrett, Charles, Gen., 58
Bataan, 8, 10, 18, 24, 265
Bayler, Walter J. L., Col., 368
Beebe, Lewis, Gen., 361
Beightler, Robert S., Gen., 281
Betio, see Tarawa
Biak, New Guinea, 180, 181, 244
Bismarck Islands, 112
Bohol, Philippines, 245
Bonin Islands, 188
Borneo, 18, 245, 262, 355
Bougainville
  Airstrip for Marine planes, 106, 107
  Ambushed by Japs, 97
  Americal Division, 35, 102
  Base for raiding Rabaul, 98
  Bayonets bared in mopping up, 98-100
  Bomb dump, 107
  Campaign, 92-109
  Casualties removed, 106
  Cemetery, 108, 109
  Conquest isolates Japs in Solomons, 102
  "Corduroy" road, 96
  Counterattack by Japs, 102
  Dogs in combat, 104, 105
  Empress Augusta Bay, 91, 98
  Landing, 91, 92
  Landing techniques perfected, 92
  MacArthur plans assaults, 98
  Marine flyers use Russells strip, 69
  Mud clogs advance, 95, 103
  129th Infantry, 101
  132nd Infantry, 102
  143rd Infantry, 102
  Preliminary landings, 90
  Raided from Guadalcanal, 57
  Religious service, 108, 109
  754th Tank Battalion, 102
  "Tarawa," art., 112, 113
  3rd Marine Division, 91, 92
  13th Air Force, 106
  37th Infantry Division, 98, 101-103
  "War in the Solomons," art., 34, 35
Bourke, Thomas, Gen., 124
Boyington, Greg, Lt. Col., 379
Breeches buoy transfers, 360
Brereton, L. H., Gen., 8
Britain, 2, 182
British Navy, 357, 360, 369
Brown, Joe E., 57
Bruce, A. D., Gen., 220
Buckner, Simon B., Gen., 143, 336
Buna, New Guinea, 66, 174, 244
Burgin, Henry L., Gen., 143
Burma
  Airbase taken after mountain march, 187
  Allies copy Japanese tactics, 170
  Border sign, Ledo road, 282, 283
  Bridge over Salween river, 187
  Burma road, 182, 185
  Casablanca conference, 182
  Casualties, 183
  Gen. Stilwell, see Stilwell
  Invaded by Siamese troops, 16
  Irrawaddy river, 183
  Japs advance through, 1942, 16, 17
  K-rations passed out, 185
  Ledo road to help retake Burma, 173
  Marauders barbecue deer, 185
  Mongyu, 185
  Myitkyina, 182, 183, 186, 187
  Naubum, 185
  Offensive begun, 185
  Outflank Japanese, 170
  Overrun by Japs, 1941, 2, 16, 17
  Rangoon, 17, 183
  Salween river, 173, 182, 187
  "War in the CBI," art., 182
Burma Road, 182, 185, 282-284
Butaritari Island, see Makin, 120
Byrnes, James F., 359

C

Cagayan Valley, Luzon, 276, 278
Calcutta, 182, 183, 185
Callaghan, Daniel, Adm., 55
Canadian troops, 13
Canton, 183
Cape Torokina, 35, 92, 98
Carabao, Philippines, 274, 275
Carigara, Leyte, 250

Carlson, Evans F., Gen., 53, 217
Caroline Islands, 112, 169, 188
Casablanca conference, 182
Casualties
  Bougainville, 106
  Corregidor, 270
  Guadalcanal, 43
  Guam, 142, 220
  Iwo Jima, 308
  Leyte, 247
  Okinawa, 143, 342, 347
  Saipan, 142, 206
  Tinian, 215
  Total American, 388
Catabato, Philippines, 245
Cates, Clifton B., Gen., 40, 213, 298, 299
Cavite, 10, 15, 265
Cebu, 245
Celebes, 20
Cemeteries
  Bougainville, 108, 109
  Guadalcanal, 44, 45
  Iwo Jima, 309
  New Georgia, 84, 85
  Okinawa, 343
  Tarawa, 134
Chaplains
  Bougainville, 108, 109
  Guadalcanal, 44, 45
  Iwo Jima, 303, 309
  Tarawa ship service, 126
Chennault, Claire, Gen., 17, 61, 172, 182
Chiang Kai-shek, 25, 182, 183
Chiang Kai-shek, Mme., 22, 23
China
  American airfields, 82, 83
  Blockade broken, 82
  Border sign, Ledo road, 282, 283
  Burma road, 82
  Canton, 183
  Chennault, Claire, Gen., 61
  China Air Task Force, 61
  Chungking, 22
  Command split after reverses, 183
  Final drive against Japan, 350
  1st Marine Division, 330, 380
  Flying Tigers, 61
  14th Air Force, 61
  Hong Kong, 13, 61
  Hukwang valley, 182, 183, 185
  "Hump," The, 182, 183, 185
  Hunan Province, 183
  Isolated, nearly, by Japs, 185
  Kumming, 61, 285
  Kweilin, 183
  Land route to China cleared, 183
  Ledo road, 173, 185, 282-284
  Lend-Lease, 182
  Liaison with United States, 2
  Liuchow, 183
  Needed supplies to stay in war, 185
  Occupation by Marines, 330, 380
  Peiping, 380
  6th Marine Division, 330, 380
  Stilwell road, 183, 186
  "Superfort Warfare in the Pacific," art.
    311, 312
  Supply lines, 182, 183
  Tientsin, 380
  Training of troops, 173, 182, 186
  Tsingtao, 380
  Tushan, 183
  Wanting, 282, 283
  "War in the CBI," art., 182
  Yunnan, 182, 185
China-Burma-India Theater, art., 182
Choiseul, 35, 90, 98
Chungking, 22
Churchill, Winston, 182
Citations, 68, 130, 202, 295
Clement, William T., Gen., 369, 374, 379
Coast Guard, U.S.
  "Coast Guard, The U.S.," art., 65
  Rendova, landing boats, 74, 75
  Ships of, 65
  "Your Navy in Action," art., 2
Cochran, Philip C., Col., 182
Cogon, Luzon, 258
Congressional Medal of Honor, 47, 119, 158,
  379
Coral Sea, Battle of the
  Chart, tracks of forces, 27

Coral Sea, Battle of the (cont'd)
  Jap carriers hit, 28
  "Lexington" sinks, 26, 28, 29
  Results, 1, 29
  "War in the South Pacific," art., 244
  "Yorktown" planes score, 26
  "Your Navy in Action," art., 1, 2
  "Corduroy" road, 96
Corlerr, Charles H., Gen., 161
Corregidor, 9, 10, 15, 19, 24, 245, 265, 270

D

Dakeshi Ridge, 316
Davao City, Philippines, 14, 245
Davidson, Howard, Gen., 182
DeHaven, Louis, Col., 154
Denfeld, Louis, Adm., 287
Denig, Robert L., Gen., 347
Devereaux, James, Col., 379
Digos, Philippines, 245
Dogs in combat, 104, 105
Donovan, Leo, Gen., 201
Doolittle, James H., Gen., 22, 312
Dulag, Leyte, 248-250
Dutch Harbor, 33

E

Ebeye, Marshall Islands, 153
Edson, Merritt, Gen., 47, 58, 124
Efate, 34
Eichelberger, R. L., Gen., 244, 370
Eighth Army, 244, 245
8th Marine Regiment, 49, 116-134, 209
18th Marine Regiment, 130
81st Infantry Division, 143, 230-243
11th Airborne Division, 244, 245, 280
XI Corps, 244
Empress Augusta Bay, 91, 98
Engebi, Marshall Islands, 163-165
Engineers, U.S. Army
  Guam rebuilt into base, 229
  Ledo road, 173, 182, 183
  Makin, lay screen mat, 111
  New Georgia corduroy road, 85
  "War in the CBI," art., 182
Eniwetok, 142, 163-165, 188
Enubuj, Marshall Islands, 148-150
Erskine, Graves B., Gen., 305, 307, 310
Espiritu Santo, 34

F

Fenton, Francis I., Col., 341
Fifth Air Force, 137, 244, 252
Fifth Corps Scout Company, 163
5th Marine Division, 130, 287-314
5th Marine Regiment, 141, 242
58th Bombardment Wing, 311
503rd Parachute Regiment, 245, 258, 265
Fiji Islands, 34
Filipino troops, 9, 15, 18, 19, 24, 245, 258, 259, 280
1st Cavalry Division, 244, 245, 371
I Corps, 244, 245
1st Marine Air Wing, 380
1st Marine Division
  China occupation duty, 380
  Cited by President, 68
  1st Regiment, 136
  Guadalcanal, 34, 38, 39
  New Britain, 135, 136, 138, 244
  New Guinea, 135
  Occupation duty in China, 330
  Okinawa campaign, 295, 314-347
  Palau Islands campaign, 230-243
  7th Regiment, 136
  Tulagi, 34
  "War in the Central Pacific," art., 143
  "War in the Solomons," art., 34, 35
  "War in the South Pacific," art., 244
1st Marine Regiment, 136, 137
1st Provisional Marine Brigade, 142, 189, 217-226
Flag, U.S.
  Aleutian Islands, 72
  Guam, 226
  Iwo Jima, 228, 305
  Marshall Islands, 161
  New Britain, 141
  Okinawa, 342, 344
  Tarawa, 124
  Tokio, 370
  Wake Island, 368
Florida Island, 39
Flying Tigers, 17, 61
Formosa, 143
Forrestal, James V., 287
4th Infantry Division, 71, 73, 83
4th Marine Air Wing, 368

4th Marine Division
  Citation, 202
  Iwo Jima, 287-314
  "Marianas Campaign," art., 188, 189
  Marshall Islands, 145, 152
  Saipan, 142, 188, 189, 200-206
  Souvenir hunt on Saipan, 207
  "Tarawa," art., 112
  Tinian campaign, 208-215
  22nd Regiment, 165
  23rd Regiment, 153, 202
  24th Regiment, 155, 202
  25th Regiment, 202
  "War in the Central Pacific," art., 142
4th Marine Regiment, 330, 360, 369, 372, 379
Fourteenth Air Force, 182
XIV Corps, 34, 245
14th Marine Artillery Regiment, 154
40th Infantry Division, 245, 270, 271
41st Infantry Division, 178, 180, 244, 245
43rd Infantry Division, 34, 83, 244

G

Gavutu, Guadalcanal, 39
Geiger, Roy S., Gen.
  I Marine Amphibious Corps, commands, 97
  "Marianas Campaign," art., 189
  "Okinawa Campaign," art., 315, 316
  Okinawa flag-raising, 344
George, H. H., Gen., 8
Gilbert Islands, see Tarawa, Makin
Gilbreath, Frederick, Gen., 143
Gloucester, see New Britain
Green (Nissan) Island, 35, 98, 171
Griffith, Sam, Col., 81
Griswold, Oscar W., Gen., 34
Guadalcanal
  Aerial view, 159
  Americal Division, 34, 35, 38, 39, 49
  Base for Marianas campaign, 188
  Bathing in guarded stream, 48
  Bridge survives flood, 56, 57
  Camouflaged Jap gun, 159
  Casualties, 43
  Cemetery, 44, 45
  Commanders inspect, 58
  1st Marine Division, 34, 38, 39
  Florida Island, 39
  Gavutu, 39
  Hara-kiri by Japs, 50
  Henderson Field, 46
  Japs move to New Georgia, 68
  Jap prisoners, 45, 51
  Landing, 38-40, 44, 56, 57
  Map, battle points, 41
  Mortar firing, 43
  Naval battle, 55
  Religious service, 44, 45
  Results of victory, 48, 57
  2nd Marine Division, 34, 39
  Tanambogo, 39
  Telephone line, 49
  Tenaru river, 45
  Tide of war turns, 189
  Tulagi, 34, 38-40
  U.S.O. entertainment, 56, 57
  "War in the Solomons," art., 34, 35
  "Your Navy in Action," art., 1, 2
Guam
  Agana, 226
  Artillery fire, 224, 225
  Assault delayed by Saipan, 142
  Banzai charges, 224, 225
  Campaign, 217-226
  Casualties, 142, 220
  Cave defenses, 222, 223
  Chonito cliffs, 223
  Coral reefs, 219
  Dead Japanese, 235
  1st Provisional Marine Brigade, 142, 217-226
  Headquarters for Army Air Force, 311
  Jap flag hoisted on, 11
  Landing, 217-220
  Map, direction of invasion, 190
  "Marianas Campaign," art., 188
  Orote airstrip, 229
  Orote Peninsula, 219-224
  Seabees rehabilitate, 226, 227, 229
  Seventh Air Force, 217
  77th Infantry Division, 217-226
  Space ample for artillery, 194
  Sumay, 219, 226
  Task Force 58 air raid, 169
  3rd Marine Division, 142, 217-226
  27th Infantry Division, 142, 217-226
  U.S. flag rises, 226
  "War in the Central Pacific," art., 142
  Wounded Marine treated, 223
  "Your Navy in Action," art., 1, 2

H

Halsey, William F., Adm.
  Bougainville strategy, 98
  "Surrender of Japan," art., 350
  Truk raid by Task Force 58, 166, 167
  "War in the Solomons," art., 34, 35
Hara-kiri, 48, 125, 212
Harmon, Millard F., Gen., 34
Hawaii, 2, 143, 188, 386, 387
Hawkins, Wm. D., Lt., 119
Haynes, Caleb V., Col., 61
Henderson Field, Guadalcanal, 46
Hill, Harry W., Adm., 116, 207
Hiroshima, 296, 358
Hodges, John R., Gen., 143, 319, 344
Holcomb, Gen. T., 40, 58
Hollandia, 136, 178-180, 244
Holtz Bay, 71
Hong Kong, 13, 61
"Hornet," 22, 23
Hull, Cordell, 359
Hukwang Valley, China, 182, 183, 185
"Hump," The, 61, 182, 183, 185
Hunan Province, China, 183
Huon Peninsula, New Britain, 244

I

Ie Shima, 143, 316, 341
Ilagan, Luzon, 278
Imphal, India, 172
Impulatao, Philippines, 245
India
  Air superiority of Allies, 172
  Assam, 173, 182, 185
  Calcutta, 182, 183, 185
  CATF Raid on Victoria Harbor, 61
  First convoy to China arrives, 285
  Gen. Chennault at command post, 172
  "Hump," The, 61, 182, 183, 185
  Imphal, 172
  Indian troops, 182, 183
  Invaded by Japs, 172
  Invasion thrown back, 183
  Ledo road bridge, 173
  Mountbatten, Adm., 183
  "Superfort Warfare in the Pacific," art., 311, 312
  10th Air Force, 61
  "War in the CBI," art., 182, 183
Irrawaddy river, Burma, 183
Iwo Jima
  Amphtracs pass a control boat, 291
  B-29 lands, crippled, 310
  B-29s dedicated to divisions, 310
  Base for Japan landing, 350
  Booby trap unearthed, 304
  Casualties, 308
  Caves protect defenders, 297
  Cemeteries, 309
  Central Field, 313
  Chaplains' role, 303
  Command post, 23rd Marines, 299
  "Courageous battle vow," of Japs, 306
  Damaged little by bombardment, 294
  Dead Marines lie where they fell, 294
  Duration of hostilities, 287-314
  5th Marine Division, 287-314
  5th Pioneer Battalion, 314
  4th Marine Division, 287-314
  Flag raising, Mt. Suribachi, 228
  Gen. Cates comes ashore, 299
  Japs fight after capture, 314
  Landing, 290-294
  Map, landing point, 289
  Map, island hopping progress, 286
  Memorial to men killed, 308
  Mt. Suribachi, 289, 301, 305, 314
  Negro Marines, 8th Field Depot, 314
  "New York" bombards, 288
  Note to Japanese defenders, 307
  Reasons for assault, 293, 310
  Religious services, 303
  Rocket firing trucks, 298, 299, 304
  Seabees build cemetery, 309
  7th Fighter Command, 312
  Strategy of Japs, 294
  "Superfort Warfare in the Pacific," art., 312
  Tanker flames offshore, 261
  Tracers streak night sky, 300
  12th Marines Artillery, 305
  28th Marine Regiment, 228, 308
  U.S. flag rises, 228, 305
  Value to Japs, 293
  "War in the Central Pacific," art., 142
  Wounded receive whole blood, 302
  Wreckage piles up on beaches, 294
  "Your Navy in Action," art., 1

J

Jaluit, Marshall Islands, 163
Japan
  Atomic bomb shatters Hiroshima, 358
  Blockade by U.S. Navy, 1, 2, 363
  Bombing of aircraft plant, 351
  Cabinet resigns over Saipan, 206
  Chiefs-of-Staff ousted for Saipan naval defeat, 169
  Defeat caused by isolation, 1, 363
  Demobilization of troops, 382
  Empire pierced in Marshalls, 161
  Entertainment for U.S. troops, 381
  Evacuation from islands, 80
  5th Marine Division band, 374
  1st Cavalry Division, 371
  4th Marine Regiment, 369, 370, 372
  Girls stroll in kimonos, 378
  Hiroshima, 296, 358
  Kobe, 22
  Invasion of, plans for, 245
  Kure, 357
  Landing of American troops, 350
  Map, early conquests, 20, 21
  Map, empire, war's end, 366, 367
  Map, territory held July 1944, 203
  Marines' chow line, 381
  Nagasaki, 296, 374
  Nagoya, 312, 351
  Naval power broken, 251-253
  Naval strategy, 1, 2
  Occupation troops briefed, 369, 372
  Occupation scenes, 370-385
  Osaka, 22, 354
  Pearl Harbor attack, see Pearl Harbor attack
  Propaganda by, 8, 11
  Roi first pre-war territory to fall, 145
  Sasebo, 330, 374
  2nd Marine Division, 374
  Surrender document, 363
  "Surrender of Japan," art., 350
  Tokio, 22, 23, 245, 312, 350
  U.S. Embassy, Tokio, 370, 371
  U.S. flag rises in Tokio, 370
  Yokohama, 22, 245, 379
  Yokosuka, 330, 350, 374, 379
Jarman, S. B., Gen., 143
Java, 20
Joint Chiefs of Staff
  Coordination of Armed Forces, 1, 2
  Leyte landing changed from Yap, 143
  Offensive assumed in Pacifiic, 142
  "Superfort Warfare in the Pacific," art., 311,312
  "Tarawa," art., 112, 113
  Truk, decides to bypass, 142
  "War in the Central Pacific," art., 142, 143
  "War in the Solomons," art., 34, 35

K

K-9 Corps, 104, 105
Kakaban, Philippines, 245
Kamikaze planes, 261, 336
Kananga, Luzon, 258
Katchin Peninsula, 315
Kavieng, 35
Kerama Retto, 143
Kiangan, Luzon, 281
Killed and wounded
  American
    Iwo Jima, 294
    Munda hospital, 86, 87
    New Britain, 138
    New Georgia, 78, 79, 84, 85
    Okinawa, 336, 343
    Okinawa wounded 331, 335, 336
    Tarawa, 122, 125, 126, 193
    Tinian, 213
  Japanese
    Bataan, 18, 19
    Bougainville, 101
    Guadalcanal, 45, 50
    Guam, 235
    Iwo Jima, 306
    Marshall Islands, 157
    New Guinea, 66, 67, 174
    Okinawa, 328
    Saipan, 202, 204, 205
    Tarawa, 120, 127
King, Edward, Gen., 18
King, Ernest, Adm., 1, 2
Kinkaid, Thomas C., Adm., 244
Kiriwina Islands, 244
Kiska, 70
Kobe, Japan, 22
Kodiak Island, 72, 73
Kolombangara, 34, 90
Kongauru, Palau Islands, 242

Korea, 350
Krueger, Walter, Gen., 255
Kula Gulf, 89
Kumming, China, 61, 285
Kunishi Ridge, 316, 340
Kure, Japan, 357
Kwajalein, 145, 150, 152, 153, 188
Kweilin, China, 183

L

Lae, New Guinea, 174, 176, 178
Landings
  Aleutian Islands, 70
  Bougainville, 91, 92
  Coast Guard, role of, 65
  Gloucester, 135, 136
  Guadalcanal, 38, 39, 40, 56, 57
  Guam, 189, 217-220
  Iwo Jima, 290-294
  Japan, 350
  Leyte, 248-250
  Luzon, 258, 259
  Makin, 111
  New Britain, 135-138
  New Georgia, Choi River, 78, 79
  New techniques, Marshall Islands, 145, 152, 154
  Okinawa, 143
  Palau Islands, 230-232
  Rendova, 74, 75, 76, 77
  Russell Islands, 68
  Saipan, 142, 188
  Tarawa, 116-120
  Tinian, 189
  "War in the Central Pacific," art., 142
  "War in the Solomons," art., 34, 35
  "Your Navy in Action," art., 1, 2
Landrum, Eugene M., Gen., 71
Lantap, Luzon, 278
Leahy, William D., 359
Ledo Road, 173, 185, 282-284
"Lexington," 26, 28, 29
Leyte
  Carigara, 250
  Casualties, 247
  Convoy approaches, 246, 247
  Dulag, 248-250
  8th Army, 244
  Jap resistance stiffens, 254, 255
  Landing, 248-250
  Landing changed from Yap, 143, 248
  Leyte Gulf, Battle of, 1, 252, 253
  112th Cavalry, 244
  MacArthur, Osmena land, 250
  Ormoc Bay, 252
  Paratroopers, 59
  Pawing, 255
  San Jose, 255
  7th Cavalry Regiment, 255
  77th Infantry Division, 244, 259
  6th Ranger Battalion, 244
  Tablas Strait, 253
  Tacloban, 247
  32nd Infantry Division, 244
  34th Infantry Division, 255
  12th Cavalry, 255
  XXIV Corps, 143
  "War in the South Pacific," art., 244, 245
LeMay, Curtis, Gen., 311, 312
Lingayen Gulf, 14, 245, 258
Liuchow, China, 183
Liversedge, Harry, Col., 81, 292
Lockwood, Charles A., Adm., 348
Loran stations, 65
Lorengau, 171
Los Negros Island, 171
Lunga Point, 34
Luzon
  Americal Division, 245
  Aparri, 278
  Baguio, 272, 273
  Balete Pass, 272, 276
  Bambam, 258, 259
  Bataan, 8, 10, 18, 24, 265
  Bridge blown up by Japs, 280
  Cagayan valley, 276, 278
  Chutists drop on Corregidor, 265
  Clark Field, 8, 245
  Cogon, 258
  Corregidor, 9, 10, 15, 19, 24, 245, 265, 270
  Death march from Bataan, 18
  8th Army, 245
  11th Airborne Division, 265
  XI Corps, 245
  1st Cavalry Division, 265
  40th Infantry Division, 244
  41st Infantry Division, 245
  43rd Infantry Division, 258, 273
  Ilagan, 278
  Isolated Japs keep on fighting, 280

Luzon (cont'd)
  Japs sweep over, 1941, 8, 14, 15, 18
  Kananga, 258
  Kiangan, 281
  Landing, 258, 259
  Lantap, 278
  Lingayen Gulf, 14, 245, 258
  Manila, see Manila
  Mariveles, 265
  Nasugbu, 244, 265
  90th Field Artillery, 276
  149th Infantry Regiment, 278
  128th Infantry Regiment, 272
  186th Infantry Regiment, 245
  Paulili river, crossing, 276
  Propaganda leaflet from Japs, 8
  Samar, 245
  San Juan, 273
  San Pablo, 14
  77th Infantry Division, 258
  775th Tank Battalion, 278, 279
  Subic Bay, 265
  Tagaytay Ridge, 265
  32nd Infantry Division, 272, 281
  33rd Infantry Division, 276, 277
  34th Infantry Division, 245
  37th Infantry Division, 244, 245, 272, 273, 280
  37th Infantry Regiment, 278
  33th Infantry Division, 245, 265
  24th Infantry Division, 245, 258
  25th Infantry Division, 272, 276
  209th Anti-Aircraft Battalion, 280
  U.S. commanders, 281
  Valencia, 258
  Villa Verde Trail, 272
  "War in the South Pacific," art., 245
Zambales, 244

M

MacArthur, Douglas, Gen.
  Assumes all Army commands in Pacific, 143
  Bougainville strategy, 98
  By-passes Wewak, 178
  Demobilization by Japan, 382
  "I shall return," 247
  Japan, sets up government, 359
  Leyte landing, 143, 250
  New Guinea coast, off, 175
  New Guinea, heads Anzac troops, 174
  Palau Islands statement, 230
  Roosevelt, Nimitz, with, 216
  Surrender document, signs, 365
  Surrender instructions, 361
  "Surrender of Japan," art., 350
  Tokio flag-raising, 370
  "War in the Central Pacific," art., 142, 143
  "War in the Solomons," art., 34
  "War in the South Pacific," art., 244
  "Your Navy in Action," art., 1
Makin, 53, 111-113, 118, 142
Majuro, Marshall Islands, 163
Malaya, 2
Maloelap, Marshall Islands, 163
Mandalay, 20, 21
Manila
  Avenida Rizal, 269
  11th Airborne Division, 267
  1st Cavalry Division, 244, 267
  48th Infantry Division, 266
  Harbor raid on Jap ships, 256, 257
  House to house fighting, 266-269
  Iniramuros section, 15, 266, 267, 269
  Occupied by Japs, 1941, 15
  Pace section, 268, 269
  Paranque, 244
  Pasig river, crossing, 260, 267
  Snipers rooted out, 263
  37th Infantry Division, 266, 267
  "War in the South Pacific," art., 245
Manus Island, 171
"Marianas Campaign, The," art., 188
Marianas Islands, see Guam, Saipan, Tinian
"Marianas Turkey-Shoot," 191
Marine Corps, see articles, division headings
Mariveles, Luzon, 265
"Mars Task Force," 182
Marshall Islands
  Air strikes from Kwajalein, 163
  Ammunition dump explodes, 156
  Banzai attacks, 158
  Base for 7th Air Force, 162
  Bombardment heaviest yet, 145, 155, 162
  Bombers based on Roi, 145

Marshall Islands (cont'd)
Campaign, 144-165
Casualties, 142
Communications lines strung, 158
Communications unit barricade, 155
Congressional Medal awarded, 158
Ebeye, 153
Engebi, 163-165
Eniwetok, 142, 163-165, 188
Enubuj, 148-150
Fifth Corps Scout Company, 163
4th Marine Division, 145, 152
14th Marine Artillery Regiment, 154
Gas drum tunnel defense, Engebi, 165
Gen. Corlett surveys, 161
Gen. Smith inspects Roi-Namur, 157
Jaluit, 163
Japanese casualties, 151
Jap machine-gunners die, 157
Kwajalein, 145, 150, 153, 157, 162, 188
Landing craft, aerial view, 145
Majuro, 163
Maloelap, 163
"Marianas Campaign," art., 188
Mille, 163
Namur, 145, 150, 152, 154, 155, 158
New landing techniques, 145, 152, 154
106th Regimental Combat Team, 163
Operation Flintlock, 146
Parry Island, 165
Perimeter of Japanese empire, 161
Roi, 145, 150, 152
Roi first pre-war Jap territory to fall, 145
Rujiyoru, 165
Seabees extend airstrips, 145
Surrender to United States, 350
"Tarawa," art., 113
Tarawa lessons applied, 152
Tractors fire from water, 152
Traffic jams beaches, 155
22nd Marine Regiment, 163, 165
23rd Marine Regiment, 153
24th Marine Regiment, 155
U.S. flag rises, 161
"War in the Central Pacific," art., 142
Wotje, 163
Yeiri, 165
"Your Navy in Action," art., 1, 2
Martin, Wm. I., Capt., 167
"Maryland," 5
McBride, Robert B., Gen., 281
Medical care
Guam, splint applied to leg, 223
Iwo Jima, whole blood transfused, 302
Munda hospital on LST, 86, 87
Okinawa, stretcher bearers work, 331
Tarawa, sulfa dressing, 122
Tinian, blood plasma given
Melbourne, 135
Merchant Marine, 65
Merrill, Frank D., Gen., 170, 182, 185
"Merrill's Marauders," 170, 182, 185, 186
Midway, Battle of
Damage by Jap bombs, 30
Map, tracks of forces, 31
Results, 2, 32
Unique because ships never met, 32
"War in the South Pacific," art., 244
"Yorktown" sinks, 32, 33
"Your Navy in Action," art., 1, 2
Mille, Marshall Islands, 163
Mindanao, 14, 244, 245, 248, 270, 273
Mindoro, 258
"Missouri," 60, 245, 364, 365
Mitscher, Marc, Adm., 167, 169, 191
Mongyu, Burma, 185
Moore, James T., Gen., 241
Morobe, New Guinea, 176
Morotai, 230, 244, 247
Motubu Peninsula, 315, 321
Mountbatten, Lord Louis, Adm., 170, 182, 183
Mulcahy, Francis, Gen., 57, 316, 325
Munda
Airstrip captured, 80, 82
Bomb raid on airstrip, 80
Capture ends 1st phase of Solomons campaign, 90
Cave defenses, 86, 87
Evacuation by Japs, 80
43rd Infantry Division, 79, 83
Kokengolo Hill, 86, 87
Landing at Rendova, 74, 75, 76, 77
145th Infantry Regiment, 81
Pillboxes cleaned out, 83
Preparation for landing, 34
Raided from Guadalcanal, 57
Rendova landing, 34, 74-77
Ruins on Kokengolo Hill, 81
Seabees build road to airfield, 87
Shelled by Navy ships, 82

N

Nadzab, New Guinea, 178
Nagasaki, 296, 374
Nagoya, 312, 351
Naha, Okinawa, 315, 316, 331-338
Namur, Marshall Islands, 145, 150, 152, 154, 155, 158
Nasugbu, Luzon, 244, 265
Naval Air Corps, U.S.
Carrier landings, 93
Catalina patrols northern waters, 59
Coral Sea, Battle of the, 1, 26-29
Japan, raids on bases, 357
Kwajalein bombardment heaviest, 145
Leyte, hitting Jap ships, 252, 253
Makin dive-bombing, 111
Manila harbor raid, 256, 257
"Marianas Turkey-Shoot," 191
Marshall Islands, 162
Midway, Battle of, 30-32
Okinawa statistics, 338
Saipan action, Task Force 58, 169
Seaplanes near tender, Saipan, 191
"Surrender of Japan," art., 350
Truk raid, 167
"War in the Solomons," art., 35
"War in the South Pacific," art., 244
"Your Navy in Action," art., 1, 2
Navy, U.S.
Air Corps, see Naval Air Corps
Asiatic Fleet, 2, 10
Breeches buoy transfers, 360
Carrier deck, off Saipan, 168, 169
Coordination with other services, 1, 2
Coral Sea, see Coral Sea
Historical role, 1
Importance to nation, King on, 1, 2
Jap pilots "Ozark," Tokio harbor, 372
Kamikaze attacks off Okinawa, 336
Kwajalein bombardment heaviest, 145
Leyte Gulf, Battle for, 252, 253
Marshall Islands, loses no ships, 161
Midway, see Midway
Medical personnel, 86, 87, 122, 213
Okinawa, forces used at, 326
PT boats, 10, 55, 59, 176, 177, 227
Pearl Harbor attack, see Pearl Harbor attack
Philippine Sea, Battle of the, 1, 2, 251
Saipan, Battle of, 168, 169
Seabees, see Seabees
Shakedown cruise, "Missouri," 60
Ships of
"Argonaut," 53
"Arizona," 4, 6
"Cassin," 7
"Downes," 7
"Hammon," 32
"Hornet," 22, 23
"Lexington," 26, 28, 29
"Maryland," 6
"Missouri," 60, 245, 364, 365
"Nautilus," 53
"Neosho," 29
"Nevada," 4, 6
"Neville," 111
"New York," 288
"Oklahoma," 4, 6
"Ozark," 360, 369, 372
"Pennsylvania," 7
"Shaw," 5
"Sims," 29
"South Dakota," 349
"Tennessee," 6, 7
"Vestal," 6
"West Virginia," 6, 7
"Yorktown," 26, 32, 360
Submarines, 348, 349
"Surrender of Japan," art., 350
Task Force 58, 166-169, 191
Truk raid avenges Pearl Harbor, 166, 167
Vella Lavella, Battle of, 89
"War in the South Pacific," art., 244
"Your Navy in Action," art., 1, 2
Naubum, Burma, 185
"Neosho," 29
Netherlands East Indies, 2, 244
Netherlands East Indies troops, 274
"Nevada," 6
"Neville," 111
New Britain
Arawe, 244
Captured Jap equipment, 141
Disease afflicts Marines, 137
Eating K-rations, 138
Fifth Air Force, 137
5th Marines, 141
1st Marine Division, 135, 136, 138, 244
1st Marine Regiment, 136, 137
Gloucester, 135, 136, 244

New Britain (cont'd)
Huon Peninsula, 244
Japanese prisoner, 140
Kiriwina Islands, 244
Landing, 135-138
Landing-site surprises Japs, 137
Map, early Jap conquests, 20, 21
Nisei helps intelligence, 140
Rabaul, 34, 35, 91, 136, 244
Salamaua, 244
7th Marine Regiment, 136, 137
Sixth Army, 244
U.S. flag rises, 141
"Walt's Hill," 141
"War in the Solomons," art., 34, 35
"War in the South Pacific," art., 244
Woodlark Islands, 244
Wounded Marine on stretcher, 138
Writing letters before landing, 136
New Caledonia, 34
New Georgia
Assault near Munda, 78, 79
Bombardment by Navy, 57
Dragon's Peninsula, 81
Engineers build corduroy road, 85
43rd Chemical Warfare Service, 85
Japs move from Guadalcanal, 68
Landing at Choi River, 78, 79
Marine flyers use Russells strip, 69
Munda, see Munda
9th Marine Defense Battalion, 76, 77
103rd Artillery, 76
172nd Infantry, 79
172nd Regimental Combat Team, 76
169th Infantry wounded, 78, 79
Rendova landing, 74-77
Russells, capture of, 76
Seabees clothe Marine raiders, 80
Segi, 34, 80
37th Infantry Division, 79
25th Infantry Division, 79
Viru, 34, 80
"War in the Solomons," art., 34
"Washing Machine Charlie," 87
Wickam's Anchorage, 34
New Guinea
Aitape, 178, 244
Americal Division, 68
Arare, 180
Australian, New Zealander troops, 174
Biak, 180, 181, 244
Buna, 66, 174, 244
503rd Parachute Regiment, 244
1st Marine Division, 135
41st Infantry Division, 178, 180, 244, 245
43rd Infantry Division, 244
Hollandia, 136, 178-180, 244
Lae, 174, 176, 178
Map, early Jap conquests, 20, 21
Marching infantry, 36, 37
Morobe, 176
Nadzab, 178
Natives on PT boat, 176
Noemfoor, 180, 181, 244
126th Infantry, 174
158th Infantry Regiment, 180, 181, 244
162nd Infantry Regiment, 178
163rd Infantry Regiment, 178, 180, 244
Owen Stanley Range, 244
Paratroopers jump, 62, 63
Port Moresby, 62, 63, 244
Saidor, 178
Salamaua, 174, 178, 244
Sanananda, 174, 244
Sansapor, 244
Seizure by Japs, 34
6th Infantry Division, 244
Tanahmerah, 178
32nd Infantry Division, 244
Toem-Sarmi, 244
Wakde, 178, 180
"War in the Solomons," art., 34, 35
"War in the South Pacific," art., 244
Wewak, 178, 180, 244
Yangdar river crossing, 174
New Hebrides Islands, 112
New Ireland, 35
"New York," 288
New Zealand, 48, 114
New Zealand troops, 98, 174
Ngesebus, 242
Nimitz, Chester A., Adm.
Changes to offensive in Pacific, 142
Leyte landing, recommends, 143
Moves headquarters to Guam, 219
"Surrender of Japan," art., 350
"Tarawa," art., 112, 113
Tarawa, visits ruins, 133
Truk raid, statement on, 167
"War in the Central Pacific," art., 132, 133

Nimitz (cont'd)
"War in the Solomons," art., 34, 35
"Your Navy in Action," art., 1, 2
9th Marine Defense Battalion, 76, 77
90th Field Artillery, 276
93rd Division, 35
Noemfoor, 180, 181, 244

O

O'Brien, Wm. J., Col., 197
Okinawa
Air support of ground troops, 321, 325
Artillery use heavy, 334
Baka suicide plane, 261
Base for B-29s, 354
Base for Japan landing, 350
Campaign, 315-347
Capital city leveled, 337
Casualties, 143, 342, 347
Cemeteries, Marine, 343
Christian church hides sniper, 340
Col. Fenton's son buried, 341
Commanders convene, 345
Dakeshi Ridge, 316
"Dash Rite Inn," air raid shelter, 325
Dead Japanese litter field, 328
Doolittle heads B-29 base, 22
8th Marine Regiment, 336
Ernie Pyle, 341
1st Marine Division, 314-347
Flame thrower assault, 295
Funeral services, 341, 343, 345, 346
Gen. Buckner dies, 336
"Grasshopper" scout planes, 337
Hospital under canvas, 336
Initial lack of Jap resistance, 321
Japanese planes knocked out, 342
Kadena airfield, 325
Kamikaze attacks on Fleet, 336
Katchin Peninsula, 315
Kerama Retto, capture of, 143
Kunishi Ridge, 316, 340
Landing, 319-324
Little known of enemy defenses, 331
Map, island hopping from New Guinea, 286
Map, relation to Ryukus and Japan, 317
Motubu Peninsula, 315, 321
Mount Yaetake, 315
Naha. 315, 316, 331-338
Naval shells rise offshore, 322
96th Division, 143, 331
"Okinawa Campaign, The," art., 315, 316
Oruku Peninsula, 316, 340
2nd Marine Air Wing, 342
7th Infantry Division, 143, 316, 331, 344
77th Division, 143
Shuri castle ruins, 340, 342
Shuri Defense Line, 143, 315, 316, 337
6th Marine Division, 143, 314-347
Size of invading force, 323, 326
Strategic importance, 315
Sugar Loaf Hill, 315, 316
"Superfort Warfare in the Pacific," art., 312
Supply lines extended, 321, 332
Tanks bring out wounded, 336
Tenth Army, 143, 315, 320-347
Torii Gate, Naha, 332
III Amphibious Corps, 143
Trucks cut distances for troops, 332
XXIV Corps, 143, 315, 316
27th Infantry Division, 315
U.S. flag rises, 342, 344
Victory celebration, Hill 89, 344
Wana Draw, 340
"War in the Central Pacific," art., 142
"War in the South Pacific," art., 245
Wounded Marine borne on stretcher, 331
Yontan airfield, 320, 325
"Your Navy in Action," art., 1
"Okinawa Campaign, The," art., 315, 316
"Oklahoma," 4, 6
Olangapo, Luzon, 265
103rd Artillery, 76
106th Infantry Regiment, 142, 163
112th Cavalry, 244
124th Cavalry, 182
126th Infantry Regiment, 174
128th Infantry Regiment, 272
129th Infantry Division, 98, 101
132nd Infantry Division, 102, 103
145th Infantry Regiment, 81
147th Infantry Regiment, 34, 35
148th Infantry Regiment, 81, 102
149th Infantry Regiment, 278
151st Infantry Regiment, 274, 275
162nd Infantry Regiment, 178, 179
163rd Infantry Regiment, 178, 180

164th Reg't, Americal Division, 34
165th Infantry Combat Team, 111
172nd Regimental Combat Team, 76
185th Infantry Regiment, 270, 271
186th Infantry Regiment, 245
Operation Flintlock, 146, 147
Ormoc Bay, 252
Orote Peninsula, Guam, 189, 219-224
Oruku Peninsula, 316, 340
Osaka, 22, 354
Osmena, Sergio, 250
"Ozark," 360, 369, 372

P

Pacific area, map, 366, 367
Pagan, 191
Palau Islands
Airbase, 241
Amphtrac spits fire, 239
Angaur, 230, 233, 240
Belly-tank bombing, 240
"Bloody Gulch," 235
"Bloody Nose Ridge," 238, 240, 241
Campaign, 230-243
Casualties, 238
Cave defenses, 239, 240, 243
Construction of Jap defenses, 242, 243
Cub scout planes, 241
Dog in action with Marines, 237
81st Division, 230-243
5th Marine Regiment, 242
1st Marine Division, 230-243
81st Infantry Division, 143
Hoisting a howitzer, 239
Intelligence information, 242
Kongauru, 242
Landing, 230-232
Map, island hopping to Iwo Jima, 286
Morotai, 230
Ngesebus, 242
Peleliu, 233, 236-243
Reconnaissance on ground, 234
Second Wing, Marine aviation, 240, 241
"Shortest bombing hop," 240
Surrender to United States, 350
Ulithi, 143, 235
Umurbrogal Mountain, 242
"War in the Central Pacific," art., 142, 143
Palawan, 245, 270
Palompon, 258
Panay, 245, 270, 271
Parry Island, Marshall Islands, 165
Patch, Alexander M., Gen., 34
Pawing, Leyte, 255
Pearl Harbor Attack
Bombing scenes, 4-6
Casualties, 5
Leads Germany, Italy to war on U.S., 121
Map, position of ships, 3
Results, King on, 1, 2
Truk raid avenges, 166, 167
Wrecked ships, 7
"Your Navy in Action," art., 1, 2
Peiping, 380
Peleliu, 233, 236-243
"Pennsylvania," 7
Philippine Islands
Bataan, 8, 10, 18, 24, 265
Bohol, 245
Bomb raids by Japs, 296
Carabao, 274, 275
Catabato, 245
Cavite, 10, 15, 265
Cebu, 245
Corregidor, 9, 10, 15, 19, 24, 245, 265, 270
Davao City, 14, 245
Death March, 18
Digos, 245
11th Airborne Division, 244
Filipino troops, 9, 15, 18, 19, 24, 245
40th Infantry Division, 271, 272
Guerillas, help from, 276
Impulatao, 245
Jap forces split in two, 247
Japanese losses, 280
Japanese surrender, included in, 250
Kakaban, 245
Leyte, see Leyte
Los Negros, 171, 245
Manila, see Manila
Map Battle of the Philippine Sea, 251
Map, island-hopping progress, 286
"Marianas Campaign," art., 188
Mindanao, 14, 244, 245, 248, 270, 273
Mindoro, 258
Palawan Island, 245, 270
Palompon, 258
Panay, 245, 270, 271
Paratroopers, 59, 245

Philippine Islands (cont'd)
Philippine Sea, Battle of the, 1, 2, 251
Surigao Strait, 253, 258
Surrender by Yamashita, 281
31st Infantry Division, 245
24th Infantry Division, 245
"War in the South Pacific," art., 244
"Your Navy in Action," art., 1, 2
Zamboanga Peninsula, 245
Pick, Louis A., Gen., 183, 285
Ponape, 167
Port Moresby, New Guinea, 62, 63, 244
"President Coolidge," USS, 64
Prisoners
American
Corregidor, 24
Japan, 361, 379
Japanese
Bataan, 19
Guadalcanal, 45, 51
Iwo Jima, 307
New Britain, 140
Saipan, 197, 198
Tarawa, 127
PT boats, 10, 55, 59, 176, 177, 227
Pyle, Ernie, 341

R

Rabaul, 34, 35, 91, 136, 178, 244
Rangoon, 17, 183
Rendova, 34, 74-77
Richardson, Ralph C., Gen., 142, 143
Rockets, 160, 262
Rogers, W. W., Col., 202
Roi, Marshall Islands, 145, 150, 152
Roosevelt, Franklin D.
Casablanca conference, 182
Joint Chiefs of Staff, forms, 1
MacArthur, Nimitz, with, 216
Tokio raid announces, 22
"War in the CBI," art., 182
Ross, R. P., Col., 342
Rota, 191
Royal Air Force, 16, 182, 183
Rujiyoru, Marshall Islands, 165
Rupertus, Wm. H., Gen., 135
Russell Islands, 34, 69, 76
Russia, 2, 183, 363
Ryukyu Islands, 143, 188, 317

S

Saidor, New Guinea, 178
St. Matthias Islands, 35
Saipan
Aerial approach, 191, 195
Aslito airfield, 188, 200
Banzai charge, 204, 205
Base for Japan landing, 350
Battle of the Philippine Sea, 189
Bomber base, 188
Camouflaged howitzer, 200, 201
Campaign, 188-206
Casualties, 142, 206
Charan Kanoa, 195
C tation to 4th Marine Division, 202
Civilians emerge from hiding, 207
Counterattack by Japs, 189, 204-206
Dead Japanese, 202, 204, 205
4th Marine Division, 142, 188, 189, 200-206
Garapan, aerial view, 195
Iwo-bound troops swim off ship, 287
Japanese cabinet quits over loss, 206
Jap prisoner questioned, 197, 198
Landing 142, 188, 192
Map, direction of invasion, 190
"Marianas Campaign," art., 188
Marine Division command post, 202
Mount Tapotchau, 188, 189, 191
Nafutan Point, 191
Native religious shrine, 207
Natural hazards, 199
Opposition on, 142
Orote peninsula, 189
Pier, traffic artery, 195
Reinforcement by Japs too late, 188
Seaplanes sit near tender, 191
2nd Marine Division, 188, 189, 200-206
77th Division, 142
Souvenir hunt, 207
Strategic importance to Japan, 105
Sugar-cane fields, 199, 200
Suicide charge knocks out tank, 202
Tanapag harbor, 197
Task Force 58 sea-air attack, 169
23rd Marine Regiment, 202
24th Marine Regiment, 202
25th Marine Regiment, 202
27th Infantry Division, 188, 189, 192, 197, 200-206

3rd Marine Div. (con't)
"War in the Central Pacific," art., 142
"Your Navy in Action," art., 1, 2
Salamaua, New Guinea, 174, 178, 244
Salween river, Burma, 173, 182, 187
Samar, Luzon, 245
Samoa, 34
San Pablo, Luzon, 14
San Juan, Luzon, 273
San Jose, Leyte, 255
Sanananda, New Guinea, 174, 244
Sanderson, H. M., Gen., 368
Sansapor, New Guinea, 244
Sasebo, Japan, 330, 374
Savo Island, Battle of, 55
Schmidt, Harry, Gen., 202, 294
Seabees
Guam rebuilding, 226, 227, 229
Iwo Jima, build cemetery, 309
Marshall Islands, extend airstrips, 145
Munda, road built to airfield, 87
New Georgia, clothe Marines, 80
Second Air Force, 311, 325
2nd Marine Division
Cemetery on Tarawa, 134
Cited by President, 68, 130
8th Regiment, 130, 209, 336
18th Regiment, 130
Guadalcanal, 34, 39
Japan occupation duty, 330
"Marianas Campaign," art., 188, 189
Occupation of Japan, 374
Okinawa campaign, 314-347
Saipan, 188, 189, 200-206
2nd Regiment, 209
6th Regiment, 130, 209
Tarawa, 114-134
"Tarawa," art., 112, 113
10th Regiment, 130
Tinian campaign, 209-215
"War in the Central Pacific," art., 142
"War in the Solomons," art., 34, 35
2nd Marine Regiment, 116-134, 209
Segi, New Georgia, 34, 80
Seventh Air Force, 162, 217, 294
7th Cavalry Regiment, 255
7th Fighter Command, 312
7th Infantry Division, 142, 144-165, 316
7th Marine Regiment, 136, 137
77th Infantry Division
Guam campaign, 142, 189, 217-226
Ie Shima, 143, 316, 341
Kerama Retto, 143
Luzon, 258
"Marianas Campaign," art., 188
Okinawa, 143
Ormoc Bay, 244
"War in the Central Pacific," art., 142, 143
775th Tank Battalion, 278, 279
Shepherd, Lemuel, Gen., 226, 315, 336
Sherman, F. C., Capt., 29
Shoup, David, Col., 119, 121
Siamese troops, 116
Singapore, 2, 244, 288, 364
Sixth Army, 136, 143
6th Infantry Division, 245
6th Marine Division, 295, 314-347, 380
6th Marine Regiment, 130, 209
Smith, Holland M., Gen.
Commands Fleet Marine Force, 213
Commands largest Marine expeditionary force, 188
Guam flag-raising, 226
Iwo Jima, briefs correspondents, 287
Iwo Jima flag raising, 305
"Marianas Campaign," art., 188, 189
Roi-Namur, inspects, 157
"Tarawa," art., 112, 113
Smith, Julian C., Gen.
Tarawa, with Bourke, Edson, 124
Tarawa, with Nimitz, 133
"Tarawa," art., 112, 113
Uses new tactics for Tarawa, 114
Watches Tarawa action from ship, 116
"You will quickly overrun . . ." 121
Smith, Ralph C., Gen., 111, 120, 142
Society Islands, 34
Solomon Islands
Arundel, 34
Baanga, 34
Blocking running by Japs, 89
Bougainville, see Bougainville
Cape Torokina, 35, 92, 98
Choiseul, 35, 90, 98
Cemetery, Guadalcanal, 44, 45
"Corduroy" road, 96
First phase of campaign ends, 90
Guadalcanal, see Guadalcanal
Japs isolated by defeats, 102

Spaatz, Carl A., Gen., 312
Spars, 65
Spruance, R. A., Adm., 112, 167, 188, 226, 319
Stilwell, Joseph W., Gen.
Leads 140-mile march from Burma, 25
Mountbatten, confers with, 170
Myitkyina airstrip, Burma, 187
Okinawa, takes over command, 336, 345
Trains Chinese troops, 173
"War in the CBI," art., 182, 183
Stilwell Road, 183, 186
Stratemeyer, George E., Gen., 182
Subic Bay, 265
Suicide planes, 261, 336
Sultan, Dan I., Gen., 183
Sumatra, 20
Sumay, Guam, 219, 226
"Superfort Warfare in the Pacific," art., 311
Surigao Strait, 253, 258
Surrender document, 363
"Surrender of Japan, The," art., 350
Sutherland, Richard K., Gen., 364, 365

T

Tablas Strait, 253
Tacloban, Leyte, 247
Tagaytay Ridge, Luzon, 265
Tanahmerah, New Guinea, 178
Tanambogo, Guadalcanal, 39
Tanapag Harbor, 197
Tarakan Island, 274
Tarawa
Airport seized, 116, 121
Amphtracs hit at beach, 129
"Battle for Tarawa," painting, 193
Beach jammed, 123, 125
Casualties, 113
Cemetery, 134
Commanders watch, 116
Dead Japs, 120, 127
Dead Marines, 126, 193
Defending Jap guns, 132, 133
Duration of battle, 116-134
8th Marine Regiment, 116-134
18th Marine Regiment, 130
Gilbert Islands, start offensive, 111
Hand-to-hand fighting, 125
Hawkins, Wm. D., Lt., 119
Jap prisoners, 127
Lessons for later landings, 113
Map of atoll, 128
Missionary nun by grave, 134
Relax after victory, 125
Religious service, 126
Ruined guns and tanks, 129, 133
2nd Marine Division, 116-134
2nd Marine Regiment, 116-134
Shocks United States, 122
6th Marine Regiment, 130
10th Marine Regiment, 130
Value of intelligence data, 113
Wading from reef, under fire, 193
"War in the Central Pacific," art., 142
Wounded treated and evacuated, 122
"Your Navy in Action," art., 1, 2
Task Force 58, 166-169, 191
Tenaru river, Guadalcanal, 45
"Tennessee," 6, 7
10th Air Force, 61
10th Marine Regiment, 130
Thai troops, 116
3rd Marine Division
B-29 dedicated on Iwo Jima, 310
Bougainville, 91, 92
Guam campaign, 142, 217-226
"Marianas Campaign," art., 34, 35
3rd Regiment, 92
9th Regiment, 92
"War in the Central Pacific," art., 142
"War in the Solomons," art., 34, 35
3rd New Zealand Division, 34
Thirteenth Air Force, 106, 355
31st Infantry Division, 245
32nd Infantry Division, 244, 272, 281
33rd Infantry Division, 276, 277
34th Infantry Regiment, 245
37th Infantry Division, 34, 97, 98, 101-103, 245, 272, 273, 280
37th Infantry Regiment, 278
38th Infantry Division, 245, 265
Tientsin, China, 380
Tinian
Aerial survey helps landing, 209
Aerial view, Ushi airfield, 215
Airfields cleared of snipers, 211, 212, 214
Assault delayed by Saipan, 142
Base for B-29s, 214
Campaign, 208-215
Casualties, 215

Toem-Sarmi, New Guinea, 244
Tojo, Hideki, 169
Tokio, 22, 23, 245, 312, 350
Treasury Islands, 35, 98
Truk, 112, 142, 166, 167, 192, 350
Truman, Harry S., 359
Tsingtao, China, 380
Tulagi, Guadalcanal, 34, 38, 39, 40
Turner, R. K., Adm., 34, 112, 148, 188, 287
Tushan, China, 183
12th Cavalry, 255
XX Bomber Command, 311, 312
XXI Bomber Command, 311, 312
22nd Marine Regiment, 165
22nd Marine Regimental Combat Team, 163
23rd Marine Regiment, 153, 202, 299
XXIV Corps, 200, 319
24th Infantry Division, 245, 258
24th Marine Regiment, 155, 202
25th Infantry Division, 34, 272, 276
25th Marine Regiment, 202
27th Infantry Division
Guam, 142, 217-226
Makin, 111, 112, 142
Okinawa campaign, 143, 315-347
Saipan, 142, 188, 189, 192, 200-206
"Tarawa," art., 113
"War in the Central Pacific," art., 142, 143
27th Marine Regiment, 292
28th Marine Regiment, 228
209th Anti-Aircraft Battalion, 280
Twining, Nathan F., Gen., 312

U

Ulithi, 143, 235
Underhill, J. L., Gen., 154
U.S.O. (United Service Organizations), 57, 381
United States
Coordination of armed forces, 1, 2
International liaison, 2
Leadership, military and naval, see Joint Chiefs of Staff
Strategy at war's beginning, 2
War effort, 2

V

Valencia, Luzon, 258
Valle, Pedro del, Gen., 340
Vandegrift, A. A., Gen., 58, 95, 97
Vella Lavella, 34, 89, 90
Vila, 89
Villa Verde Trail, Luzon, 272
Viru, New Georgia, 34, 80

W

Waesche, Russell R., Adm., 65
Wainwright, Jonathan, Gen., 19, 361, 365
Wakde New Guinea, 180
Wake Island, 12, 14, 350, 368
Walker, John T., Col., 165
Wait, L. T., Col., 141
Wanting, China, 282, 283
"War in the Central Pacific, The," art., 142, 143
"War in the CBI, The," art., 182
"War in the Solomons, The," art., 34, 35
"War in the South Pacific, The," art., 244
War Shipping Administration, 64
Wedemeyer, Albert C., Gen., 183
"West Virginia," 6, 7
Wewak, 178, 180, 244
Wickam's Anchorage, New Georgia, 34
Wingate, Orde C., Gen., 182
Winn, H. S., Col., 206
Wolfe, Kenneth B., Gen., 311
Woodlark Islands, 244
Woods, Louis, Gen., 325
Women's Reserves, 2, 65
Wornham, Tommy, Col., 292
Wotje, Marshall Islands, 163

Y

Yamashita, Tomoyuki, 255, 281
Yap Island, 143, 244
Yeiri, Marshall Islands, 165
Yokohama, 22, 245, 379
Yokosuka, 330, 350, 374, 379
"Yorktown," 26, 32, 360
"Your Navy in Action," art., 1, 2
Yunnan, China, 182, 185

Z

Zambales, Luzon, 244
Zamboanga Peninsula, 245